The Estranged God

The Estranged God

Modern Man's Search for Belief

by Anthony T. Padovano

SHEED AND WARD : NEW YORK

© Sheed and Ward, Inc., 1966

Library of Congress Catalog Card Number 66–14154

Nihil obstat:
    Very Rev. Msgr. William F. Hogan
    Censor Librorum
Imprimatur:
    †Thomas A. Boland
    Archbishop of Newark
    December 22, 1965

Manufactured in the United States of America

To my Mother, Father, and Sister

Preface

If there is one thing which characterizes theology today, it is pastoral concern. Theology may be the science of God but it is for man. We are involved today in what we might call a consensus theology. It is a theology which seeks to emphasize the things which bind men together rather than those which divide us. This does not mean that we take the distinctive or the challenging or the crucifying factors out of Faith. It means rather that we strive mightily to understand before we differ. It means that we try to absorb everything good in the world of non-belief not only in order to bring the world to belief, but also to Christianize the goodness that Christianity has not previously encountered. The imperative which drives us to this is not only the phenomenon of Vatican II. We are impelled to this task by the theology of the Incarnation and by the influence of the Spirit in this century. We are led to this task by the theology of the Incarnation. For Christ comes as one of us and in compassionate concern before He tells us of the difference His Presence must make and of the greater things He calls us to achieve by the surrender of what is lesser in us. One has the impression that the contemporary of Christ never felt his humanity threatened by Christ. Christ did not try to disregard our humanity but to challenge it.

We are also led to do what we are doing today by the influence of the Spirit in this century. For this is the century when the Church tells us that clergy and laity must cooperate more effectively not only in the government of the Church but even in the celebration of her liturgy. It is the century when Protestant and Catholic call each other Christian; when Jew and Christian see each other as men of faith; when men of good will cooperate on all those issues of vital importance for man. This nostalgia for unity comes, as we have been reminded, from the Holy Spirit.

These influences lead us to what we have called consensus theology. Such a theology offers us new opportunities, wider vistas, more expansive evangelical possibilities, fresher insights, brighter visions. It is in the spirit of this new age that these pages are written. They are written to understand better the world in which we live, the men we love, and the problem of God we must all face. They are written also not only to remind us of what is contemporary and twentieth-century about our profession of faith. They are written also to help us appreciate what is traditional, time-honored, perennial, unchanging, and inherited in our Faith. They are written to remind our contemporaries that we do not only understand and love, but that we preach an approach to life which is distinctive and demanding. They are written to remind us that the greater mystery of Faith lies in what we receive (the Incarnation, the Church, grace, the Eucharist, the Scriptures, an imperishable message) rather than in what we contribute (though this is not without significance; in fact, it is indispensable). We come into the world as Christians not only to understand our situation and approve all in it but to transform the world and to preach to it even as we bless it.

This book has been written within the structure of what Catholic theology calls the course on the One God. It is an experiment in what dogmatic theology can do and might be today. It is the sort of a book which could only have been written in this century and yet it unsays nothing of what was said so splendidly in centuries before our own. It is an attempt to tell all men of the theology of God and of the Church's love for the God who made men and for the men who seek God.

December 20, 1965   Rev. Anthony T. Padovano
                                    Immaculate Conception Seminary
                                    Darlington, New Jersey

Contents

Contents

The Problem

There is no human problem more primitive or more confusing than the relationship of man with something greater than himself. Man, in spite of all his loudly-declared autonomy, never accepts himself as the highest or the best form of life. Individual men cannot give themselves in entire devotion only to themselves. Nor can any of us give himself to humanity in general without a tinge of dissatisfaction and disappointment. Man is forever disillusioned with himself, with the world he makes, with the thought that there is nothing more to serve except man. And so he looks elsewhere and beyond. He is not sure but he is compelled to search. There is always the conviction that a deeper love, a greater freedom, a fuller life exists somewhere or somehow. Nothing ever convinces the memory of man that this conviction must be forsaken and forgotten. And so he lives —with human life the only thing he is absolutely sure of and with the realization that human life is not enough.

This primitive problem of man and mystery is still with us. It is a primitive problem and yet a contemporary concern of sufficient magnitude to warrant our attention. We shall try in the course of these pages to answer some key questions. How does a Catholic priest or a Christian layman or a religious man talk to those of our fellow-men who sense the mystery but give it no name, who feel a greater power but grant it no personality? What does one say to those who deny the problem and live with man alone, gaining a measure of happiness but tortured by the brittle fragility and senseless destruction of human life?

The problem of atheism has been called "a problem of the utmost importance . . . a fearful danger overshadowing all mankind."[1] Paul VI expressed concern about atheism in his first encyclical:

> We do not consider the world a stranger. . . . All things human are our concern. We share with the whole of mankind a common nature, human life with all its gifts and problems . . . we are aware . . . that there are many who profess themselves, in various ways, to be atheists. . . . *This is the most serious problem of our time* . . . we are moved by our pastoral office to seek in the heart of the modern atheist the motives of his turmoil and denial. . . . We see these men full of yearning, prompted sometimes by passion and desire for the unattainable, but often also by great-hearted dreams of justice and progress.[2]

How then are we to approach this magnificent creature of God who is modern man? We must approach him, above all else, in love and freedom.

We must approach modern man in love. Our task is to make ourselves, to come to be. Nothing we say of ourselves or of others has any meaning until we begin to give ourselves in love. As an individual I never reach reality unless I love. I never know who my fellow-men are or who I am unless I love. Love is the supreme value on earth and in heaven. God comes to know himself only if He gives to Other in Love. Man must follow the same pattern. We cannot reach modern man unless he can see the Gospel incarnate in us. And the essence of the Gospel is love.

We must approach modern man in freedom as well. Freedom must become so identified with Christianity that men will not be able to think of one without the other. Striving for freedom is fraught with danger and peril. For men too often perpetrate tyranny in the name of freedom and license under the banner of liberty. Our freedom and our love are never sinless. Yet we must labor for both since it is impossible to be sinless without them.

We are to approach modern man then in love and freedom. We are not to laugh at him when he cannot think as we do. We need not argue with him because he cannot conclude as we have. We cannot write off his agony and his struggle as only self-seeking.

By the force of our faith, we are compelled to see him as made in the image and likeness of God. And we, who believe so passionately and deeply in God, cannot be indifferent to what God has made like Himself. Modern man is the product of a world that has moved too quickly for him to assimilate, a lonely creature who wants so much to communicate and to have someone understand him, a rebel without a cause, a lover who finds no one to love. He is perplexed by his world, paralyzed with doubt, filled with fear, alienated from a God grown, it seems, silent. He has run to sex, to narcotics, to alcohol, to violence, to suicide. He is the perpetual man in need, beaten by robbers for a meaningless possession. He is wounded by the wayside. He knows not how to heal himself or to find his way again. And some of us have passed him by. We have passed him by because we thought he was different from us, a Samaritan, an atheist. We passed him by without remembering that Christ told us it was our brother whom we left alone and in pain.

NOTES

[1] Paul VI: Address to Jesuits in Rome (May 7, 1965).

[2] Paul VI: *Ecclesiam Suam* (NCWC translation), pp. 38–41. Italics not in original text.

The Estranged God

I
MODERN MAN IN SEARCH OF SELF AND MEANING FOR HIS LIFE

1 Existentialism and Religious Belief: The Mood of the Age Is Set

INTRODUCTION: WHAT IS EXISTENTIALISM?

Existentialism is an extremely difficult thing to define. It is both elusive and pervasive. It has influenced our lives on every level. It has given a different emphasis to atheism and theology, to literature and Catholic spirituality. Existentialism embraces so much that every definition of it misses the point. Thus, *Webster's New World Dictionary:*

> Existentialism: a literary-philosophic cult of nihilism and pessimism popularized in France after World War II, chiefly by Jean-Paul Sartre: it holds that each man exists as an individual in a purposeless universe, and that he must oppose his hostile environment through the exercise of his free will.

Existentialism is something that cannot be ignored. As every other system man has devised, it has its pros and its cons. We must not fear to study Existentialism. It is wrong to assume its thought is disturbing or its insights worthless. No longer is it possible or desirable to cut ourselves off from our contemporaries. To do this is to develop our faith in a world of artificial security, a world so safe that it is unreal, so protected that it is oppressive. The faith that issues from this atmosphere is a faith

5

irrelevant and so delicate that it must forever protect itself from alien influences. A faith built on fear is not belief but escape. Is our faith strong enough to stand today? We must not fear to ask ourselves this question. If we fear the question then we are men without courage and our faith is inauthentic and dead. For a man of faith, nothing human is fearful or unworthy. His faith has given him security; freedom, strength to love, and given him God Himself. What is there to fear? Who is there to despise? Should our answer not be, "No one, Lord"? Pope John once said it so well: "We have no reason to be afraid. Fear comes only from a lack of faith."[1]

The generation of Vatican II must be convinced of the nobility of its cause and the inevitability of its success. Cardinal Newman described his day and ours in courageous words:

> The cause of truth . . . has its ebbs and flows. It is pleasant to live in a day when the tide is coming in. Such is our own day; and, without forgetting that there are many rocks on the shore to throw us back and break our advance for the moment . . . still we may surely encourage ourselves by a thousand tokens all around us now, that this is our hour, whatever be its duration, the hour for great hopes, great schemes, great efforts, great beginnings. We may live indeed to see but little built but we shall see much founded. A new era seems to be at hand and a bolder policy. . . .

A somewhat better definition of Existentialism than the one previously cited is given in *Webster's New Collegiate Dictionary:*

> An introspective humanism or theory of man which expresses the individual's intense awareness of his contingency and freedom, a theory which stresses the individual's responsibility for making himself what he is.

Dictionaries are hardly primary philosophical sources. If one must define Existentialism, however, they do serve a purpose. Existentialism, however, is better described than defined. In describing Existentialism, a word about its objective, characteristics, and weaknesses may help us to evaluate it properly.[2]

The objective which Existentialism pursues is an analysis of man's concrete existence. It hopes to achieve many things as it seeks this objective. It is thus at times a ringing protest against every intellectual, social, or even pseudo-ecclesiastical force which would destroy genuine freedom. It is a clarion call summoning us from the stifling abstraction and deadening conformity of modern life. It is a modern philosophy for modern men who fear or fail to face life's most basic problems. What does it mean to be a human being or to be myself? What does it mean to give love and feel freedom? How can we find and keep the courage to be and the fortitude to face death? Every man must wrestle with these problems. The answers to them must not only be accepted from others but formed in one's heart of hearts. They must be not only this man's answers or that man's answers or even the answers of all men. They must be *my* answers as well. As I answer these questions, I grow into what I was meant to be. And even if I cannot find the answer early in life or easily, even if I am annoyed at feeling the need to respond at all, yet I must at the very least listen to the questions and recognize their urgency.

Existentialism then calls man to a spiritual struggle with himself. It is discounted as philosophy by many since it seeks at times not an answer but a phenomenology of experience. Philosophy or not, however, it has set the mood for our age. It speaks for millions of our contemporaries for whom God is dead. It can speak for all of us who know that God lives and that man cannot make God die.

One of the most refreshing aspects of Existentialism is its honesty. Unfortunately some have been bewitched by Existentialism's insistence on honesty and authenticity; and they have used the labels to mask fanaticism and egomania. At its best, however, Existentialism is sternly honest. It tears away the masks of complacency, hypocrisy, and indifference. It says what it thinks. And if it says it believes in God, we know that this is so.

The characteristics that Existentialism manifests in the search for its objective are diffuse:

Existentialism is a protest against all forms of rationalism.

No matter how impressive reason may be, it is not man. Therefore, human truth is not the result of logic and reason but of all that is man. Truth is not a system but a total experience. A man does not live and die for a conclusion. There is no cost too great, however, for truth. For something someone lives by, death is not too precious a price. Truth does not live alone in the mind of man. It reaches his will where he must choose it. It captures his emotions so that he lives passionately in its power. It incarnates itself in his action and experience. If truth does not do this, it may remain truth but I have missed it; I may recognize it, admire it from a distance, even proclaim it in the hearing of my fellow-men, but I have still missed it. Truth was never meant to be a possession or an achievement. It is, like grace, something that possesses me. It is a discovery that demands and excites, an uncharted ocean whose waters are never fully known but whose beckoning call makes voyagers of us all.

Existentialism is a protest against all views which tend to regard man as if he were a thing.

Existentialism is committed to the sacredness, the perilous unpredictability, and the infinite possibilities of human life. In this fundamental attitude Christianity has much to give Existentialism. For Christianity senses the sacredness of human life so deeply that it calls men to see in all human life the vestigial signs and gracious Presence of God. Man is the first temple in which God chooses to dwell. When God regards human life he forever sees His own life therein. It is man's burden and glory to recognize the fact that he is God's image. It is the vocation of Christianity to make man realize this.

Christianity emphasizes too the perilous unpredictability of human life. Anything might happen to us: redemption or perdition, worship or blasphemy. And what happens to us happens not only for time but forever. Christianity is committed too to the infinite possibility of human life. So rich is human life that, in grace, it can bear the sonship of God which is bestowed upon us. And it never ceases to be human life in the process. So inexhaustible is the mystery of human life that an Eternal Word can speak and take flesh in it and God's only Son can live this life without offending the majesty of His divinity or our humanity.

To see man as a thing or an object is to un-man man. It is to frustrate not only his human potential but his divine possibilities. Man is not to conform ever to what men arbitrarily choose to make him. He cannot be servant to capitalism, nor slave to Communism, nor pawn in any economic or social enterprise. He is center of all things earthly. All that we do must take the dignity of man first into account. For man who was not made by God to give his devotion even to the creatures God made cannot be compelled to bend his knee before the alien gods men make in one generation and discard in the next. Man must serve the human life God gave him. If he serves this in all the range and magnitude God gave to it his hands always reach out, find God, and address Him in prayer.

Existentialism makes a drastic distinction between subjective and objective truth.

Existentialism does not deny that science, common sense, and logic give men genuine objective truth. But it insists that in connection with ultimate matters it is impossible to lay aside the impassioned concerns of the individual. It is not a question as to whether the objective order exists or is essential. This must be taken for granted. The task of Existentialism is not to deny the objective order but to disclose its insufficiency. Had the objective order been enough God need never have made man. For man is subject and person. The objective order must cede to the properly understood subjective personality of man. The objective order is indispensable and—it is secondary.

When Existentialism builds the distinction between objective and subjective truth into a disparity, then it betrays man. Objective and subjective truth are a complement, a harmony, and a deeply humanizing process.

Existentialism regards man as fundamentally ambiguous.

Existentialism sees the human situation as filled with contradictions and tensions which cannot be resolved by means of exact or consistent thinking. Man is free—yet his whole life seems to determine him. Man is finite—and impatient with his finitude he senses a strange kinship with eternity. Seen from outside, man is but an episode in the vast process of nature. Seen from within, each man is a universe in himself with a dignity that touches us poignantly and sometimes makes us speechless in reverence.

In all his ambiguity, man finds himself in a world not yet fully created, in the midst of his fellow-men who bewilder him and themselves, before a God whom he never understands but cannot fail to serve. Existentialism examines in great detail these polarities of man's brief days: man and the world, man and his fellow-man, man and God.

Man comes into life unfinished. He is a minimum of fulfillment and all promise. He dies with most of his promise still within him, promise so endlessly deep that all eternity alone can fully redeem it.

Christianity preaches to man in his ambiguity a world that is God-made. Christianity tells him in the midst of his fellow-men there was once God. And that God Himself was finite in Christ. Christianity does not make life unambiguous. It gives life some definition and ambiguity some clarity. It gives an answer to the mystery of human life without taking away the mystery or cheapening the solution. Darkness does not become brighter because someone tells you there is light and points the way. But it is good to know that light there will be and that the path is the right one and that the darkness is only a phase. The crucifixion did not hurt less because it was the beginning of the Resurrection. The Resurrection made the crucifixion meaningful, not painless.

There are then no simple answers for man. Existentialism tells us this. Christianity tells us this. Everything would be so simple if we could become either animals or God. We are, however, both and neither.

Existentialism is a system not only of objectives and characteristics but of failures as well. It does not reach all facets of reality. In fact, it sometimes endangers values which must be affirmed for a complete picture of man. These weaknesses in Existentialism have already been implied in what we have said. It might aid our evaluation of Existentialism to single out some of these for more specific consideration.

Existentialism sometimes so stresses the subjective that the objective is disregarded.

Man is not just a series of subjective responses to the objective order but a creature who must come to terms with that order. Man does not make reality. He recognizes and utilizes it. He creates his personality not only in the inner recesses of his unique mystery but in his external relationship with what is outside of him. Man is that strange being who attains self-consciousness only by being conscious of something other than himself, who deals with himself by occupying himself with something else, who catches sight of himself only by perceiving an object. He must go out of himself in order to enter into himself. Man is at home with himself only by being with others and accepting them.[3]

In its stress on the subjective, Existentialism sometimes emphasizes emotion and experience to the exclusion of judgment. Man, we must remind ourselves, is a creature not only of passion but also of intellectual discernment. Man's heart may be his greatest treasure, but the problem with man's heart is that it leads in different directions all at once. It illuminates all values but it does this indiscriminately. Man's heart makes him restless, brings him to tears, renders him speechless in wonder and glorious in sacrificial love for others. Man's heart forever betrays his desire to create a fully rational universe. It leads man continually in search of a greater justice, a deeper truth, a richer love.

The intellect, however, is part of man too. And the intellect's final service to the heart is one of purifying criticism. If man were without intellect, he would lose control of himself. Without reason man would waste his energy and life in misdirected and self-contradicting strivings. "A hierarchy must be established on the basis of objective importance. What counts here is not the mere force of feeling, but how it is interpreted; not the brute tug of a particular good, but the meaning it has for our total being."[4]

Existentialism can so isolate the individual that he becomes preoccupied with his own concerns.

The misguided existentialist searches only for *my* freedom, is involved only in *my* struggle for authenticity, is lost only in *my* inner conflicts. This is not Existentialism but selfishness which seeks a noble name. It is egoism that uses Existentialism as the vehicle of its expression.

This over-concern with self can cut man off from fruitful contacts with nature, other men, and God. Personal dignity is not the total possession of any one man. It is something we share with each other and ultimately with God.

The great task of Existentialism is to carry us in the direction of a restored and purified conception of community. If it cannot do this, it will destroy us. If it can do this, it will give mankind a benefit that will lead future generations to rise up and call it blessed.

Existentialism then is a phenomenon of our times. So is Christianity. Vatican II has given us a conciliar mandate to express Christianity in existential, concrete terms. This reminds us of that even more traditional evangelical mission given us in the Person and Message of Christ. Christianity has always expressed itself in concrete and almost painfully personal terms. Divine love expressed itself concretely in the flesh of Christ. Divine forgiveness expressed itself concretely in the crucifixion. Divine glory expressed itself concretely in the Risen Body of the Lord. Christianity, then, cannot be at odds with genuine Existentialism. Even the Church expresses itself best concretely; in Bread made Christ, in water that sanctifies, in oil that gives growth and heals, and with words which minister pardon.

If we succeed in post-Vatican II Christianity, if we give vitality again to Christianity's existential concern, then we shall have fulfilled the purpose for which our generation was given to the Church. If we succeed, then we shall pass from the Church visible knowing that unworthy servants though we were, we served Christianity when it needed us. And the words of Henry V on the eve of Agincourt may not be overly-pretentious:

> From this day to the ending of the world,
> But we in it shall be remembered . . .
> And gentlemen in England now a-bed
> Shall think themselves accurs'd they were not here.

JEAN-PAUL SARTRE

Our task is now to examine the thought of some of the main existentialists. We shall not try to explore or expose the philosophical state of the question on these men. Rather we shall attempt to choose those conclusions and insights which deal with the problem of modern man and his relationship with God. We shall proceed from those thinkers farthest removed from theism to those who are Christian and Catholic. We shall not try to criticize but to emphasize instead an understanding of what these men have said.

Of the existentialists, Jean-Paul Sartre is perhaps the most uncompromisingly atheistic. In our study of Sartre's thought, the themes of freedom, interpersonal relations, and God's existence will preoccupy our attention.

Freedom

Man, as Sartre understands him, is born into a world that has no meaning. He is not *l'en-soi*, i.e., being-in-itself. For this is inactive and unconscious being. Rather he is *le pour-soi*, i.e., being-for-itself.[5] Because he is active being he is doomed to live with no permanence. He can never achieve a static, finished situation. And because he is conscious, he is tormented by the need to search constantly for an impossible goal. The world is meaningless and so is man. Yet he strives to discover meaning. Hence he is a perplexed and desperate creature, unfortunately conscious and inescapably senseless.

As man becomes aware of the lack of meaning in the world, he is filled with nausea.

> . . . I knew it was the World, the naked World suddenly revealing itself, and I choked with rage at this gross, absurd being.

You couldn't even wonder where all that sprang from or how it was that a world came into existence, rather than nothingness.[6]

Nausea then is the disgust man feels at the lack of meaning in existence. It is a sickening realization of the complete contingency of everything. Man with fortitude must face these facts. Though the world has no meaning, man need not suffer the same fate. A certain intelligibility can be given his life. He can do something since he is conscious and free. He is *le pour-soi*. How can man give meaning to his life? He can do this by his freedom of choice. Freedom of choice then becomes the essence of life. Yet to choose is a dreadful burden. For once man begins to choose he becomes something. He is responsible for what he makes himself to be. Everything derives from his power of choice: the value he attaches to things, the opinions he has of himself, all that he is. Man is really inanimate until he chooses. When he chooses, he is responsible for the entire world of meaning he creates for himself. He knows today that all could be different. For if he made another set of choices, his being and his world would not be the same. Hence, everything is arbitrary and precarious.

> Man can count on no one but himself: he is alone, abandoned on earth in the midst of his infinite responsibilities, without help, with no other aim than the one he sets himself, with no other destiny than the one he forges for himself on this earth.

Man is completely alone "with no excuses behind us or justification before us." Nor can man escape from the conflict by not choosing. The very pressure of life forces man to choose. He is, in Sartre's phrase, "condemned to be free." He cannot *not* be free.[7] In his choices, he begins to feel terribly abandoned. There are no standards or guides to help him. He knows he must choose but not how to choose or what to choose. He is alone.

He realizes also that, as he chooses, he is confronted with an absurd world and circumstances beyond his control. He chooses; he feels alone; and then despairs as he sees a world of absurdity conflicting with his choices. He asks himself at times in his life: "What has become of me? Who am I? What have I made of myself? I do not want to be this." Yet man must go on choosing and learn to act without hope. Not individual man alone but the entire human enterprise is doomed to failure. For the goal of man is the achievement of complete and perfect being. To be a man is to try to be God. Human nature is characterized by a futile and yet undying thirst to be God. Since this cannot be done, "man is a useless passion."[8]

> All human activities . . . are doomed to failure. Thus it amounts to the same thing whether one gets drunk alone or is a leader of nations.

It becomes apparent then that, as man creates himself, he creates his own standards of right and wrong. The only thing that seems really to be wrong is "bad faith." "Bad faith" means inauthentic existence. It means accepting the world and one's self as given realities rather than as things which must be created in choice. Man must reject "bad faith" and act only in "good faith." He must accept his condemnation to freedom in a meaningless universe, his sentence to live forever alone in his freedom. No one else can touch him, reach him, or love him. If man lives in "good faith," accepting courageously his agonizing situation, choosing always authentic existence, some values will come to him. He will become aware of who he is and of his responsibility for his own situation. If he runs from freedom, he does and becomes nothing. As man lives in "good faith," he overcomes indifference in "engagement." "Engagement" means choosing a positive part in human affairs and wanting freedom for others. No man must be without freedom. Man, then, must choose "engagement" for the benefit of mankind.

Thus, if we might summarize the situation before us, Sartre has given us this picture of man:

man is born into absurdity and feels nausea as he realizes this;

he can overcome some absurdity by choosing to be himself;

as he chooses, he feels his alone-ness and despairs;

yet he must go on choosing authentic existence and engagement: there is no other way;

man must look for no one, not even God, to help: no one can help man;

what then does man gain from life? He creates himself authentically and he engages himself for the benefit of others.

The picture we have of man then is that of an individual committed to a solitary struggle. If we follow out this idea of man's alone-ness, of his inability to receive help anywhere or from anyone, we cannot but ask ourselves: "What of the other people in the world?" The world, after all, is not empty but filled with others like myself. As Sartre completes his description of man the individual, he must consider what this individual does in the midst of others. What happens to man, or at least, what must man do in the experience of interpersonal relationships?

Interpersonal Relationships

It is clear that man's burden of freedom is absolute. No one can lift it from him. What surprises us is that Sartre insists that the other not only cannot help but is a threat. Man's estrangement is radical. He is estranged not only from the nauseous world but also from his threatening fellow-men. In fact, it is an indignity for man to find himself circumscribed by a physical world and other selves.

What precisely is the threat my fellow-men pose for me? They make me conscious of my contingency and they limit my freedom. They must be kept at a certain distance. The loneliness of man is complete and almost unbearable. This should not deter us since courageously we can live through this dilemma. All of us might prefer that things were different but to live with the thought that there is a way out is to live in fantasy.

We can never make others incapable of threatening us because the freedom and selfhood of the other are not accessible to us. To love the other is to make a costly mistake. For if ever I overcome the separation and love another, I sooner or later destroy him. I begin to control his liberty and I keep him from making choices alone, in authenticity. He begins to choose for my sake and thus never becomes himself. Once I love another, I am no longer engaged in his struggle for freedom. Instead I work against it. This is why "Hell is other people."[9] I must hate the other and fear him. He seeks to limit my freedom. I may destroy his freedom. Therefore we cannot understand or reach each other. Yet there is a certain dedication to other people since I give my life struggling for their freedom. The other must be hated. And if God did exist, since he is Absolute Other, he would be most hated. But God, of course, does not exist.

The very notion of God must be rejected since it is not reconcilable with human freedom. God is the greatest threat of all to the supreme value of freedom. If God did exist, then what it means to be human would be determined by God. Man would have an essence. God, not man, would make man. And God would give all the answers, thus destroying our liberty. Sartre finds it distressing that God is dead because it means that anything can happen to man. But this fact must be faced. That is the way things are. It is useless to want them any other way.

"God does not exist . . . it is necessary to draw the consequence of his absence right to the end."[10]

Sartre does just this. His philosophy is a faith without belief in a free will to no purpose set adrift in an absurd and meaningless universe.

There is, then, no God and there must be no idea of God if man is to face all the facts. This idea of God has a way of persisting even if God does not exist. It shows itself in many forms and must be avoided at all costs.

Man must resist the temptation to think he or all men are God. He must not strive for this. He is a useless passion and nothing more. He cannot be God. "To be man means to reach toward being God. Or if you prefer, man fundamentally is the desire to be God."[11]

One of the basic reasons why the idea of God is all wrong is because it frees us from *nausea*. It can deceive us into thinking there is meaning for ourselves or in our world. It can make us depend on the freedom and power of Another for solutions. But He cannot help us since He is not there. To depend on illusion is to live in "bad faith" or inauthentic existence. This is the worst of all evils.

> We have lost religion but we have gained humanism. The ideal now is to liberate and to help emancipate mankind with the result that man becomes really an absolute for man.

These then are some basic ideas from the philosophy of Sartre. He represents, as we have said, the most uncompromisingly atheistic position taken by our contemporaries. In spite of his many defects, there is a certain grandeur and a certain value in Sartre. He portrays well the emotions we feel when we see existence as contingent, fragile and absurd. He insists that we can remain ourselves even in a situation where all meanings are threatened or undermined. He shows the precariousness of all human values and the dignity of freedom and honesty. He insists, finally, that faith cannot be an escape from the insecurity and frustration of life.

Though Sartre does say some things well, he still leaves us unsatisfied. He takes too much for granted. His atheism is not something he proves but rather something he presupposes. He asks us to face the facts of our situation but one does not feel certain that Sartre has faced all the facts about man or that his "facts" are really facts. Freedom so often, it seems, is not liberty but a desire to do what man desires to do. How does one ever know when his freedom is not selfish choice or stubborn intransigence? Sartre asks us to be brave in spite of all. Bravery, however, is not accepting absurdity unflinchingly but affirming meaning against everything that threatens it.

One cannot help asking himself as he reads Sartre: "Has this man really caught the human person in all his values? Has he given us a workable philosophy of life? Can one really live this and be humanized in the process? Is Sartre perhaps just slightly passé? Was his call to courage in the face of ruin on every side not better suited to the despair of war-torn Europe of the 1940's than to the confidence and energy of the 1960's?"

Sartre does though, in spite of all, remain consistent.

> . . . salvation and immortality are going to pieces; the edifice is going to rack and ruin . . . atheism is a cruel and long-range affair. I think I have carried it through.

Perhaps. But has Sartre carried through what must be carried through? One shudders at his conclusions not because they are grim but because they do not seem to be true.

> Every existing being is born without reason, prolongs itself out of weakness, and dies by chance.[12]

MARTIN HEIDEGGER

With Martin Heidegger we deal with a thinker whose difference from Sartre is not only apparent to the reader but insisted upon by Heidegger himself. The difference between these two men highlights the difficulty of grouping any more than one individual under the label: *existentialist*. In Heidegger's own words Sartre's philosophy has "not the slightest thing in common" with his own. For Sartre, man is everything. For Heidegger, Being counts most of all. For Sartre, freedom explains and creates all. For Heidegger, Being is needed to give intelligibility to human freedom. Nor does Heidegger envision man as alone in a senseless universe. Man is not alone. Being is his element. The philosophical center of gravity then is not man but Being. Thus, what matters most of all is not an analysis of man's subjective state but his bond with Being itself.

In an attempt to put Martin Heidegger into perspective for our purposes, we shall say a few words about his thought on Being, authentic human concerns, the world itself, and, finally, God.

One of the great tragedies of contemporary life is the fact that Being has fallen into oblivion.[13] This situation condemns man to confusion. For Being is the altogether transcending reality. It is Being which conditions the things that are and yet is not created by them. It is Being which calls man to itself and places man where he is. Man is the place where Being manifests itself in the world. He is *Da-sein* (Being there). But man is not just *Da-sein* in the way Sartre erroneously interprets Heidegger. Man is not just *there* in the sense that he has been hurled up (*geworfen*) without purpose on the beach of that-which-is. Man is *there* for Being, a temple where Being builds a shrine for itself in the world. Man is not the most important thing there is. Being (*Sein*) is more important. But man is Being-in-the-world. He is, as we have said and as Heidegger calls him in his novel terminology, Being-there (*Da-sein*). Though man may not be the most important thing there is, still man is a starting point for philosophy since man is the only way to reach Being. Man is thrown into existence but for Being. He has a vocation to Being. He is to be the shepherd of Being, accepting his destiny of guardianship for Being.

Since man is free, he can refuse his destiny and become deaf to his vocation. Every man has a choice to make. He may make himself just one thing among others, subordinating his selfhood to thinghood. Or he may choose himself authentically, struggling always not to become inauthentic, never to be a thing. He may accept his calling to Being. He may sacrifice himself for Being and live with a hidden act of thanksgiving for Being.

The problem with modern man is that too often he loses himself in the complexity and superficiality of modern life. He becomes preoccupied with everyday concerns, lost in the anonymity of the things which are. No one knows who the other is or even cares. What is even worse, he does not know who he is himself and he does not care about himself. He has replaced care or concern for self with inauthentic preoccupation. What can he do? What material or economic purpose does he serve? How much can he earn, own, and enjoy? He is preoccupied with things and gradually, imperceptibly but tragically he becomes like the things with which he is preoccupied. He loses care for self, for the dignity of what he is, for the only genuine concerns of life. He surrenders his selfhood to thinghood. Modern man becomes so caught up in external anonymity that his joys and sorrows are at the mercy of the way things happen. Hope and despair do not come from himself but with the way things are going.

The insidious thing about this situation is that everything seems all right because all other modern men appear to be living the same way. But this is bondage; this is slavery; this is loss of self. Man is alienated from his authentic possibilities. He is enslaved to his fake self—continually falling away from the true self hidden in him, which he might be realizing. He shows his inauthenticity especially in superficial activity:

Zweideutigkeit (ambiguity) is the surrender of man to the practical necessities of life.

Neugier (curiosity) is the fascination men find in information about life rather than in fundamental questions.

Gerede (chatter) is the useless talk which so often replaces thoughtful silence or meaningful communication. Heidegger makes much of the value of silence, the experience of speech-lessness, the realization of the nameless in life. Heidegger's thought here is not unsimilar to Hammarskjold's complaint that we must spend our lives "Jabbering away about this or that, slouching along the bypaths of gossip . . ."[14] "to talk merely because convention forbids silence . . . exhausting . . . like any improper use of our spiritual resources."[15]

Man, Heidegger insists, is made for more than this. He is Being-in-the-world. His dignity is beyond exaggeration. It is, however, a dignity that can only exist in relationship with Being. All human interest must be sacrificed for the sake of preserving the truth of Being. There is no other way—except superficiality, inauthenticity, thinghood. All of us are pilgrims in search of a homecoming, wanderers in the neighborhood of Being. We must come home, although we can, since we are free, prefer homelessness. If man refuses the grace of Being's calling, he is forever a voyager. Though Being is always a mystery, though it never fully reveals itself, still it is not forever hidden. The only way to bring modern man to an awareness of his vocation is to create in him a concern about the right things.

There are times when a total boredom affects man—times when he is bored not just with someone or something but with life itself. Everything withdraws from us, turns against us, and threatens us. All attempts to say "yes" to life in the presence of this boredom are powerless. If, in those moments, we become

concerned and anxious only about things and not about ourselves, then we forsake the call to authenticity. If we can learn,
when all our ties with superficiality are broken, to come to
genuine concern (*Sorge*), then we are on the way to liberty and
selfhood. Coming to terms with self is a coming to terms with
Being in its magnitude.

Our concern or anxiety (*Angst*) is not fret about some one
thing (this is fear) but a concern about life in general, its contingency and the nearness of non-being. In *Angst*, man is no
longer concerned with the everyday world but he begins to experience human existence itself and the thrilling reality of freedom.

But what was it that convinced man he had to be concerned?
What persuaded him of the nothingness of the everyday occur-
rences and spoke of a deeper meaning and a nobler endeavor?
Ultimately it is, of course, Being. Proximately, however, it is conscience, that force in man which calls him from the things men
generally regard as normal and acceptable. Conscience shows
man how inadequate, how passing, how unworthy the commonplace is.

Conscience gives man a feeling of guilt. It is a guilt he must
accept. Conscience accuses men of not having become what they
might have been. As conscience calls man beyond the everyday, as guilt fills him with sadness for not having realized himself, he is led to *resolve* and faces "the courage to be" and to be
true to whatever he is.

In the experience of *resolve*, human fellowship develops. One
individual understands himself and thus is able truly to understand another. Now men deal with each other not in superficial
social settings but with deep personal concern for self and
other. Concern and anxiety, conscience and guilt deepen man
and open him to Being, to his true self, to his every fellow-
creature.

As Heidegger deals with the factors which are worthy of man's concern and which force us to liberating anxiety, he reminds us that not conscience alone makes us anxious. There are other factors as well: the briefness of time and the threat of death.

Man must face time with the proper attitude. Conscience and guilt, death and non-being press in upon man in time. He has only so much time in which to be himself. If he lives inauthentically, then the future means nothing more than what will happen and the past means only what is done with, lived through, forever over. When the future is seen only as *coming* and the past only as *gone*, there is no resolve in the present.

When man faces time properly, however, the future for him is not what will happen but the time left in which to find himself—and the past is not over with but influences his realization that he is and was guilty. If the past speaks to man of guilt and the future, of challenge, then the present is filled with resolve. This is how things must be. For man is not a substance only but a center of responsibility for his own nature. He is only truly human when he accepts the responsibility for developing into maturity. His most critical concern must be this solicitude to become truly human.

Man then develops in the midst of these authentic concerns: life is more than its everyday existence; conscience and time restrict and encourage man. As man lives, he realizes that death is ever near, that man is a being meant for death (*sein zum Tode*). Death is to be his inevitable experience. And it is an experience that *he* must personally undergo. There comes a moment when man cannot say "not yet," "another time," "much later," "another one," "not I."

Death, the World, and God

Death is another of man's authentic concerns. It too can lead him to self-discovery. But the way modern man faces death is wrong. He says continually "people die" without identifying people, whereas he should say "I," i.e. "I die." Where death is concerned, no one can take my place. I have to do my own dying. And death means being no more. It cuts me off from all relation to the world and other human beings. It hurls me into non-being. Death teaches me that just as other things have ceased to be, so must I. Death tells me that all life is a flight to non-being. Human existence is a brief moment of light, something Being has employed to be here. Being hurled man into existence, made him Being's guardian, called him to authentic life, filled him with fear of death, and then passed from man leaving him in a void of non-being.

Death then is a puzzling reality. It is my supreme possibility (for it leads me to authentic concern about the things which really matter) but it is also the limit of all my possibilities. A man who realizes he is to die cannot give supreme concern to any other event. Man must face death every moment and every day. He must stand before Nothingness, knowing one day he will be nothing, no-thing, non-being. Unexpectedly death comes upon man. Therefore he cannot postpone his concern about death. He must be concerned about it always. To live this way is to preserve oneself from ever being lost in ambiguity, curiosity, and chatter.

This whole drama of man that Heidegger has so carefully described enacts itself on the stage of this world. The world, however, is not only the place where man happens but it makes man what he is. Man never loses the world. For he is Being-in-the-world. He is in the world. He alone, of all things in this world, knows what Being is and what it means to be in the world. The world makes man and man makes the world. In his consciousness, man is in constant dialogue with the world. Man then is never alone. He is surrounded by Being and influenced by the world. He is in communion with his fellow-creatures who know too that Being is and who also feel the world's influence.

Man can be lost. He can betray himself. He can turn traitor before Being. Alone, however, he can never be.

If only man could capture again his sense of wonder and mystery before Being and before the world, he would be healed and saved. Scientific knowledge of the world is not enough. This leads to indifference and estrangement. It alienates man from Being, distances him from Being, and ultimately de-humanizes him. It is not that science is not good. It is simply not enough. It never tells him what what-is is. It fills him with knowledge of a thousand different objects but tells him nothing of Being. Man cannot live by facts alone. He must live also in wonder, dread, reverence, and mystery before Being. Man then is not only for Being but also for the world. He is a creature of time, a conscience-ridden, death-destined, world-making, glorious moment of Being. Beyond the world and time, there is no man. Except for man, there is no Being-in-the-world. Of all things we know, nothing is more important than that man be man.

A final theme from Heidegger's thought now demands recognition. What of God? Is there God? What can God do for man? Heidegger refuses to answer this question. God, he claims, is given to man in religious experience, not in philosophical analysis. Philosophy can never name any Absolute it finds, God. The philosopher simply does not know of God. God is forever hidden to philosophy. Philosophy claims God is not Being; that if He does exist, He is more than and different from the Being which is philosophy's province. The God of Aristotle and Thomas is not the God of Abraham, Isaac and Jacob. Heidegger never asks himself a question philosophy must ponder: Is there a relationship between the religious and metaphysical view of God? He does not ask himself if there might not be many approaches to the same reality. He concludes that "Being itself is finite in essence,"[16] and excludes God from his consideration.

This much, however, is certain. If God exists, contemporary

man cannot find Him. For modern man has lost his sense of the holy. He has refused to live in reverence; he has not lived life as a consecration; and what is holy has withdrawn and hidden itself. Man needs the holy to live fully and thus he is confused. What-is-holy is not entirely absent but man is not aware of what is there or of how much he needs it. The contemporary crisis comes, in part, from a loss of faith. The twentieth century is caught between a dead world and a new world yet unborn. The old gods have left us and the God of the future has not yet come to us. This tension between the "no longer" and the "not yet" characterizes our time, its culture, its religion, its philosophy. In the midst of this age, destiny has assigned us four tasks: to recover again the true meaning of Being; to sense again holiness in life; to search after divinity; to define the word *God*.

There are then many virtues in the thought of Heidegger. He has shown us that existence is a pilgrimage and vocation. He places freedom in a saner perspective than Sartre did. Not freedom alone but time, death, guilt, conscience, and the world help man to find himself. Heidegger incisively indicts the pettiness of so many of man's unreal concerns and the emptiness of modern man's pretense. He gives us an intriguing analysis of contemporary man and twentieth-century problems. And he speaks in a way that convinces us that Christianity can express itself easily in Heidegger's categories.

One demurs at times before the thought of Heidegger. His concept of death is too definitive and too destructive for a Christian to accept. His unawareness of God disturbs a Catholic convinced that man need not be philosophically ignorant nor metaphysically crippled before God. Yet it is refreshing to see Heidegger insist that God is not only the superlative of that which is, not just another being but distinctive and divine. As one reads Heidegger he cannot help but wish he had employed the concept of analogy in his discovery of Being. Yet, in spite of all his silence and ambiguity concerning the existence of God, there seems to be not agnosticism really but expectancy in his thought. It is not Good Friday but Advent in the world of Martin Heidegger.

KARL JASPERS

Karl Jaspers, as all the existentialists, incorporates into his philosophy a study of modern life. His extensive scientific and psychiatric background gives his thought a consistency, restraint, and psychological perception not found in Sartre, Heidegger, or even Marcel.

Modern life is a life of uprootedness and insecurity. There is an emptiness to our existence because we live without spiritual purpose or belief. We have lost our sense of individual worth and of genuine community with each other. Thus we, men of the Twentieth Century, feel a loneliness that never existed before, a dissatisfaction with all our achievements, a void that our technology never quite fills.[17]

In our few words on Jaspers' thought, we shall explore some of his key themes: boundary situations, shipwreck, transcendence, and existential communication.

The situation in which man today finds himself is not accidental to the thought of Jaspers. Empirical being is always being-in-a-situation. Most of the situations we face are not of critical consequence. They do not engage us at a level deep enough to threaten or penetrate our entire way of being. Some situations, however, reach the very fundamentals by which men live. It is important to realize that, even though existence as we know it is always being-in-a-situation, Being itself is not in any one situation. Being is beyond all horizons and situations. It is only its empirical manifestation which is situational in an exclusive sense.

The most important moments of life are those in which man experiences what Jaspers calls boundary situations.[18] Among these situations, Jaspers lists suffering, guilt and death. These experiences serve an important purpose. The obstacles that life throws in my path, the suffering I feel, the guilt I live with, the death I fear, these keep me from passive and indecisive existence. As these boundary situations challenge me they deepen my decisiveness and humanity. They tell me that I, a suffering, sinful, mortal man, must do something with my life.

Of all boundary situations, death is the most important. It makes me decisive, formed, resolute, and reconciled to finitude. It keeps the important questions before me. If life were endless and its possibilities infinite, I would never become decisive or develop. It is restriction and limitation which tells me I must decide. I must be myself. For I do not have forever.

One is reminded of the words Robert Frost wrote so well and President John F. Kennedy was so fond of recalling:

> The woods are lovely, dark and deep
> But I have promises to keep,
> And miles to go before I sleep
> And miles to go before I sleep.[19]

Boundary situations are indispensable for me not only that I might come to be what I must but also because they enable me to see beyond myself and beyond the life I know. There is something beyond the boundary of my being-in-a-situation. There is Transcendence which calls to me and draws me most forcefully to itself when I suffer, bear guilt, and fear death. These experiences bring me to the end of myself and yet I sense still something more. What is beyond the boundary and beyond man? Jaspers does not think there is life but neither does he think there is nothing. Man knows there are some values and decisions he makes in life that are of indestructible significance. These must manage to survive him. Anyone, for instance, who has entered into existential communication with another person knows that what was important in the life of the other cannot be annihilated by death. He senses too that there are some things in his own life which cannot die.

When man is involved in boundary situations, there is still some intelligibility to his life. There are, however, moments when everything is lost—even minimal intelligibility. This is the situation Jaspers calls "shipwreck." It occurs when all the approaches to Transcendence are taken away.

Shipwreck

To understand fully what Jaspers means by shipwreck, one must appreciate his thought on what he calls "ciphers." A "cipher" is any ordinary finite event which points beyond itself. If an ordinary finite event suggests Transcendence, it is a cipher. The cipher then in a symbolic manner leads to Transcendence. When one reflects on it he realizes that only part of a cipher's significance falls into our ordinary experience.

As one thinks over Jasper's analysis, he realizes how often in his own life a word, a gesture, a tear or a halting attempt at articulation put him in touch with the heart of the matter. Hammarskjold seems to speak of what Jaspers calls a cipher when he writes of "a shared, timeless happiness, conveyed by a smile, a wave of the hand."[20] Graham Greene seems to be searching for a cipher into Transcendence when he writes, "If one knew the facts . . . would one have to feel pity even for the planets? if one reached what they called the heart of the matter?"[21]

"Shipwreck" is the situation which occurs when all the ciphers are silent. Man searches for intelligibility and finds chaos. His freedom destroys freedom. His religious or philosophical quest leads him to silence and emptiness. Nothing helps. Something should happen and it does not. This is "shipwreck" indeed. Nothing is left to man except Being itself.[22]

What purpose does "shipwreck" serve? Is it merely tragedy or can man gain from this dread experience? Actually, Jaspers insists that "shipwreck" is the most compelling call we ever receive from Being. "Shipwreck" proves to us that our destiny is beyond the empirical. It keeps us from being so domesticated in the world that we think there is nothing else. "Shipwreck" can be man's finest hour. For through it, he discovers Being. In this discovery, a new kind of strength is given man. The greatest moment man knows is when he can say sincerely to himself: "It is enough that Being is."

Even though "shipwreck" serves so nobly, it is something man must never choose or want. This is a failure not to be planned, a disaster we must seek to avert. "Shipwreck" will come to all of us at Being's choosing or, better, from life's inevitability. Finite man is doomed to "shipwreck" since he cannot for long embrace the Infinite in time. When it comes he must face it authentically. But we must struggle against it, even if we realize it cannot be avoided. This is defeat before which there must be no surrender even though it be defeat before which there can be no victory. We must really care about the values which are destroyed in "shipwreck" and yet face the destructibility of everything we have learned to cherish. It is when in struggle and sadness we have let go of everything temporal and finite that the Eternal comes to man in temporality and finitude. Man then in "shipwreck" finds a kind of faith for life. Before we consider this, however, a word about Jaspers' thought on existential communication is in order.

Jaspers differs strongly from Sartre in his insistence on the need for existential communication. In existential communication, the uniqueness of each participant is fully revealed and recognized. Yet each retains his independence and solitude. Existential communication stands between the extremes of isolation (what Kierkegaard called "shut-upness") and total loss of independence in another.

In existential communication or communion a person not only reveals what and who he is but he becomes someone new. He achieves openness in love. But this love must be neither sentimental nor uncritical. Rather this love is fashioned within a solidarity which cannot be broken and which enables two people to speak full truth to each other. Such a relationship, marked by honesty and awareness of limitations, rises above competitiveness and resentment to deep abiding love.

Modern man too often sees communication with another as purely superficial. It is at its maximum when individual differences are smoothed over, defects overlooked, emotions suppressed. Everything is rational, planned, right. This is not person meeting person but image meeting image or type meeting type.

Now that we have explored Jaspers' thought on boundary situations, "shipwreck" and existential communication, we can return to a theme we touched on a moment ago, namely the faith man needs for life.

A Faith for Living

According to Jaspers, man today cannot come to any genuine faith until he has passed through despair and nihilism. He must pass through these, not around them. He must undergo "shipwreck," not achieve security. Yet despair cannot be man's constant companion. If this happens, it is because man is not sincere with himself or transparent to himself. Contemporary man must face the world, not perish in it. He must see himself without friends or belief, without values or love before he can know what it means to have faith in something. The void is that which man must overcome and leap across. Despair and nihilism are inverted witnesses to the faith value or religious significance life ought to have. Faith alone can bring man out of despair, across the void, and beyond nihilism to the Absolute.

At the height of his freedom, man faces himself and life, chooses a faith to live by, and feels something inescapable and compelling at the basis of life's meaning. He begins to understand that, "Where I am completely myself, I am no longer only myself." This thought of Jaspers is reminiscent of what Catholic theology calls grace.

Man then must see himself as a being who needs freedom and faith, as a being who is called to something beyond self. As one suffers in the tragedy of "shipwreck," he chooses freedom and belief, and he finds a kind of faith for life. This is a philosophical rather than a religious faith. Man sees that there are no remedies for evil, guilt, or suffering. Yet he trusts in Being, confident that life can be made worthwhile. He does not use a God to hide behind in timidity and dishonesty. He faces life without craven capitulation and yet he gives himself to Being in hopefulness.

Jaspers differs from Sartre in his judgment that religion has a value for man. He adds, however, that religion's role is secondary and that philosophical faith is superior. More than on any other issue, Jaspers shows here the dilemma of his thought: he is caught between religion and atheism. He is unable to solve the equation harmoniously. He sees God as an intrusion, a threat to freedom; yet he insists on a relationship with Transcendence, a faith in Being, a type of revelation (ciphers) and providential care ("shipwreck") from Being. Jaspers in all his fascination with Transcendence never clearly explains what the Transcendent which creates a need for Transcendence is. He believes a Fall keeps us from seeing things as we must. He tells us we are harmed by Being so as not to forget the other. Everything points to Transcendence and yet Being is impersonal. All of man's personal values depend, it seems, on a very impersonal Reality. Man ultimately is asked to place his faith in the Faithless, to transcend his personhood for the Impersonal, to recover from shipwreck to attain something which can neither rescue nor finally harbor him. Man is asked to hear a Being which reveals and speaks but knows not itself, to answer when Being calls even though Being lacks itself the eloquence of wisdom or sufficient self-perception to name man and itself. Jaspers, therefore, preaches a heroic effort on the part of man in the face of inevitable defeat. Man, it seems, must overcome the void of this life to encounter tragically a yet greater void in death. Ultimately one suspects that Being in spite of all its meaningfulness is fundamentally meaningless. It is there without purpose, existing without perception, calling without object, reaching man without healing him, asking man to give himself to it even if there is no promise of salvation. Yet Jaspers insists we must live by faith and go on philosophizing (which is a kind of prayer).

What then must be said of the thought of Karl Jaspers? Is he an atheist or a believer in search of Belief? Is he a religious thinker or a philosophical humanist? Is he closer to theism than Heidegger or as far removed from God as Sartre? The answer is not simple. Perhaps this is due to the fact that Jaspers is in the midway point between atheism and God where one is not quite sure of either.

Jaspers' thought on the Incarnation is a typical case. He rejects the Incarnation on a number of counts. If Being were incarnate, this would destroy its Transcendence. It would no longer be beyond us but in our midst. If there were an Incarnation, this would threaten our authenticity. For we would have a perfect model of Manhood and therefore never really choose ourselves. Furthermore, Being Incarnate would be sinless and the sinless would never really share our dark and tragic history. Yet in spite of all this, the spirit of Christ must be preached and preserved. In this spirit, selfhood can be achieved.

Such then is the thought of Karl Jaspers. He has a number of virtues in spite of the difficulties we have cited. He gives us an insight into human tragedy and into Transcendence that is both poignant and persuasive. He has achieved an effective analysis of how Being touches us: in boundary situations, ciphers, and shipwreck. His philosophy has a structure capable of bearing many Christian concepts. When man is most free, he is no longer himself, Jaspers says. And the Christian thinks of grace. In the midst of our everyday history, Transcendence speaks in ciphers. And the Christian thinks of Revelation. We must believe in Being if life is to have dignity or meaning. It is not easy to believe in Being but there is no other way. Jaspers speaks in this fashion and the Christian thinks of faith. One must trust Being, even in shipwreck, with a confidence deep enough to gain serenity in the mere thought that Being, at least, is. As Jaspers describes this brave surrender, a Christian thinks of hope.

In the thought of Karl Jaspers, Being continually calls us to dialogue with itself. If only Being were a Word one wonders, what would this mean? If Being would not only call but speak. . . . But Being, one realizes, must wear a human face and have a human voice before we can understand its Word. Man needs more than a call from Being. He needs an answer also.

SÖREN KIERKEGAARD

Sören Kierkegaard cannot be called a philosopher as easily as others we have so far considered. He is the only thinker we deal with in this first chapter who is not a twentieth-century figure. Yet Kierkegaard's thought has so influenced both philosophy and the twentieth century that he somehow belongs in this survey.

Kierkegaard once made a statement that rather significantly sums up what most of his thought and life tried to express. "Luther has ninety-five theses," he once reflected. "I have only one. Christianity has not been made a reality." His every energy was bent upon making people realize (in the Newman sense of the word) their Christian vocation.

Many of the themes from his work which we shall explore will seem familiar in the light of all we have thus far treated. It is important, however, to appreciate the freshness of Kierkegaard's insights at a time when so few others spoke in this fashion. The influence he has had on subsequent existentialism will be obvious.

Since our purpose here is not detailed analysis, we shall presuppose the reader's acquaintance with Kierkegaard's pathological melancholy and with his vitriolic reaction to Hegelian thought. These are factors which influenced his writing considerably, although Kierkegaard would not be the great figure he is today if one could ascribe too much of his contribution to emotional depression or philosophical counter-attack. These factors remain, in the last analysis, factors which occasion rather than cause or explain. They are accidental to the substance of his thought, important though they be. Accidental features are seldom unimportant. His alienation from himself could become so deep at times that he would write in his *Journal:*

> I have just returned from a party, of which I was the life and soul; wit poured from my lips, everyone laughed and admired me—but I went away . . . and I wanted to shoot myself.[23]

From early childhood, the figure of Christ on the cross haunted Kierkegaard, reminding him that the world slaughters love.

We shall study Kierkegaard's thought in two main areas. His exploration of human concerns (the typical existential problems of freedom, anxiety, dread, and decision) and his reminder to us of what should be Christian concerns (God's existence, faith, salvation, prayer and the Incarnation). It is immediately evident that we have reached a point where we are studying not atheistic or agnostic but rather religious and Christian existentialism. The common denominator in all the thought we have considered is that the concern is always man. The difference comes in as-

signing him an ultimate value. For Sartre, the ultimate value is
man alone; for Heidegger it is Being; for Jaspers, it is Transcendence; for Kierkegaard, it is Christ.

Kierkegaard wrote in his *Diary* on May 12, 1839:

> All of existence intimidates me, from the tiniest fly to the
> enigmas of incarnation; as a whole it is inexplicable, my own
> self most of all. . . . [Editor's note explains word incarnation as
> "assuming bodily form, especially about Christ's incarnation."][24]

Life then is not a trivial game. It is an experience tensioned
with anxiety and guilt, blessed and burdened with freedom, demanding decision and accomplishment. It is an experience lived
by this creature man who is always being and yet ever surrounded by non-being; it is an experience endured in bondage
and responsibility by this mystery man who somehow manages
to be both limited and limitless. Life is horizoned by the boundary man never surmounts, the frontier where his ignorance begins and his understanding is rendered conceptionless. Man
stands immobile and questioning when he reaches the limit of
himself and wonders what is beyond the horizon.

Human life is lived on one of three levels.[25] They are stages
in the growth of mature personality. At any level, growth may
cease if we refuse to face life or utilize our freedom. On the
esthetic level we really choose nothing; on the ethical level, we
choose ourselves; on the religious level, we choose God.

The esthetic stage is the one in which man makes no decisions.
He lives only in the present. He looks for all the answers of life
in things outside of himself.

One is reminded of the words John Henry Newman (a contemporary of Kierkegaard) once addressed to his first students at
the Catholic University of Ireland:

> Gentlemen: if I am called upon to state the difference between
> a boy and a real man, I should say this—that a boy lives on

what is without and around him: the one depends upon others for instruction and amusement; the other is able in great measure to depend upon himself. You come here to learn to pass from the state of boys to the state of man.

The ethical state is not fully liberating. It bespeaks a certain heroism but it also leaves one enslaved to the social and the legal. The ethical level of existence is law's level and duty's level. It forever indicts and accuses man, making him more aware of failure than of rebirth and new life. The ethical stage of life gives man a type of salvation, but it is a salvation of fortitude and resistance rather than of personal encounter. Ethics gives man a sense of stern dignity but too often its stoical victory seems unworthy of the effort. It is quite different from faith where a concrete individual does not so much overcome himself as come to know the Eternal in time.

The man of faith lives on the religious level. He lives not unmindful of self nor preoccupied with self. The remarkable thing about the man of faith is that he renounces the finite and the temporal only to get them back again. He breaks with the world and is returned to the world. This is the type of man we shall be dealing with as we study Kierkegaard. The man of faith, Kierkegaard reminds us, might be anyone. He might be the neighborhood grocer—a man who realizes that his wife, family, or daily tasks are not "the answer." The religious man knows that in faith alone are the sublime and pedestrian fused (Christ and the neighborhood grocer), in faith alone are the unconditional and the relative united (God and managing a store). Every human concern is meant ultimately to be a faith-concern.

Of all human concerns, none are more decisive than freedom and yet the great temptation in life is to abandon freedom. Because we have a kinship with Nothingness as well as with Eternity, our freedom can move us in either direction. It is our freedom which is a determining factor. Thus we have a hand in making ourselves what we become. Freedom perishes at the point where we choose only the secure and visible things of life, forsaking the risk-laden invisible. Faith's function is to proclaim the security of the irremedially uncertain. It is to name as man's destiny not the temporal but the Eternal, which has entered into and transformed the temporal.

Despair

As man freely chooses and creates himself, he must avoid despair. Despair comes from within a man and is due to unsettling the balance within us between finitude and infinitude. We can easily delude ourselves into thinking we are infinite or only finite. God destroys, as He must, our illusions of being infinite. We must destroy our own illusions of being only finite, i.e., creatures of conformity with no individuality.

Man's delusion that he is infinite can lead him into what Kierkegaard calls the "despair of possibility." The individual lives with all his imagined possibilities. He is a man who lacks maturity because he fails to discover which of his possibilities are attainable and which are not.

If there is anything one might term a characteristically American temptation, it is what Kierkegaard calls "the despair of possibility." The American creed is that the individual can do anything if he tries hard enough. He is a creature with no limits. Americans subtly proceed from the enviable notion that man ought to be free to do all he should, to the unreal notion that he *must* do anything he can do, to the ultimate fiction that there is nothing man cannot do. This leads us so often not to genuine liberty but to the compulsory freedom demanding we do everything and filling us with guilt at every failure. Thus we ignore our limitations and defy them. We are convinced we are infinite. The old think they are young; the indecisive imagine themselves to be leaders of men; the ordinary man thinks himself an intellectual. Everyone feels guilty about not having enough talent. Everyone has to do everything every time. No one seems willing to be just something or someone. This is what Kierkegaard would call "the despair of possibility."

Man then can delude himself into thinking himself infinite in the "despair of possibility" or only finite in the "despair of necessity." Here man lives fatalistically. This is a life of mute submission, of spiritual suffocation, of tired thought and tedious platitude. This is a world in which one never finds an individual, including himself. It is a world of human bondage and slavery peopled with a race of men, whose language knows not the vocabulary of freedom. Here liberty has neither a name nor a home.

Man living his life in either "the despair of possibility" or "the despair of necessity" is trying to solve life on his own terms. Thus, he despairs. He knows he is not infinite nor only finite. He needs help from outside. He needs a God to show him his infinite potential and to reveal to him his finite structure. Without God, man turns to despair, then to defiance, finally to hate. Without God, a man might defiantly try to realize himself but he must do this in torment and with no hope of either success or salvation.

Christian Concerns

Sören Kierkegaard is unmistakably and completely a Christian. He cannot therefore be content with a study of human concerns unless these are related to Christ and thus become Christian concerns. Kierkegaard does his most brilliant writing in this area. In the process, he gives us a perennial insight into the predicament of what we call "modern man," his anguish and aspirations. When Kierkegaard wrote in his diary on May 12, 1839, that all existence frightened him, he included in the range of existence the mystery of the Incarnation. He insisted always that if man was to be saved from despair, from the sickness unto death, he would have to discover God in the very temporal process in which human development takes place. Ultimately, Kierkegaard will demand, as every Christian must, that God be discovered not only in the world of contingency but in the person of Jesus Christ.

Kierkegaard was not a Christian because he fancied Christianity a simple solution or Christ an easy escape. "I felt a dread for Christianity," he confesses, "and yet felt myself so strongly drawn towards it."[26] On another occasion he admits "In Christianity itself the contradictions are so great. . . ."[27]

It might suit our purpose best to take from Kierkegaard's reflections a number of themes a Christian should consider, without trying to weave these into an artificial unity. Hopefully, from this choice a mosaic of Kierkegaard's thought will be pieced together, sufficient to acquaint the reader with the direction taken by Kierkegaard, and sufficient also to inspire the reader with the vitality of Kierkegaard's approach.

Fundamental to any Christian consideration is the existence of God. God is found, Kierkegaard argues, not in proofs but in a struggle between God's will and man's. God's existence as well as truth's discovery is a matter of personal commitment, not objective demonstration. Some truth evidently can be appropriated without personal commitment: thus, science, mathematics, and logic. This truth is true regardless of who thinks it. But the truths men live by are of a different order. God then is found only in personal surrender. So necessary is this personal dimension for Christianity that Christianity never does exist until someone embodies it in his life. Christianity is never really true until it transforms someone.

When a man accepts God in his life, when he lives by personal commitment to truth, he is a man of faith. Faith is the realization that the ultimate question concerning the meaning of life is beyond our control. It is a leap made by man with freedom, from himself to God. It is a risk, a perilous venture, a courageous gesture, a personal engagement when one is not sure of the cost, a donation of all that one has to a God one never understands. A modern novelist describes well what Kierkegaard would mean by faith.

> What is faith? A blind leap into the hands of God. An inspired act of will which is our only answer to the terrible mystery of where we came from and where we are going. What is hope? A child's trust in the hand that will lead it out of the terrors which reach from the dark.[28]

Faith is that in which man is infinitely interested because his eternal salvation depends upon it.[29] It is something which is not objective. It does not even depend upon correct Biblical exegesis for its existence. If this were true, a man's faith would somehow be different as Biblical exegesis advanced. To think in this fashion is to confuse faith with science. No, faith is not an objective experience. Faith rather is a subjective response. It exists only when a man will sacrifice and die for Christianity. In fact, risking one's life is the only ultimately convincing proof of Christianity's truth. Faith is not born in objective security or in unshakable certitude but in fear and trembling. So important is the subjective response that *how* a man believes means much more than *what* he believes. Faith then asks much of man. "To become subjective is the most difficult of all tasks"[30] and subjectivity is the only way to approach a divine object.

Kierkegaard realizes that his stress on subjectivity is so strong that he might jeopardize Christianity in his very effort to save it. He tries to correct this by reminding his reader that subjective Christianity is not the same as immanent religion. Immanence claims that man's religious instincts and the object of his faith are from man. Kierkegaard never claimed this. The object of man's faith is God, not man. Immanence does not require an order beyond man to explain man's religious striving. Kierkegaard, on the other hand, always insisted on man's need to refer to a transcendent order. This order is personal, divine, and temporalized in Christ.

This leads us logically to the concept of salvation in Kierkegaard. The man who accepts God's existence and lives personally by faith does so not only out of a need for God but in the hope of salvation. Before God, man realizes there is a weakness in his soul and that he is powerless to cure it.[31] He realizes he has sinned and that he will sin again. A man who looks at himself only philosophically never comprehends the seriousness of the human predicament or the miraculous love by which God rescues us. The first act of redemption is an accusation against us. We are sinners and need divine forgiveness.

> To the sinful woman . . . everything had become indifferent: the hostility of the environment . . . the opposition of the Pharisees . . . their cold derision . . . and yet she dared this because one thing was absolutely important to her: to find forgiveness.[32]

Eternity breaks through time in an Instant and declares the whole of temporality sinful. And yet Christ dies for our forgiveness. In Christian forgiveness, dread and hopelessness are taken away. Christian, then, can cry to Christian the saving words of the Gospel: "Thy sins are forgiven." This saving forgiveness is purchased at the cost of suffering love and is totally undue to man. Splendid though salvation is, man can still reject it. And he does. So often Christians ask themselves whether or not God wills their salvation. In reality, the question ought to be whether we shall will our salvation. God always does.

A Christian who believes in God, lives by faith, accepts forgiveness, must also spend a lifetime in prayer and love. Prayer seems so simple but since it involves transparency and honesty in man's relationship with God, its task is really endless. So often we pray hoping God will hear us, forgetting that the finest prayer is that we might hear God. Prayer should be a supreme admission of our helplessness. It ought to be a plea not that things go as we wish nor that the world be made in our image but that we be transformed in God. The trouble with our prayer so often is that we wish to go to a certain point with God. God, however, is just the opposite of what goes only to a certain point.

A Christian is asked, finally, to accept the commandment of love and to fulfill it. There is no norm that demands more from a man than love itself. For love knows no limits. It is forever dissatisfied with what it accomplishes. What Christianity demands is not really that we love any more deeply than those who do not know Christ. The depth with which men love is not a sectarian accomplishment. Even love of enemies is not distinctively Christian love. What is distinctive about Christian love is the relationship it has to one's love for God. Love for one's fellow-men is the surest and most Christian sign I have that my love for God is real. As my love for my fellow-men grows, my capacity for Christianity increases.

From love, I know how to suffer. Some think themselves courageous when they suffer. In reality, many of us suffer not because of some noble motive but because we have pursued selfish ambitions. Frequently the deepest sorrow we know is not the sorrow of failing in responsibility or in love for others but the sorrow that comes from not having what we want. There was a time when to be a Christian was to know persecution and to leave all. Now Christianity has become a new worldliness, a secularized, routine religion. Now Christians consider suffering and disappointment the greatest evils they endure. One wonders if there are any Christians left in Christendom!

The Incarnation

The summation of all Kierkegaard's thought on Christian concerns expresses itself in the mystery of the Incarnation.[33] Despite the total otherness of sinful man, God enters our history and takes his place beside us. This is *the* Instant of human history. And man's intelligence tells him that Christ at this Instant is incomprehensible. For Christ is God and man; he is the Eternal in time; the unchangeable God made a creature. Christ is the absolute Paradox. Intelligence cannot help here. All that intelligence does is to help us see more clearly that Christianity is beyond understanding. Christ then can only be reached in a passionate decision of faith. And reaching Christ is everything. Faith in the Incarnation means that we accept the incredible paradox of Christ as credible; the supreme possibility as real.

The Incarnation is Love made flesh. It is a gesture on the part of God meant not to demonstrate the greatness of man but the greatness of God's love. We do nothing to merit the Incarnation. God alone decides the Instant when Eternity becomes time. For us, the Incarnation is a mere fact. It happens not because we do anything but because God has decided to do everything.

The Incarnation is proof that God is love and that God will pursue man until He overtakes man in his sin. The Incarnation is both a judgment and a redemption for sinful man. On the night Jesus was betrayed, we learned we were all sinners. Christ is the only man who has the right to demand that all men feel guilt over his death. The cross in this sense of its being a universal indictment against us proves better than any miracle the divinity of Christ.

The cross which accuses is also the cross from which Christ prayed for his enemies. Not only the death of Christ but also this pardoning prayer belongs to the Gospel. Christ gave his life not only for the truth of our wickedness but for the truth of his forgiving love. Thus before Christ we are rejected and accepted, judged and redeemed, declared unworthy and made His brethren.

We are then loved by God in Christ with a love that surpasses all understanding and with a love which is the death knell of our sinful state. In Christ, God came into this world for each one of us.

These then are some insights into the thought of Kierkegaard which might help us to appreciate modern man and the God he seeks. The value and virtues of Kierkegaard are so clear that a justification of them seems hardly necessary. There are two aspects of his thought, however, which seem to be weaknesses.

One problem with Kierkegaard is his evaluation of reason's role in the process of man's being Christianized. One almost gets the impression from Kierkegaard that the *concept* of God and Christ does not matter. We agree with Kierkegaard that a person-to-person relationship is at the heart of Christianity. We agree that this relationship cannot be produced by thought. We can even accept the fact that a person who has passion in his atheism may be closer to God than one who toys with theism as an hypothesis. Yet to say this much is not to say everything. It is difficult to agree that the right concept of God is not liberating. It is impossible to see why the right relationship with God must be opposed to right reason. One suspects that even in Christianity man needs his intellect to keep him from nonsense. Perhaps Kierkegaard's contention (and here we can accept him) is not that faith conflicts with reason as such but rather with reason which has forgotten its proper limits. A man has to give Christ not only reason's service but passion and personal interest as well.

A second problem Kierkegaard poses is one which disturbs Catholic theology more than its Protestant counterpart. Catholic theology feels uneasy with Kierkegaard's exaggerated individualism. Each man seems alone in his act of faith. Newman also demanded personal involvement in faith but not quite so introspectively or subjectively as Kierkegaard. For Newman, history and the Church had an influence in faith so that man in his search for God was not alone and anguished. He is in the com pany of God's people, enlightened by God's Word which the Church has kept faithfully, strengthened by sacramental encounter. For Newman, man finds Christ in Faith, Word, Church, and Sacrament. Seen in this light, the lyrical, isolated grandeur of Kierkegaard somehow seems a little less grand in its inability to provide a solid foundation for Christian community.

GABRIEL MARCEL

There are many similarities between Sören Kierkegaard and Gabriel Marcel. Both existentialists evolve their thought in terms of fidelity to God and Christian commitment. Marcel tends to be less subjective and less individualistic than Kierkegaard. Thus, he proves to be a more satisfactory thinker in those areas where Kierkegaard seems to be at his weakest.

Marcel makes a distinction between problem and mystery in man's approach to reality.[34] A man who works in the area of problem seeks pragmatic intelligence in the world. His object is technical control and scientific certitude of reality. This is a necessary part of man's knowledge and life. It is not, however, everything. Man lives not only by certitudes but also by intuition. Intuition makes man aware of his situation in existence. It reveals to him aspects of reality which science cannot reach. Intuition cannot take the place of scientific knowledge. It does not preclude further analysis. It is not a retreat into anti-intellectual fantasy. Intuition is simply a way of reaching Being on another level. Being cannot be comprehended by science alone. What can science tell me of the sacredness of a sleeping child? What can science tell me of the sanctity and elusive mystery of life which all of man's instruments never measure?

The proper object of metaphysics is not problem knowledge but mystery. Man lives by intuition and mystery—no other creature man knows functions on this level. Man is the only creature who can evaluate his life. He is the only creature who questions himself. In fact, he is the creature who calls his whole life into question, the being who demands to know what Being is.

Marcel, as we have said, is not as subjective as Kierkegaard. He does not demand what Kierkegaard called "the crucifixion of understanding" before man can know Being, mystery or subjective truth. Intuition may not be empirical knowledge but it is experiential, probative, and fundamentally intellectual. Marcel does not retreat into agnosticism or nescience before the reality of Transcendent Being. Man, he insists, can know something of every type of being, God included.

Before man can understand Being, however, something is demanded of him. He must make an act of trust in Being. He must grant the validity of intuition and the presence of mystery. If he does not do this, he is condemned to live his life with thing and problem knowledge.

To the man who gives himself to Being in fidelity a certain comprehension of life's mystery is granted. He begins to appreciate the fact that he is an incarnate being and one who does not understand himself. He does not understand himself because he is never fully present to all of himself. For example, I might grasp the past and see the things I did as a child. I can understand them better now because I am older. Yet as I do this I do not know all I was as a child because I cannot appreciate exactly how a child sees and feels unless I am a child. Thus there is something of me which I have lost and cannot grasp. The full meaning of my life transcends my conscious awareness of all of it at any given moment. I remain always a partial stranger to my own depths. I need someone else to bring me to a fuller vision of myself. For man is not only incarnation of Being. He is also made for communion, that is, for going beyond himself to the whole of Being. All are given a call to presence with other people. This is a call to overcome the pride of thinking I can draw all my strength from myself. To be proud is to have communion with no other. In pride, I fear relationship with others because others make me aware of my imperfections.

If I can overcome pride and respond to the call of communion, I enter into presence with other people. Presence with another is not physical presence but communion. A man in the same room with me may be quite alien and aloof. I cannot feel his presence. I cannot be myself with him. When he listens to me, he is not attentive. He withholds himself.

Marcel then differs completely from Sartre. Sartre demands that man keep to himself. Marcel sees this as self-destruction. The more ego-centric I am, the less I exist. The deeper my communion with others, the closer I am to the mystery of Being and the surer is my intuition into its structure. I can trust Being if I can trust my fellow-men.

Marcel insists that man has not been made only to be Being's incarnation nor only for communion with others. He is made for Transcendence and for God.

A man begins to realize as he discovers himself and others that life must have a meaning beyond this. Even if life is pointless, the very fact that I can raise the question makes it possible that life might have a point. As man searches for the point of life, he is looking for something he can live and die for. This is his call to Transcendence and to an ultimate Presence—a Presence giving life its sacredness, a Presence partially perceived in oneself and gradually deepened in the others I meet. It is this Ultimate Presence alone which can heal man's emptiness with wholeness, which can humanize him again as he begins to lose his grip, which can fill him with a hope more powerful than despair.

We have been given the dreadful power of keeping ourselves from this Ultimate Presence which is a divine reality. But we cannot do this without losing ourselves. We have been made to give faithfulness and creative fidelity to God.

The positive and trustful response to Being which Marcel envisions includes many factors. It demands, for example, our ability to distinguish between "being" and "having" in life.[35] "Having" occurs when I possess and control the things by which I live. They are possessions that belong to me and from which I remain somewhat aloof. "Having" becomes all wrong when I begin to use people as I use possessions. I have "business" to do with people but I am never at their disposal or in communion with them. "Having" is furthermore all wrong when I give my selfhood to things. My very being becomes vulnerable when I surrender that being to objects and when I compromise its dignity by a concern over the order of having. Christian poverty is a safeguard against this betrayal of being to objects.

The order of "being" is man's proper realm. We participate in being and yet we can lose control over it. For created being is constantly threatened. Our being is saved only by our creative fidelity to Being. Creative fidelity is opposed to dead conformism and to fatalistic freedom. Freedom is not for freedom's sake but for the sake of Being. Thus before Being we must stand in wonder and humility, freely choosing Being, not to use it or remain aloof from it but to serve it. Being is not something that belongs to me but rather something which is a part of me.

This is the vast difference between suicide and martyrdom. One who commits suicide uses Being as a possession. He relegates Being to the order of "having." He feels life is at his disposal. Life, however, is not property but a devotion to Being in freedom. Martyrdom is totally different. The martyr too chooses to let life be taken from him. He does not, however, dispose of his life. He offers it to God in dedication for the sake of his fellow-men. The martyr reminds us that we were made for "being" and not for "having." In his blood and suffering, he tells us that our loyalty belongs to God.

Likewise, the saint, who knows not martyrdom, exists to remind us of the Being for whom we were made. The saint does not withdraw from the world but only from "having" the world that he might be at Being's service in the world. The saint reminds us that our primary trust must be given to a Person and not to a world: we give our first fidelity to a Presence, not to a creature. Actually the saint unites himself deeply to the world but he does this in union with the world's creative source, i.e., from a divine perspective. This is why, as Kierkegaard reminded us, those who surrender the temporal and finite for Christ receive them back more richly.

Man's creative fidelity to Being then is a consecration in freedom. Like a vow, it proves to all that there is a permanence to man and to Being. In spite of the changeableness of life, man has constancy and Being has durability. Like a vow, creative fidelity is an appeal to God for strength amidst the uncertainties of life. It is an act of hope that man will not fail since God does not fail.

Thus life is a grace and a gift. Its sanctity and dignity are forever ennobled in freedom and fidelity. Life, however, can only redeem its fullest promise if we believe in God. Being is not enough unless Being has personality, divinity, and is worthy of our communion with it. Our belief in God, however, cannot be contingent upon our demands. It must be a faith that draws its strength not from an idea of God nor from a formula which explains God but from a perception of God's Presence. Only the Presence of God, never our idea of Him, proves stronger than the catastrophes of life.

Marcel feels, as Kierkegaard does, that having witness to faith is far more convincing than proofs. Thus Marcel has some difficulty in accepting the Thomistic proofs as strict demonstrations of God.[36] They do not seem sufficiently existential for him. Nor do they prove irrefutable since they fail to convince so many. We shall examine the import of the Thomistic proofs for contemporary man in our theological section of this book. Marcel insists that faith or unbelief is preceded by man's general approach to Being. If man mistrusts and refuses Being, if life is a problem rather than a mystery, if "having" is the only order he knows, then man can never accept Thomistic proofs or the God whose existence they demonstrate.

A living witness to faith and God is the most impressive thing man can do. There is an intriguing aspect of witness to God. Some truth, for example mathematical truth, does not need constant witness. Once mathematical truth is discovered, all subsequent reporters of it are, in a sense, superfluous. But no past witness to God or Christ can make a present witness to God or Christ superfluous. Christianity, and all men, are in constant need of sanctity and martyrdom or at least of consecration in witness.

The Presence of God and the truth of eternal life must ever remain if the sacredness of human life is to continue. It is unexpected but ever true that when men abandon the idea of eternal life, they are led not to more care for life in this world but to less. Nazism and Communism are a twentieth-century proof of this.

Man, finally, must live by hope in Being and in God. Hope is the driving force behind what it means to be human.[37] It is not just a biological urge to survive. It is not a trust that such a thing will occur. Rather, it is confidence in God and in His Presence. It gives meaning to everything human.

Too often we confuse hope with desire and illusion. Desire is directed to the finite and sometimes to the impossible. Hope is directed to the infinite and the real. I might, for example, "hope" that a friend will live in spite of every evidence to the contrary. This is not hope but intense desire and noble sentiment. But to know that my friend's life has value and that his importance cannot die, this is hope. The hope Marcel speaks of is not a stoical search for meaning in life, a meaning one seizes after a struggle against impossible odds. Hope, rather, is serene and creative. It convinces us that some things do not depend upon us and yet will succeed. It convinces us that life is a gift and Being, trustworthy. It tells us that tragedy is never the final word on man.

Because I trust Being, I come to trust myself and my fellow-men. I am filled with hope, knowing that I am worthwhile and that life is good. Hope enables me to see that I have a purpose and a mission, that the substance of my life will benefit my fellow-man and please God. In hope, I enter into deep communion with those about me. In hope, I find Being and rely upon God.

These then are some aspects of Marcel's thought which may prove helpful for the purpose we have in mind. Marcel convinces us that our need for a Transcendent Presence is deep and irradicable. We cannot live only with the presence of ourselves and each other. Human life, rather, seems to be embraced by a living reality more dynamic and free and meaningful than we are. There is a Presence which always makes itself known and yet which never appears, an Encompassing Reality from which everything comes to us and to which we owe all that we are. In fact, every human life seems to be a temple enshrining this Gracious Presence.

CONCLUSION: WHERE IS OUR PHILOSOPHICAL THOUGHT TAKING US TODAY?

A number of things seem to characterize the way we are thinking today. All of these endeavors are encouraging. We are engaged in a massive effort to know man. This is helpful for Christianity. It is only when man forgets man that we must fear. If man is concerned with man, he will eventually find God. What are some of these characteristics?

In an age of bewildering technology our philosophers insist that science must not be worshipped. It must not become a new idolatry. Science serves man best when it does what science was meant to do. Sometimes, however, the reaction against scientism becomes so severe that objectivity itself seems to be under attack.

Another characteristic of contemporary thought is its insistence on our coming to terms with the real issues of life: God, death, conscience, time, self-hood. A Christian sympathy with the human concerns which make us one family is a powerful pre-evangelical situation for the preaching of Christ's message. If we have not suffered with our fellow-men, we have no right to preach to them. We are not above our fellow-men but at their service. We have all suffered frightfully in this century and we do not know why. We have all sinned when we did not really want to. We all feel the fascination with the things man has made. We have all feared so much and so many that we have become afraid of each other, at times distrustful of the entire human venture.

A concern with freedom is another value spoken of frequently today. The question does not seem to be, as it was some decades ago, whether we are free or not. The question grants freedom's existence and asks whether freedom is a curse or a gift and how it is to be used. Christianity's function is to prove that self-affirmation in freedom need not lead to a denial of God. In fact, Christianity's message will seem most relevant today when it shows modern man that freedom has little purpose and lesser creative value apart from Christ.

Existentialism makes it clear that twentieth-century man is desperate in his search for love and personal communication. We are a generation which has lost each other. We must destroy the barriers we have erected in ignorance and fear. This has always been Christianity's function. It was never more needed than today when our mistrust of each other can lead us to destroy all human life.

A final characteristic of today's thought is its constant reference to Transcendence. We seem to understand better now Pascal's comment "The last proceeding of reason is to recognize that there is an infinity of things which are beyond it." Christianity preaches a Transcendence beyond reason and preaches also that Being has a human face and a gentle heart.

Our task today then is to understand the men we must reach. We must show we can identify with those who do not know who they are, who feel the terrible cross of uncertainty about life's meaning, those for whom God is not life and salvation but a question mark. We too must be modern men who see a broken and tragic world—men who have no final answer but preach a Way, men who cannot say anything worthwhile when they see a child die in pain or a young President assassinated in the streets of Dallas. We must ever be men who never explain the cross but accept it and live by it. We are convinced that there is something meaningful beyond the tragedy we endure. This much we know and not very much more.

No man is an Island, entire of itself;
every man is a piece of the continent,
a part of the main;
if a clod be washed away by the sea,
Europe is the less . . .
any man's death diminishes me because I am involved in Mankind;
And therefore never send to know for whom the bell tolls;
It tolls for thee.

NOTES

[1] Address of Cardinal Suenens in St. Peter's on October 28, 1963, the anniversary of the election of John XXIII.

[2] I have found *Existentialism and Religious Belief* by David E. Roberts (Oxford University Press, 1959) especially helpful for this entire first chapter.

[3] Karl Rahner, *Theological Investigations* (Baltimore, Helicon Press, 1963), vol. II, p. 269.

Existentialism and Religious Belief 57

4 Robert O. Johann, *America* (September 5, 1964), p. 234.

5 Jean-Paul Sartre, *Being and Nothingness,* trans. H. E. Barnes (New York, Citadel Press, 1964). Hereafter referred to as *Being.*

6 Jean-Paul Sartre, *Nausea,* trans. Lloyd Alexander (New York, New Directions, 1959), pp. 180–181. Copyright © 1965 by New Directions. Reprinted with permission of the publisher, New Directons Publishing Corp.

7 *Being,* p. 439.

8 *Ibid.,* p. 615.

9 Jean-Paul Sartre, *No Exit,* trans. S. Gilbert (New York, Knopf, 1948), p. 61. Copyright 1946 by Stuart Gilbert. Copyright 1948, 1949 by Alfred A. Knopf, Inc.

10 Jean-Paul Sartre, *Existentialism,* trans. B. Frechtman (New York, Philosophical Library, 1947), p. 25.

11 *Being,* p. 566.

12 *Nausea,* p. 180.

13 Most of the thought herein referred to comes from Heidegger's classic work *Sein und Zeit* (English trans., *Being and Time*).

14 Dag Hammarskjold, *Markings,* trans. Leif Sjoberg and W. H. Auden (New York, Knopf, 1964), p. 46. Translation Copyright © 1964 by Alfred A. Knopf, Inc., and Faber & Faber, Ltd. Forward Copyright © 1964 by W. H. Auden.

15 *Ibid.,* p. 63.

16 Martin Heidegger, *Existence and Being,* trans. D. Scott, R. Hull, and A. Crick (Chicago, Regnery, 1949), p. 377.

17 Karl Jaspers, *Man in the Modern Age,* trans. E. Paul (London, George Routledge and Sons, 1933).

18 Jaspers' thought on boundary situations is elaborated in his three-volume opus *Philosophie* (Berlin, Springer-Verlag, 1932).

19 From "Stopping by Woods on a Snowy Evening" from *Complete Poems of Robert Frost.* Copyright 1923 by Holt, Rinehart and Winston, Inc. Copyright 1951 by Robert Frost. Reprinted by permission of Holt, Rinehart and Winston, Inc.

20 *Markings, op. cit.,* p. 96.

21 Graham Greene, *The Heart of the Matter* (New York, Viking, 1948), p. 128. Copyright 1948 by Graham Greene.

22 Jaspers writes of "shipwreck" (*Scheitern*) in the final pages of *Philosophie.*

23 *The Journals of Søren Kierkegaard,* trans. Alexander Dru (New York, Harper Torchbooks, 1959), pp. 50–51.

24 *Diary of Søren Kierkegaard,* trans. Greda M. Anderson, ed. Peter C. Rhodes (New York, Philosophical Library, 1960), p. 19.

25 One can find a brief outline of Kierkegaard's thought on three levels of existence in *Concluding Unscientific Postscript,* trans. David Swenson and Walter Lowrie (Princeton University Press, 1944), pp. 261–265. A more complete presentation of the same thought is available in *Stages on Life's Way,* trans. Walter Lowrie (Princeton University Press, 1940).

26 *The Journals,* entry 841.

27 *Ibid.,* entry 16.

28 Morris L. West, *The Devil's Advocate* (New York, Dell, 1964), p. 86. Copyright © 1959 by Morris West. Words addressed by Bishop Aurelio of Valenta to Monsignor Blaise Meredeth.

29 Much of Kierkegaard's thought on faith is contained in his work *Concluding Unscientific Postscript* which he wrote under the pseudonym Johannes Climacus.

30 *Concluding Unscientific Postscript, op. cit.,* p. 116.

31 Most of Kierkegaard's thought on sin is contained in *Concept of Dread,* trans. Walter Lowrie (Princeton University Press, 1944) and *Sickness unto Death,* trans. Walter Lowrie (Princeton University Press, 1941).

32 "Two Discourses at the Communion on Fridays," in *For Self-Examination,* trans. Walter Lowrie (Princeton University Press, 1944), p. 265.

33 The reader can find Kierkegaard's thought on the incarnation chiefly in the following works: *The Works of Love,* trans. David F. and Lilian M. Swenson (Princeton University Press, 1946); "Judge for Yourself," in *For Self-Examination, op. cit.; Training in Christianity,* trans. Walter Lowrie (Princeton University Press, 1944); *Concluding Unscientific Postscript, op. cit.;* and the four volumes of *Edifying Discourses,* trans. David F. and Lilian M. Swenson (Minneapolis, Augsburg, 1943–1946).

34 Marcel's thinking on this issue can be found in his *Metaphysical Journal,* trans. B. Wall (Chicago, Regnery, 1952), and in "Reflection and Mystery," *The Mystery of Being,* trans. G. Fraser (Chicago, Regnery, 1951), vol. 1.

35 Gabriel Marcel, *Being and Having,* trans. K. Karrer (Boston, Beacon Press, 1951).

36 In his *Journal,* Marcel examines the Cartesian proofs of God's existence. In *Being and Having,* he examines the Thomistic proofs.

37 Gabriel Marcel, *Homo Viator: Introduction to a Metaphysic of Hope,* trans. Emma Craufurd (Chicago, Regnery, 1951).

2 The Literary Expression of Modern Man's Values and Problems

In any attempt to understand modern man fully, one must look to not only the philosophers but also to those who write the enduring literature of any particular period. We are convinced that every effective insight into man's nature brings one to God. A perennial philosophical intuition, therefore, can always serve Christianity to some degree. Likewise, every true artistic expression of the universe, can bring one to God. In choosing the literary spokesmen whose message rings true, one must leave out so many others he would like to include. This is, however, not a work of literary analysis but one in which we attempt an appreciation of our contemporaries to whom the Gospel of Christ must be preached. In our survey, we shall deal mostly with men who give indications of no clear religious loyalty. We shall not exclude, however, those who are convinced Christians or Jews. One regrets that the present purpose of this book does not permit a study of William Faulkner, Ernest Hemingway or Tennessee Williams. Perhaps a later book or another study may permit us to return to these authors. If we are not content with what must always be a partial study, we shall never finish.

It is not certain that all the conclusions we draw are conclusions the authors under consideration would recognize. It is a fallacy to think that the author is the best judge of his work or that the author is always aware of all the repercussions of his own creative insight into reality. On the other hand, one is never justified in drawing conclusions arbitrarily from literature. They must be conclusions easily or at least convincingly justified.

FYODOR DOSTOEVSKY (1821–1881)
Faith is no longer easy for us

Before we can put the conclusions we draw into proper perspective, a brief note on biography and on the books we deal with will be necessary. With each of the authors we study, we shall try to follow the same outline: biography, notes on books, and, finally, themes.

Biography

Dostoevsky was born in Moscow. His background was a series of tortured memories. His father was killed brutally by serfs who despised his discipline. He himself was sentenced to death for anti-government activities. He was reprieved only in the final moments while before the firing squad. The suffering in his life included five years in Siberia and five years in the army. Perhaps the happiest years of his life were the last ten years he lived. Dostoevsky was a man whose most passionate loyalty belonged to Orthodoxy and to Russia. The world would one day find a new redemption, Dostoevsky dreamed, from Russian soil by means of the Russian people and in the dogma of Orthodox Christianity.

Notes

A note on each of the four books which provide the material for our discussion is now in order. The first of these is *Crime and Punishment*. Dostoevsky wrote this work in 1866 and critics

generally agree it is his most perfect work in design and execution. It is the story of a young man, Roskolnikov, whose name
in Russian means "dissenter." He is an intelligent and introspec-
tive figure who believes himself justified in murdering an old
woman for her money. While killing his victim, he is forced to
commit a second murder to escape detection. Both women are
killed with an ax. As the story progresses, Roskolnikov suffers
intense remorse. He finds redemption from his guilt only when
he confesses his crime and accepts the purifying love of Sonya.
She accompanies Roskolnikov to Siberia for a seven-year term
of imprisonment. Together they await return to Russia and a new
life. *Crime and Punishment* is remarkable for the depth and passion of its sympathy for humanity. It preaches a redemption
from guilt only in confession, suffering, and love.

The second novel is *The Brothers Karamazov* (1879–1880).
This is the most complex and the most profound of Dostoevsky's
books. It deals with the Karamazov family, Fyodor and his four
sons. Three of his sons are legitimate (Dmitri, Ivan, and
Alyosha). One, Smerdyakov, is illegitimate. The novel is an almost exclusive study of the three legitimate sons of Fyodor
Karamazov. Dmitri is the eldest son. He is a symbol of man's
need to be purified in suffering. Dmitri chooses to suffer for the
murder of his father even though he did not commit the crime.
In this pain, he seeks redemption from all his sins and guilt.

Ivan, the second son, is a journalist and an atheist. He and the
youngest son, Alyosha, are pitted against each other in the novel.
Ivan sums up his position of disbelief rather well when he says:

> It's not that I don't accept God, you must understand,
> it's the world created by Him I don't and cannot accept.[1]

Alyosha, the third son, is the symbol of goodness and belief.
He is the idealist, the lover of all humanity, the man of faith

who exercises no concern over the material. His character is
revealed somewhat in his description of one of Christ's miracles.

> . . . Cana of Galilee, the first miracle. . . . It was not men's
> grief but their joy Christ visited. He worked His first miracle to
> help men's gladness. . . . He who loves men loves their gladness
> too. . . . There's no living without joy.[2]

The last son, Smerdyakov, enters little into the story. He is an
epileptic and a mentally retarded boy. It is Smerdyakov who
kills Fyodor, his father, though Dmitri is imprisoned for the
crime. Smerdyakov hangs himself later in the story.

The Brothers Karamazov is Dostoevsky's final statement on religion, morality, sin, and suffering. The Grand Inquisitor section
of the novel, which we shall analyze later, is one of the most
powerful scenes in all literature. There are a number of recurring
Dostoevsky ideas which run through the story. Once again the
theme of redemption in suffering (Dmitri) occurs. The constant
dialogue between Ivan (evil) and Alyosha (goodness) reflects
Dostoevsky's own inner conflict. In these two figures one sees
Dostoevsky's religious temperament (Alyosha) and his skeptical
intellect (Ivan).

The Idiot (1869) is the novel most characteristic of Dostoevsky's style. It is a narrative about Prince Myshkin. The Prince is
not really an idiot at all. He is considered a fool by his contemporaries because he is so gentle, self-sacrificing, and saintly.
His great love for others is contagious and brings most to love
him in spite of themselves.

The Possessed (1871) is Dostoevsky's weakest novel. It contains a series of portraits of "possessed" men. Stavrogin is the
unscrupulous and conscienceless "hero" of the novel. Kirillov is
an insane atheist. Verhovensky is a murderer. Though the book
is not strong as a novel, it will prove quite useful for our study.

Themes

With this very sketchy background on biography and story, we proceed to our proper object, a study of the themes delineated by the author. What Dostoevsky is telling us in all his writings is that faith is no longer easy for us. He especially should know. For he is intensely concerned about the problem of belief in God, both for himself as well as for all men. "God has tormented me all my life," he writes.[3] "God torments me. I think of nothing but that."[4]

The first major theme Dostoevsky explores might be described in this fashion: Faith never fully overcomes the temptation to unfaith; nor does atheism fully overcome the tendency to faith.

There are a number of passages which illustrate this first major theme. Ivan in *Karamazov* is a case in point. He has unmistakably rejected God and yet he cannot ignore Him. Thus, he once confides to Alyosha:

> What is surprising . . . is not that God should really exist; the marvel is that such an idea, the idea of the necessity of God could enter the head of such a savage, vicious beast as man. It is such a touching, holy, wise idea and does man so much honor.[5]

Ivan, in fact, in spite of his atheism, does not only admire belief from a distance. He hopes also that belief might be one day something he can accept.

> "I've led the conversation to my despair. . . ."
> "You will explain why you don't accept the world?" said Alyosha.
> ". . . dear brother, I don't want to corrupt you or to turn you from your stronghold. Perhaps I want to be healed by you."
> Ivan smiled suddenly quite like a gentle child. Alyosha had never seen such a smile on his face before.[6]

Conversely, Alyosha, so deeply committed to faith, is not without his moments of doubt. When Lise, a fourteen-year-old paralytic, describes a dream in which she is surrounded by devils, Alyosha listens intently. The devils try to seize her, Lise explains, and she can only resist them by crossing herself. During the dream, she feels at times a desire to revile God. At these moments, the devils start to advance again. When she has completed her description, Alyosha looks at the girl and confesses he has had the same dream and experienced the same temptation.[7]

The tension and fear Alyosha finds in his faith are explained to Lise in even greater detail.

> "My brothers are destroying themselves . . . my father, too. And they are destroying others with them. It's the primitive force of the Karamazovs . . . a crude, unbridled, earthly force. Does the spirit of God move above that force? Even that I don't know. I only know that I, too, am a Karamazov . . . Me a monk, a monk! Am I a monk, Lise? You said just now that I was."
>
> "Yes, I did."
>
> "And perhaps I don't even believe in God."
>
> "You don't believe? What is the matter?" said Lise quietly and gently.
>
> But Alyosha did not answer. There was something too mysterious, too subjective in these last words of his, perhaps obscure to himself, but yet torturing him.[8]

At another point in the story, Alyosha reveals his confusion to Rakitin, an unbeliever. In this episode, Alyosha's faith is shaken because a saintly priest, Father Zossima, is not preserved from corruption after death. Alyosha expected his faith and his God to work a miracle. When they do not, he finds himself repeating his brother Ivan's words of doubt. One is reminded here of Gabriel Marcel's insistence that our belief cannot be contingent upon our demands. Rakitin senses Alyosha's torment and tries to make the most of it.

"Can you really be so upset simply because your old man has begun to rot?"

"I believed, I believe, I want to believe, and I will believe, what more do you want?"

". . . So now you are in a temper with your God. You are rebelling against Him."

"I am not rebelling against my God; I simply 'don't accept His world.'"

Alyosha suddenly smiled, a forced smile.[9]

Dostoevsky does not limit this tension in faith to only two of his characters. Sometimes the problem is shown not so much in Ivan who symbolizes lack of belief or in Alyosha who symbolizes belief but in Dmitri who is searching. Dmitri and Alyosha are here speaking.

"Rakitin explained it to me yesterday, brother, and it simply bowled me over. It's magnificent, Alyosha, this science. A new man's arising—that I understand. And yet I am sorry to lose God."

"What will become of man then . . . without God and immortal life? All things are lawful then. They can do what they like?"[10]

Dimitri continues a description of his faith-difficulty.

"It's God that's worrying me. That's the only thing that's worrying me. What if He doesn't exist? What if Rakitin is right —that it's an idea made up by men? Then, if He doesn't exist, man is the chief of the earth, of the universe. Magnificent! Only how is he going to be good without God? That's the question. I always come back to that. For whom is man going to love then? To whom will he sing a hymn . . . Rakitin says that one can love humanity without God . . . only an . . . idiot can maintain that."[11]

There is then in the writings of Dostoevsky a dialectic with
faith that functions on two levels. Ivan and Alyosha, as we have
seen, feel the tension between faith–unfaith within themselves.
Apart from the internal stress each feels, there is an external slash
between faith–unbelief, e.g.,

> Ivan vs. Alyosha (*Karamazov*)
> Shatov vs. Kirillov (*Possessed*)

This preoccupation with the tug from both sides reflects, as
we have mentioned, Dostoevsky's own problem with faith. In his
writings and his life, the cry that there is nothing mingles with a
serene and joyful affirmation that life is meaningful. He is a man
not insensible to the power of denial but one whom that power
ever taunts but never conquers.

Dostoevsky once wrote in his diary: ". . . it is not like a child
that I believe in Christ and confess Him. My hosanna has come
forth from the crucible of doubt."

"nothing but hosannah is not enough for life, the hosannah
must be tried in the crucible of doubt." — spoken by
the devil in Ivan's hallucination

Karamazov XI, 9.

The Value of Unbelief

The second major theme Dostoevsky develops comes as a bit
of a surprise to a man of faith. Dostoevsky grants no unshakable
security to either faith or atheism. Both involve a risk. Faith may
demand courage but it never gives a man so much certitude that
the struggle is forever finished. Once the mathematical truth that
two and two are four is accepted, there is never a struggle in
maintaining this acceptance. With faith, one accepts but not
without a continuing effort.

We said that the second theme is somewhat unexpected. We
might describe it with this formula: Atheism has a value.

To illustrate this thesis, we shall work mostly with *The
Possessed*. In the epilogue to the novel, Stavrogin, one of the
possessed, is in conversation with Tikhon, an elderly monk.

"Complete atheism is more honorable than secular indifference."

"So, that's how you see it; indeed you're absolutely surprising."

"The complete atheist, whatever you say, stands high up the ladder, on the rung below that which leads to perfect faith . . . but the indifferent man has no faith whatsoever except perhaps craven fear."[12]

The most effective atheist in *The Possessed* proves to be not Stavrogin but Kirillov. It almost seems that Dostoevsky uses Kirillov to rid himself of his temptations against faith. In the process, he creates a rather attractive personality. Kirillov is a mystic of sorts, a man who admires Christ, and gives himself for others. His atheism leads him, however, to commit suicide as a demonstration of the fact that man's will is totally independent. Kirillov is a strange individual who manages to reflect in his life both sanctity and atheism. He shows forth an "atheism" that is not devoid of value. In a rather moving conversation between Kirillov and Verhovensky, Kirillov gives evidence of the goodness and nihilism which co-exist within him.

KIRILLOV: If there is no God, then I am God. . . . If God exists, all is His will and from His will I cannot escape. If not, it's all my will and I am bound to show self-will. . . . I am bound to shoot myself because the highest point of my self-will is to kill myself with my own hands. . . . I am bound to show my unbelief. . . . I have no higher idea than disbelief in God. I have all the history of mankind on my side. Man has done nothing but invent God so as to go on living and not kill himself; that's the whole of universal history up till now. I am the first one in the whole history of mankind who would not invent God.

VERHOVENSKY: Do you know, to my thinking, you believe perhaps more thoroughly than any priest.

KIRILLOV: Believe in whom? In Him? . . . Listen to a great idea:

there was a day on earth, and in the midst of the earth, there
stood three crosses . . . The day ended; [all] died and passed
away . . . that Man was the loftiest of all on earth. He was that
which gave meaning to life. The whole planet, with everything
in it, is mere madness without that Man. There has never been
any like Him before or since . . . that is the miracle, that there
was or never will be another like Him. And . . . the laws of
nature did not spare even Him . . . What is there to live for?
. . . I can't understand how an atheist could know that there is
no God and not kill himself on the spot . . . Man has hitherto
been so unhappy and so poor because he has been afraid to
assert his will in the highest point and has shown his self-will
only in little things. . . . For three years I've been seeking for
the attribute of my godhead and I've found it; the attribute of
my godhead is self-will. That's . . . my new terrible freedom.
For it is very terrible. I am killing myself to prove my independence and my new terrible freedom.[13]

This dialogue contains some of Dostoevsky's most incisive
thinking on atheism. One can see in Kirillov's speeches a number
of key Existentialist themes. Once man destroys God, man must
become God. Kirillov's statement is reminiscent of Sartre's idea
that to be man is fundamentally the desire to be God. This passion makes man God when he believes there is no God.

Another point in Kirillov's argumentation is that man cannot
invent God in order to solve the problem of living. Man must
face all the facts without God. Once again one is reminded of
Sartre's insistence that man should live without looking to even
an idea of God.

Kirillov has evidently a deep respect for Christ. This we find
over and over again in atheism and in Existentialism. One recalls
Karl Jaspers' tribute to the spirit of Christ and what that spirit
can mean in man's search for genuine selfhood. So deep is
Kirillov's admiration for Christ that the thought of Christ's death
drives him to desperation. If Christ did not triumph over human

evil or nature's disregard for life, how can any of us hope to find meaning in existence?

Man then is forlorn. Kirillov gives us a grim picture of man. He has no God. He has destroyed Christ. He has only his will and his freedom to rely upon. The most man can do, Kirillov argues, is to assert that self-will even if one must take his life to prove his total mastery of himself.

Kirillov looks for a type of salvation in the existence and dominion of freedom. Exactly what this salvation offers is unclear. It leads to man's destruction. Yet it proves him divine. The attribute of Kirillov's godhead is self-will, he insists. Yet his very self-will which gives him divinity, brings him death.

Dostoevsky is not without sympathy for Kirillov. Nor would Kierkegaard have been without sympathy for Kirillov. It is better to be a committed atheist, both men would argue, than to live as an unimpressed Christian. The Christ of the Apocalypse is more severe with the lukewarm than with the violently hostile.

Atheism then has a certain value. Stavrogin recognizes this in a letter he writes later in the novel. He speaks of Kirillov, now dead.

> Kirillov, in the greatness of his soul, could not compromise with an idea, and shot himself; but I see, of course, that he was great-souled. . . . I cannot even be interested in an idea to such a degree.[14]

The Value of Faith

The third and final major theme we would like to consider from Dostoevsky's writings might be phrased simply: Faith has a greater value. The term of the comparison is, of course, atheism. Dostoevsky is not saying that atheism is nothing but that faith is more.

Dostoevsky is convinced that for life to be meaningful, a re-

ligious viewpoint is necessary. Man must begin with the conviction that there is a God and that man is immortal. When he
forever questions or finally denies these truths, he becomes less
human. To kill God is to kill man. If God is dead, so is man.

It would be too much to expect that the deeper value of faith
is something easily demonstrated. Dostoevsky seems to set about
this task in stages. First, the absolute statement: God must be
affirmed. Then, the practical directive: He is best affirmed in
intuition. Last of all, the irrefutable conclusion: God affirmed in
Christ gives faith its deepest meaning. Let us take these in turn.

First, God must be affirmed.

Zossima in *Karamazov* takes this for granted.

> Much on earth is hidden from us but to make up for that we
> have been given a . . . mystic sense of our living bond with the
> other world . . . the roots of our thoughts and feelings are not
> here but in other worlds. . . . If that feeling grows weak or is
> destroyed in you . . . you will be indifferent to life and even
> grow to hate it.[15]

This thought, that without God all is indifference, is found
continually in Dostoevsky. One sees it also in Sartre's conclusion
that since man is going to die it makes little difference if one
gets drunk alone or leads a nation. It is a thought that Camus
develops in *The Stranger*, as we shall see later. Camus says it
makes little difference if one marries or does not, if one kills or
does not. Without God, man is like a compass which has no
magnetic field.

In *The Possessed*, Stephan Trophimovitch speaks of man's
need to affirm God.

> The mere fact of the ever-present idea that there exists some-
> thing infinitely more just and more happy than I am fills me
> through and through with tender ecstasy—and glorifies me—
> whoever I may be, whatever I have done! What is far more es-

sential for man than personal happiness is to know and to believe at every instant that there is somewhere a perfect and
serene happiness for all men and for everything. [God is necessary to me, if only because He is the only being whom one can
love eternally. . . . If I have once loved Him and rejoiced in my
love, is it possible that He should extinguish me and my joy and
bring me to nothingness again?] The one essential condition of
human existence is that man should always be able to bow down
before something infinitely great. If men are deprived of the infinitely great, they will not go on living and will die of despair.
The unmeasurable and the never-ending are as essential for man
as the little planet on which he moves.[16]

In this passage from *The Possessed*, there is a somewhat different evaluation of affirming God's existence. Zossima told us of
the need to affirm God lest life become an indifferent or an intolerable experience. Here, man's need not only to affirm but also
to worship God is stressed. One must not only find God but love
Him and rejoice in this love. God is necessary not only to explain
life but to give man Someone whom he can love eternally. It is
not only man's meaning but his power to love which rests in the
affirmation of God.

This need for man to give devotion to Someone is mentioned
by Ivan in *Karamazov:*

So long as man remains free, he strives for nothing so inces-
santly and so painfully as to find some one to worship.[17]

Really, Dostoevsky insists, it is never a question of whether
man will worship but whom he will worship.

. . . to live without God is nothing but torture. . . . Man cannot
live without kneeling, he could not bear it, nobody would be
capable of it; if he rejects God, he kneels before an idol of wood
or of gold or an imaginary one. . . . They are all idolaters and
not atheists. That's what they ought to be called.

If God must be affirmed, He is best affirmed in intuition. This
is the second stage illustrating our theme of faith's deeper value.

Dostoevsky's approach to God is not objective and probative.
Rather it is subjective and necessitating. He argues to God's
existence not from intellectual analysis but from man's nature
and needs. He is unmistakably an existentialist.

Prince Myshkin in *The Idiot* speaks of affirmation in intuition.
The following passage occurs about an hour after a chance meeting with an atheist who impresses Myshkin but always seems
"beside the point" in speaking of God.

> An hour later, when I was going back to the hotel, I came upon
> a peasant woman with a tiny baby in her arms. She was quite a
> young woman and the baby was about six weeks old. The baby
> smiled at her for the first time in its life. I saw her crossing her-
> self with great devotion. "What are you doing, my dear? . . ."
> 'God has just such gladness every time he sees from heaven that
> a sinner is praying to Him with all his heart, as a mother has
> when she sees the first smile on her baby's face.' That was
> what the woman said to me almost in those words, this deep,
> subtle and truly religious thought—a thought in which all the
> essence of Christianity finds expression; that is the whole con-
> ception of God as our Father and of God's gladness in man,
> like a father's in his own child—the fundamental idea of Christ!
> A simple peasant woman! . . . The essence of religious feeling
> does not come under any sort of reasoning or atheism. . . .
> There is something else here, and there will always be some-
> thing else—something that the atheists will for ever slur over;
> they will always be talking of something else.[18]

Dostoevsky then sees "proof" for God in the simple experiences
of life rather than in elaborate demonstrations. A child's smile
can say nothing or everything.

Dostoevsky returns again to the affirmation of God in intuition
in *The Possessed*. Shatov speaking to Stavrogin observes:

Science and reason have, from the beginning of time, played a secondary and subordinate part in the life of nations: so it will be to the end of time. Nations are built up and moved by another force which sways and dominates them. . . . It is the force of the persistent assertion of one's own existence, and a denial of death. It's the spirit of life. . . . It's . . . 'the seeking for God,' as I call it more simply. The object of every national movement, in every people, and at every period of its existence is only the seeking for its god. . . . There never has been a nation without a religion, that is, without an idea of good and evil. . . . Reason has never had the power to define good and evil, or even to distinguish between good and evil.[19]

The dialogue between Shatov and Stavrogin ends quite dramatically:

STAVROGIN: . . . do you believe in God, yourself?
SHATOV: I believe in Russia . . . I believe in her orthodoxy . . . I believe in the body of Christ . . . I believe that the new advent will take place in Russia . . . I believe. . . .
STAVROGIN: And in God? in God?
SHATOV: I . . . I will believe in God.
Not one muscle moved in Stavrogin's face. Shatov looked passionately and defiantly on him . . . [and] cried at last: "I haven't told you that I don't believe."

Dostoevsky's insistence on a subjective affirmation of God's existence is reminiscent of Gabriel Marcel's thought on mystery knowledge and intuition or even of Karl Jaspers' thesis of the unexplainable call of unknown Transcendence. Dostoevsky is less objective than Marcel; yet he is more sure of his conclusions than Jaspers. Perhaps, when all is said and done, he is closer to Kierkegaard than to any other thinker. He possesses the subjective preferences and the unshakable convictions of Kierkegaard. Kierkegaard, however, sees anxiety in almost every aspect of Christian experience. Dostoevsky seems to feel that if man can only affirm God's existence boldly, the rest of Christian experience will follow rather serenely. For both men, faith in God has an insufficiency about it, apart from Christ.

The third and final stage demonstrating faith's value leads us from the affirmation of God's existence by intuition to the affirmation of God in Christ. A few passages from Dostoevsky's letters and notebooks, rather than from his novels, show his concern with this type of faith. He once wrote:

> And yet God sometimes sends me moments of complete serenity. It is in such moments that I have composed in my mind a profession of faith in which everything is clear and holy. This profession of faith is very simple. This is what it is: to believe that there is nothing finer, deeper, more lovable, more reasonable, braver and more perfect than Christ. . . . More than that: if anyone had told me that Christ is outside truth, and if it had really been established that truth is outside Christ, I should have preferred to stay with Christ rather than truth.

In another letter, written in 1871, he writes:

> This man has insulted Christ in my presence. . . . But in insulting him, he has never asked himself: 'Whom are we to put in His place?' Ourselves? No, he has never given a thought to that.

In his notebook, he observes:

> We continually go astray if we have not Christ and His faith to guide us . . . repudiate Christ and the human mind can arrive at the most astounding conclusions.

These then seem to be the major themes Dostoevsky develops on the problem of faith. In an age when men took faith so much for granted and saw it as so necessary for social acceptability, his message is both strident and vital. He sounds a note of disharmony with his surroundings, a note not so much of confusion and protest as it is a note of summons. Faith and atheism, he insists, are never fully tranquil. Each has a value. The critical question is this: Which of the two does man need more? Which of the two does man greater honor?

The Grand Inquisitor

For all practical purposes, we have completed our survey of Dostoevsky's thought. We mentioned before that the Grand Inquisitor section from *The Brothers Karamazov* is one of the finest in all literature. It has much to say to us of the problem of atheism in our day. Some notes on this chapter from *Karamazov* might prove helpful and serve as a fitting conclusion to our study of Dostoevsky.

The Grand Inquisitor section of *The Brothers Karamazov* is the title of chapter five in the fifth book. Chapter four, however, is worthy of comment before we undertake a study of chapter five proper. In this chapter, Ivan tries to give Alyosha some of the reasons why he cannot believe. He bases his atheism on three arguments.

Ivan confesses that he cannot love his neighbor at close range.

It's just one's neighbor, to my mind, that one can't love, though one might love those at a distance. . . . Christ-like love for men is a miracle impossible on earth. He was God. But we are not gods.[20]

This is not the only problem with belief. Far more difficult to accept is the horrible suffering of children who are innocent and easy to love.

But then there are the children and what am I going to do about them. That's a question I can't answer. . . . If all must suffer . . . what have children to do with it, tell me please? It's beyond all comprehension why they should suffer. . . . Some jester will say, perhaps, that the child would have grown up and have sinned, but you see he didn't grow up. . . . I want to forgive, I want to embrace, I don't want more suffering. . . . It's not God that I don't accept, Alyosha, only I must respectfully return Him the ticket. . . .[21]

This protest of Ivan is re-echoed in the writings of a modern atheist whose writings we will study in detail later. A comparison of both passages may be useful at this point. In *The Plague,* Albert Camus describes a scene in which a child dies from the plague in terrible agony. Camus writes this section of the novel with frightening intensity since it is one of the main reasons for his atheism. Paneloux, a priest, and Rieux, an unbelieving doctor, observe the child's pain.

Paneloux . . . sank on his knees, and all present found it natural to hear him say in a voice hoarse but clearly audible across that nameless, never-ending wail: "My God, spare this child!" But the wail continued without cease. . . . A gust of sobs swept through the room, drowning Paneloux's prayer, and Rieux, who was still tightly gripping the rail of the bed, shut his eyes dazed with exhaustion and disgust. . . . And now the doctor grew aware that the child's wail, after weakening more and more, had fluttered out into silence . . . it was over. . . . His mouth still gaping, but silent now, the child was lying among the tumbled blankets, a small, shrunken form, with the tears still wet on his cheeks. . . .

"Come, doctor," [Paneloux] began.

Rieux swung round on him, fiercely. ". . . that child . . . was innocent, and you know it as well as I do! . . ."

"What we'd been seeing was as unbearable to me as it was to you."

Rieux turned to Paneloux. "I know. . . . But . . . there are times when the only feeling I have is one of mad revolt."

"I understand." Paneloux said in a low voice. "That sort of

thing is revolting because it passes our human understanding. But perhaps we should love what we cannot understand. . . ."

"No, Father, I've a very different idea of love. And until my dying day I shall refuse to accept a scheme of things in which children are put to torture."[22]

The final argument Ivan offers in his witness to unbelief, is a demand that justice be given to all now, not at the end of time.

I must have justice, or I will destroy myself. And not justice in some remote infinite time and space, but here on earth and justice that I can see myself. I have believed in it. I want to see it . . . I want to be there when everyone suddenly understands what it has all been for.[23]

The conversation between Ivan and Alyosha continues. Ivan then tells Alyosha the story of the Grand Inquisitor (chapter five).

Christ reappears in human history, is recognized, and once again begins to perform miracles. An aged Spanish cardinal (the Grand Inquisitor) sees Christ and arrests Him. The cardinal explains carefully to Christ that He must be banned as a heretic. Christ is a threat to the Church. The Church has finally persuaded people, after centuries, to forfeit their freedom and to find happiness in servitude. Now Christ comes along to upset this comfortable situation in which all are reasonably content. Therefore, He must die.

Christ is a danger and a triple temptation to the Church.

The first temptation Christ represents is manifested in His willingness to feed men easily, making bread from stones if need be. The Church must feed them, the cardinal insists. If men are fed, they will not want to be free.

. . . never, never can they feed themselves without us! . . . In the end they will lay their freedom at our feet, and say to us, "Make us your slaves, but feed us."[24]

In a second way, Christ is a temptation to the Church. He intends to convince men to live in freedom and love rather than to live bewitched and docile before the awesome reality of miracles. Christ expects too much of men, the cardinal argues. Appealing to men in freedom and love, he causes unrest, confusion, and unhappiness. The Church knows better. She will substitute mystery, miracle, and authority for Christ's unreal invitation to another type of life.

The Church has accepted the third temptation, one which Christ rejected. She has responded to the devil's offer to rule all kingdoms of the earth.

The Church, the cardinal continues, is not a harsh ruler. She will allow men to work, to play, even to sin a little. But she must first dispense with Christ.

> We shall allow them even sin. They are weak and helpless, and they will love us like children because we allow them to sin.[25]

Therefore, Christ must surely understand that He must die. To save the Church, he, the Grand Inquisitor, must burn Christ.

ALYOSHA: How does your poem end?

IVAN: I meant it to end like this. When the Inquisitor ceased speaking he waited for some time for his Prisoner to answer him. His silence weighed down upon him. He saw that the Prisoner had listened intently all the time, looking gently in his face and evidently not wishing to reply. The old man longed for him to say something, however bitter and terrible. But He suddenly approached the old man in silence and softly kissed him . . . That was all his answer. The old man shuddered. His lips moved. He went to the door, opened it, and said to Him: 'Go and come no more . . . come not at all, never, never!' And he let Him out into the dark alleys of the town. The Prisoner went away.

Chapter Four then anticipates for us some of the concerns of twentieth-century atheism. Ivan's reasons are repeated today. Sartre calls us to "engagement" for mankind but to hatred for our neighbor at close range. Hell is one's neighbor at close range. Camus, as we have seen, protests bitterly at the suffering of innocent children. Marx and Communism will take Dostoevsky's plea for justice now and try to bring it to reality on this earth, in the present, and by equitable economic distribution. Chapter five, although an unfair estimate of Roman Catholicism (Dostoevsky disliked the Catholic Church strongly), is a reminder to us that Christianity has been given to men as a pledge of freedom and love.[26] Christianity is that religion which preaches Love made flesh in Christ Jesus. And the Christian Church believes herself to be the very sacrament of freedom.

Dostoevsky then gives us a remarkably complete study of man, faith, and unbelief in this contemporary era. He felt that Western atheism could endure only for a time. For man cannot live without God. Christ will come to Europe and to Russia once again.

THOMAS WOLFE (1900–1938)
Man has only man and he is oppressingly alone

With Thomas Wolfe, we deal with a writer who could hardly be more different from Fyodor Dostoevsky. Dostoevsky was a Russian, Wolfe, an American; the former was a deeply committed Christian, the latter, religiously indifferent; the one wrote creatively and gave literature a host of memorable characters, the other could write only of himself and his own life.

Thomas Wolfe was a native of Asheville, North Carolina. This became Altamont in his early books, Libya Hill in his later writings. Wolfe himself was Eugene Gant in his first works. He called himself George Weber in his final books, trying to create a character other than Eugene Gant. Wolfe changed the name of

his new protagonist but he still remains very much Thomas
Wolfe.

Wolfe attended the University of Chapel Hill, received his
master's degree from Harvard, and taught English at New York
University. He has written four important books: *Look Homeward, Angel* (1929), *Of Time and the River* (1935), *The Web
and the Rock* (1939), and *You Can't Go Home Again* (1940).
We shall deal with themes principally from two of these books.

Wolfe was a sensitive, insecure, lonely individual. He was
gargantuan in his approach to life. He was not capable of a
measured mastery of anything. He seems almost to have attacked
rather than experienced life. He possessed "an almost insane
hunger to devour the entire body of human experience." Wolfe
was unmistakably autobiographical, ever the chronicler of his
own brief days. Few have written so completely of their ad-
ventures, experiences, and feelings. He was once well described
as a novelist who writes novels about a novelist writing novels.

Books

Look Homeward, Angel was the first book Thomas Wolfe
wrote. Its original title was "O Lost." Later it was changed to its
present name, borrowing a line from Milton's *Lycidas*. In Milton's poem, Michael is invited with these words to turn from
strange lands and weep over a disaster at home; he is asked to
take pity on the drifting corpse of Lycidas.

The book describes the childhood, adolescence, and young
manhood of Eugene Gant. It closes with Eugene's decision to
leave his home in Altamont to continue his search for self.

You Can't Go Home Again was published after Wolfe's pre-
mature death. As the novel opens, George Weber has just returned from Europe. He is now a man of mature age, a man who
at last can see his limitations. He has lost what Kierkegaard
would call his "despair of possibility." On a trip back to his birth-

place, he realizes that you can't go home again to the past, to the joy and innocence of youth, to the acceptance and affection a child receives. A man must move forward. The novel has a note of sadness to it which contrasts strongly with the exuberance of *Look Homeward, Angel.*

The book describes the years of the Depression, Weber's association with his mistress Esther Jack (Mrs. Aline Bernstein) and his break with his beloved editor Foxhall Edwards (Maxwell E. Perkins of Scribner's), probably due to criticism that his books were dominated by his editor.

There are a number of themes Thomas Wolfe develops which provide an insight into modern man and into the modern American. We shall deal with five themes, four of which are typical existential preoccupations.

Five Themes

Wolfe is intrigued and pained with the experience of loneliness. *Look Homeward, Angel* deals with this theme. It is a story of what Wolfe calls, a man's hunger in his youth, unsatisfied because he is lost and has no home.

> Naked and alone we came into exile. In her dark womb we did not know our mother's face: from the prison of her flesh have we come into the unspeakable and incommunicable prison of this earth.[27]

The title of Wolfe's final novel, *You Can't Go Home Again,* suggests the same interest in home and exile as man wanders from birth to death. It is worthy of note that Wolfe's final sickness came upon him when he was alone and on a journey. His constant attempt to reconcile himself to his frightful loneliness influenced most of his emotional life and literary output. Yet, Wolfe surprises us. Though he is himself lonely and though he writes in an age when cynicism was in vogue, he never becomes pessimistic. For this reason, his insights are more enduring and more typically American than those of Eugene O'Neill, for example, or Tennessee Williams.

Eugene Gant comes to understand that ". . . men were forever strangers to one another, that no one ever came really to know anyone. . . ."[28]

Life then for Wolfe is a long journey of exile, a yearning for love and security which may never be attained, a wandering from birth to death in search of peace and fulfillment which never come.

It is not loneliness alone which occupies Wolfe's attention but something quite akin to loneliness, the search for self-knowledge. To even the most casual reader of Wolfe, this concern with identity and fulfillment is evident on almost every page. It is strange that Wolfe who wrote so much of himself found himself ever more elusive and self-contradictory. The lyric, for example, which runs all through *Look Homeward, Angel* states that man is involved in a quest for "the great forgotten language, the lost lane-end into heaven, a stone, a leaf, an unfound door."

There is something typically American about Wolfe's search for an answer to himself. He speaks our idiom, articulates our fears, bespeaks optimism and restless energy, loves this land of ours, its dreams, its people, its spirit. Because of this, he has become the favorite of countless college students.

The ghost of his brother Ben tells him in *Look Homeward, Angel* that self is not found in strange lands but is hidden deep inside a man. As Michael the Angel, he is invited to weep not over distant tragedies but over the sadness inside himself. Though Eugene Gant hears Ben's observation, he still feels he must leave Altamont, and go beyond its mountains, to find himself. He senses that the world he is about to meet is chaotic and lacks universal values, yet he senses too that it is a world of challenge and opportunity. And so hopefully he sets forth.

A third theme Wolfe develops is typical of him. In spite of loneliness and self-confusion, there is a tragic grandeur about man. The greatness of man emerges undiminished in spite of all the odds against him. Man may be forever assailed. He is never overcome. Here, Wolfe might best speak for himself. In a passage from *You Can't Go Home Again,* he articulates his philosophy in words filled with power and eloquence.

For what is man?

First, a child, soft-boned, unable to support itself on its rubbery legs, befouled with its excrement, that howls and laughs by turns, cries for the moon but hushes when it gets its mother's teat; a sleeper, eater, guzzler, howler, laugher, idiot, and a chewer of its toe; a little tender thing all blubbered with its spit, a reacher into fires, a beloved fool.

After that, a boy, hoarse and loud before his companions, but afraid of the dark; will beat the weaker and avoid the stronger; worships strength and savagery, loves tales of war and murder and violence done to others; joins gangs and hates to be alone; makes heroes out of soldiers, sailors, prize-fighters, football players, cowboys, gunmen, and detectives; would rather die than not out-try and out-dare his companions, wants to beat them and always to win, shows his muscle and demands that it be felt, boasts of his victories and will never own defeat.

Then the youth: goes after girls, is foul behind their backs among the drugstore boys, hints at a hundred seductions, but gets pimples on his face; begins to think about his clothes, becomes a fop, greases his hair, smokes cigarettes with a dissipated air, reads novels, and writes poetry on the sly. He sees the world now as a pair of legs and breasts; he knows hate, love, and jealousy; he is cowardly and foolish, he cannot endure to be alone; he lives in a crowd, thinks with the crowd, is afraid to be marked off from his fellows by an eccentricity. He joins clubs and is afraid of ridicule; he is bored and unhappy and wretched most of the time. There is a great cavity in him, he is dull.

Then the man: he is busy, he is full of plans and reasons, he

has work. He gets children, buys and sells small packets of everlasting earth, intrigues against his rivals, is exultant when he
cheats them. He wastes his little three score years and ten in
spendthrift and inglorious living; from his cradle to his grave he
scarcely sees the sun or moon or stars; he is unconscious of the
immortal sea and earth; he talks of the future and he wastes it
as it comes. If he is lucky, he saves money . . . he consumes
rich food and golden wine that his wretched stomach has no
hunger for; his weary and lifeless eyes look out upon the scenery
of strange lands for which in youth his heart was panting. Then
the slow death, prolonged by costly doctors. . . , the perfumed
carrion, . . . the fast motor hearses, and the earth again.

This is man: a writer of books, a putter-down of words, a
painter of pictures, a maker of ten thousand philosophies. He
grows passionate over ideas, he hurls scorn and mockery at another's work, he finds the one way, the true way, for himself,
and calls all others false—yet in the billion books upon the
shelves there is not one that can tell him how to draw a single
fleeting breath in peace and comfort. He makes histories of the
universe, he directs the destiny of nations, but he does not know
his own history, and he cannot direct his own destiny with
dignity or wisdom for ten consecutive minutes.

This is man: for the most part a foul, wretched, abominable
creature, a packet of decay, a bundle of degenerating tissues, a
creature that gets old and hairless and has a foul breath, a hater
of his kind, a cheater, a scorner, a mocker, a reviler, a thing
that kills and murders in a mob or in the dark, loud and full of
brag surrounded by his fellows, but without the courage of a
rat alone. . . .

. . . Yes, this is man, and it is impossible to say the worst of
him, for the record of this obscene existence, his baseness, lust,
cruelty, and treachery, is illimitable. His life is also full of toil,
tumult, and suffering. His days are mainly composed of a million
idiot repetitions—in goings and comings along hot streets, in
sweatings and freezings, in the senseless accumulation of fruit-

less tasks. . . . He is the dweller in that ruined tenement who, from one moment's breathing to another, can hardly forget the bitter weight of his uneasy flesh, the thousand diseases and distresses of his body, the growing incubus of his corruption. This is man, who, if he can remember ten golden moments of joy and happiness out of all his years, ten moments unmarked by care, unseamed by aches or itches, has power to lift himself with his expiring breath and say: 'I have lived upon this earth and known glory!'

This is man, and one wonders why he wants to live at all. A third of his life is lost and deadened under sleep; another third is given to a sterile labor; a sixth is spent in all his goings and comings, in the moil and shuffle of the streets, in thrusting, shoving, pawing. How much of him is left, then, for a vision of the tragic stars? How much of him is left to look upon the everlasting earth? How much of him is left for glory and the making of great songs? . . .

. . . Here, then, is man, this moth of time, this dupe of brevity and numbered hours, this travesty of waste and sterile breath. Yet if the gods could come here to a desolate, deserted earth where only the ruin of man's cities remained, where only a few marks and carvings of his hand were legible upon his broken tablets, where only a wheel lay rusting in the desert sand, a cry would burst out of their hearts and they would say: 'He lived, and he was here!'

Behold his works:

He needed speech to ask for bread—and he had Christ! He needed songs to sing in battle—and he had Homer! He needed words to curse his enemies—and he had Dante, he had Voltaire, he had Swift! He needed cloth to cover up his hairless, puny flesh against the seasons—and he wove the robes of Solomon, he made the garments of great kings, he made the samite for the young knights! He needed walls and a roof to shelter him—and he made Blois! He needed a temple to propitiate his God—and he made Chartres and Fountains Abbey! He was born to creep upon the earth—and he made great wheels, he sent great engines thundering down the rails, he launched great wings into the air, he put great ships upon the angry sea!

Plagues wasted him, and cruel wars destroyed his strongest sons, but fire, flood, and famine could not quench him. No, nor the inexorable grave—his sons leaped shouting from his dying loins. The shaggy bison with his thews of thunder died upon the plains; the fabled mammoths of the unrecorded ages are vast scaffoldings of dry, insensate loam; the panthers have learned caution and move carefully among tall grasses to the water hole; and man lives on amid the senseless nihilism of the universe.

For there is one belief, one faith, that is man's glory, his triumph, his immortality—and that is his belief in life. Man loves life, and, loving life, hates death, and because of this he is great, he is glorious, he is beautiful, and his beauty is everlasting. He lives below the senseless stars and writes his meanings in them. He lives in fear, in toil, in agony, and in unending tumult, but if the blood foamed bubbling from his wounded lungs at every breath he drew, he would still love life more dearly than an end of breathing. Dying, his eyes burn beautifully, and the old hunger shines more fiercely in them—he has endured all the hard and purposeless suffering, and still he wants to live.

Thus it is impossible to scorn this creature. For out of his strong belief in life, this puny man made love. At his best, he *is* love. Without him there can be no love, no hunger, no desire.

So this is man—the worst and best of him—this frail and petty thing who lives his day and dies like all the other animals, and is forgotten. And yet, he is immortal, too, for both the good and evil that he does live after him. Why, then, should any living man ally himself with death, and, in his greed and blindness, batten on his brother's blood?[29]

This tribute to man is existentialistic and contemporary throughout. Man—the creature of time (Heidegger), whose freedom can do all things (Sartre)—lives ever with the fear of age and death about him (Jaspers), and yet knows there is something sacred in his very breath (Marcel). Wolfe hardly misses a defect in the human condition and yet somehow leaves us with the conviction that man is glorious. The distressing tone in the passage comes not from the fact that man has failed but from the assumption that he has no purpose. He survives but with little meaning. He wants to live from sheer refusal to die at times but he knows not what living is all about. Wolfe envisions man without God or Transcendence. And still man is a remarkable reality. As one reads Wolfe's words, he thinks of man's life and asks himself, "For what purpose was this precious possession wasted?" We have a right to expect some answer. Wolfe has described for us a phenomenology of man's experience in living. Descriptions, however, are not always enough. There are times when one is grateful for the soaring prose and the accurate description and yet feels a need for explanations and finality. We may be in Wolfe's debt for having led us as far as he does. Yet as one looks about him, he is sure that there are summits not yet reached.

A fourth theme which Wolfe deals with is the concept of time. The realization of "the bitter briefness of our days" haunts Wolfe. He is concerned that he might not have enough time to become all he must—that he might not make his mark in the short period given him. Every theme Wolfe develops increases man's loneliness: search for meaning, the tragic grandeur of man, the limit of time. Man's longing for a place in the sun and his fear he may not achieve this, the knowledge that he could ultimately fail and that life and nature will not aid his success, this increases man's loneliness. We are anxious and desperate for at a time we know not time is denied us. What is left and who remembers?

The most impressive symbol Wolfe employs to signify the

passing of time is a train journey. One can almost hear Wolfe cry out: Won't someone stop time, not forever but just long enough? Won't something give us back some of the moments we never forget and never repeat? But time, like a train, rushes across the earth, giving us only a glimmer of things we see but cannot hold in our hands. In the lonely wail of a train's distant whistle, all the nostalgia of human existence somehow comes across. In a train's sad and brief passage across the open spaces of our land, we can sometimes see ourselves.

Wolfe sees all these things. He becomes confused but never dreary. He is pained but also fascinated at "the strange and bitter miracle of life."

Once again, it might be more effective to quote the words of Wolfe himself. This passage is from his book *Of Time and the River.*

And outside there was the raw and desolate-looking country, there were the great steel coaches, the terrific locomotives, the shining rails, the sweep of the tracks. . . . And inside there were . . . people fixed there for an instant in incomparably rich and vivid little pictures of their life and destiny, as they were all hurled onward . . . to their journey's end somewhere upon the mighty continent, across the immense and lonely visage of the everlasting earth.

And they looked at one another for a moment, they passed and vanished, and were gone forever, yet it seemed to him that he had known these people, that he knew them better than the people in his own train, and that having met them for an instant under immense and timeless skies, as they were hurled across the continent to a thousand destinations, they had met, passed, vanished, yet would remember this forever. . . . For, having lived together as strangers in the immense and swarming city, they now had met upon the everlasting earth, hurled past each other for a moment between two points in time upon the shining rails, never to meet, to speak, to know each other any more, and the briefness of their days, the destiny of man, was in that instant greeting and farewell.

Therefore, in this way, they passed and vanished. . . . Then they drew away and lost the train forever. And presently their own train came in to Newark where it stopped. . . . What that astounding meeting of two black atoms underneath the skies . . . meant, he never knew; but he did not forget it.[30]

The last theme we shall draw from Wolfe's writings is his faith in the American spirit. He has a deep belief in the spiritual future of this country. He sees himself, hopefully almost, as the spokesman for his generation of Americans—a generation lost but undaunted, surrounded on all sides by temptation but not uninfluenced by virtue, a generation that sees no limit to its material potential and suspects that this is not sufficient. He sees us as rootless and isolated, a drifting people looking for an end to exile, and irrepressibly optimistic. His closing words in *You Can't Go Home Again* reflect his conception of his country: "I believe that we are lost here in America but I believe that we shall be found."

Since loneliness is so characteristic of Wolfe's approach to life, it does not surprise us to discover that this characterizes his approach to Christ. In one of his few references to Christ, Wolfe writes of "God's Lonely Man" in an essay published after his death.

What Christ is saying always, what he never swerves from saying, what he says a thousand times and in a thousand different ways, but always with a central unity of belief, is this: "I am my Father's son, and you are my brothers." And the unity that binds us all together, that makes this earth a family, and all men brothers and the sons of God, is love.

The central purpose of Christ's life, therefore, is to destroy the life of loneliness and to establish here on earth the life of love. The evidence to support this is clear and overwhelming.

. . . Such was the final intention of Christ's life, the purpose
of his teaching. And its total import was that the life of loneliness could be destroyed forever by the life of love. Or such, at
least, has been the meaning which I read into his life. For in
these recent years when I have lived alone so much, and known
loneliness so well, I have gone back many times and read the
story of this man's words and life to see if I could find in them a
meaning for myself, a way of life that would be better than the
one I had. I read what he had said, not in a mood of piety or
holiness, not from a sense of sin, a feeling of contrition, or because his promise of a heavenly reward meant very much to me.
But I tried to read his bare words nakedly and simply, as it
seems to me he must have uttered them, and . . . if the meaning
I have put upon his words seems foolish or extravagant, child-
ishly simple or banal, mine alone or not different from what ten
million other men have thought, I have only set it down here as
I saw it, felt it, found it for myself. . . .

. . . And now I know that though the way and meaning of
Christ's life is a far, far better way and meaning than my own,
yet I can never make it mine; . . . Christ himself, who preached
the life of love, was yet as lonely as any man that ever lived.
Yet I could not say that he was mistaken because he preached
the life of love and fellowship, and lived and died in loneliness;
nor would I dare assert his way was wrong because a billion
men have since professed his way and never followed it.

I can only say that I could not make his way my own. For I
have found the constant, everlasting weather of man's life to be,
not love, but loneliness. Love itself is not the weather of our
lives. It is the rare, the precious flower. . . .

. . . How or why or in what way the flower of love will come
to us, whether with life or death, triumph or defeat, joy or madness, no man on this earth can say. But I know that at the end,
forever at the end for us—the houseless, homeless, doorless,
driven wanderers of life, the lonely men—there waits forever
the dark visage of our comrade, Loneliness.[31]

FRANZ KAFKA (1883–1924)
Man is frustrated as he searches for justice and love

Franz Kafka has an ability to create a mood of desperation which few, if any, can rival. He is an author never easy to understand but one in whom it is difficult to be uninterested. Kafka is, however, important not because he is a weaver of gripping atmosphere but because he has a message to communicate.

Franz Kafka was born in Prague, of Jewish parentage. He studied law, absorbed deeply a Kierkegaardian influence in his life, and spent many of his days recovering from a weakness brought on by consumption. He died at the age of forty-two, with the request that all his manuscripts be burned. It was a refusal to accede to this wish which gave us Kafka's two great novels: *The Trial* (1925) and *The Castle* (1926).

Kafka's ability to describe a desperate situation is so effective and so typical of him that the word Kafkaesque has been added to our language. An example of a typical Kafka situation was given recently by a leading American magazine.

The automatic elevator stops with a jolt. The doors slide open, but instead of the accustomed exit, the passenger faces only a blank wall. His fingers stab at buttons: nothing happens. Finally, he presses an alarm signal, and a starter's gruff voice inquires from below: "What's the matter?" The passenger explains that he wants to get off at the 25th floor. "There is no 25th floor in this building," comes the voice over the loudspeaker. The passenger explains that, nonsense, he has worked here for years. He gives his name. "Never heard of you," says the loudspeaker. "Easy," the passenger tells himself. "They are just trying to frighten me."

But time passes and nothing changes. In that endless moment, the variously pleading and angry exchanges over the loudspeaker are the passenger's only communication with the outside world. Finally, even that ceases; the man below says that he cannot waste any more time. "Wait! Please!" cries the passenger in panic—"Keep on talking to me!" But the loudspeaker clicks into silence. Hours, days, or ages go by. The passenger cowers in a corner of the steel box, staring at the shining metal grille through which the voice once spoke. The grille must be worshipped; perhaps the voice will be heard again.[32]

Since there is a somewhat different message in each of Kafka's two chief novels, it might be well for us to vary somewhat the format we have been following. Instead of the biography-notes on books-commentary outline we have followed to date, we shall take a different approach with Kafka: biography and then capsule and commentary on each book as it comes up for consideration. The general commentary on his contribution will emerge better in this fashion.

The Trial

The Trial is the story of Joseph K., a respectable functionary in a bank, who is unexplainably arrested as he gets out of bed one morning. The opening words of the novel immediately set the mood:

Someone must have traduced Joseph K., for without having done anything wrong, he was arrested one fine morning.

Joseph K. is the symbol of the dilemma modern man faces. He does not know the reason for his arrest. His captors refuse to explain why he is in bondage. They will not even name the authorities on whose behalf they act. Joseph K. is given his freedom for a time. It is not a comfortable freedom. It is limited and ever threatened by the charge against him. Since he is a man under indictment and unable to understand what is happening to him, he cannot feel he is really free. To show his freedom is precarious and that he is not master of his own life, he is summoned before tribunal after tribunal. Once Joseph K. realizes there is a charge against him, he spends the rest of his life fighting against someone he never sees and against an accusation of which he is totally ignorant, perhaps even not responsible. If only someone would explain to Joseph K. the *who* and the *what* of his situation, he might cope with things. But to struggle when one knows not the battle or the enemy or even the cause, this is unreasonable. Joseph K. uses logic and learning to rescue himself from his predicament, but logic and learning are not enough. One finds oneself saying "This is unfair!" over and over again as he reads of Joseph K.'s plight. Who has a right to do this to a man? The least a man ought to know is *why*.

Divided between disbelief and hope, between confusion and despair, Joseph K. goes to his death. Two well-dressed and polite gentlemen come to get him one fine day. They invite him to follow them. Joseph K., hoping this might be the answer, follows. Courteously, they lead him into a suburb, put his head on a stone, grasp his throat, and thrust a knife into his heart. Before dying, Joseph K. speaks the final words of the novel:

> "Like a dog!" he said; it was as if the shame of it must outlive him.[33]

A reading of this final scene of *The Trial* in Kafka's own words will give us a better idea of the mood and message the author wants to convey.

> After an exchange of courteous formalities regarding which of them was to take precedence in the next task . . . one of them came up to K. and removed his coat, his waistcoat, and finally his shirt. K. shivered involuntarily, whereupon the man gave him a light, reassuring pat on the back. Then he folded the clothes carefully together, as if they were likely to be used again at some time, although perhaps not immediately. Not to leave K. standing motionless, exposed to the night breeze, which was

rather chilly, he took him by the arm and walked him up and down a little, while his partner investigated the quarry to find a suitable spot. When he had found it he beckoned, and K.'s companion led him over there. It was a spot near the cliffside where a loose boulder was lying. The two of them laid K. down on the ground, propped him against the boulder, and settled his head upon it. But in spite of the pains they took and all the willingness K. showed, his posture remained contorted and un-natural-looking. So one of the men begged the other to let him dispose K. all by himself, yet even that did not improve mat-ters. Finally they left K. in a position which was not even the best of the positions they had already tried out. Then one of them opened his frock coat and out of a sheath that hung from a belt girt round his waistcoat drew a long, thin, double-edged butcher's knife, held it up, and tested the cutting edges in the moonlight. Once more the odious courtesies began, the first handed the knife across K. to the second, who handed it across K. back again to the first. K. now perceived clearly that he was supposed to seize the knife himself, as it traveled from hand to hand above him, and plunge it into his own breast. But he did not do so, he merely turned his head, which was still free to move, and gazed around him. He could not completely rise to the occasion, he could not relieve the officials of all their tasks; the responsibility for this last failure of his lay with him who had not left him the remnant of strength necessary for the deed. His glance fell on the top story of the house adjoining the quarry. With a flicker as of a light going up, the casements of a window there suddenly flew open; a human figure, faint and insubstantial at that distance and that height, leaned abruptly far forward and stretched both arms still farther. Who was it? A friend? A good man? Someone who sympathized? Someone who wanted to help? Was it one person only? Or was it man-kind? Was help at hand? Were there arguments in his favor that had been overlooked? Of course there must be. Logic is doubt-less unshakable, but it cannot withstand a man who wants to go on living. Where was the Judge whom he had never seen?

Where was the High Court, to which he had never penetrated? He raised his hands and spread out all his fingers.

But the hands of one of the partners were already at K.'s throat, while the other thrust the knife deep into his heart and turned it there twice. With failing eyes K. could still see the two of them immediately before him, cheek leaning against cheek, watching the final act. "Like a dog!" he said; it was as if the shame of it must outlive him.[34]

Few books lend themselves to commentary as easily as do Kafka's. *The Trial* leaves one mystified but questioning. It is the story of man's anxious pursuit of innocence and justice. The search is marked by continual frustration and perhaps failure. K. is aware of his guilt but sees no way out of it. He is in need not really of exoneration but of intelligibility and adequate retribution. Relief from guilt is not as easy in Kafka as it is in Dostoevsky. Dostoevsky, it is true, demanded much. One had to accuse himself, confess to others, accept suffering. But in Dostoevsky, man at least knows what must be done. He may lack courage to see his conversion through, but he at least knows why he is guilty and how to gain pardon. Kafka, however, creates a far more bewildering situation—if not an entirely hopeless one. There is no way out of guilt except in death. Man is conscious he is criminal but he does not know the crime or the manner in which he might be rescued. There is, as Sartre would say, no exit. Man exists in a totally unredeemed and, one suspects, unredeemable situation. Because he knows he is guilty, he cannot say he has no right to suffer; yet justice demands not indiscriminate suffering but punishment measured by the gravity of the offense.

Joseph K.'s story does not seem to be a search for human justification alone. He is looking for supra-human acceptability also. Therefore, we really do not know if Joseph K.'s failure is complete. Divine justice may appear unjust to us. From the human viewpoint, Joseph K. never has a chance. But *The Trial* does not make it clear what justice itself is or what type of justice man needs. It is not, it seems, some deed that Joseph K. is called to account for; rather, his whole life and his very being are called to reckoning. As the book progresses, the center of attention moves from Joseph K. to the invisible Court of Justice and its unfathomable demands. What is the Court asking? What will please the Court? What right has the Court to act as it does? Why does the Court not reprieve? Does the Court have any interest in man? Is its objective torture or salvation?

The Court's procedure is even more mystifying as one realizes that it makes no accusation. Joseph K. is arrested. The Court never tells him he is guilty. But K. feels guilty in the realization that the Court has confronted him and arrested him. At times, one almost receives the impression that the Court only reflects K.'s own accusation of himself without ever issuing an accusation of its own.

This idea is hinted at in the scene where Joseph K. speaks with a priest about his predicament. From a pulpit in the cathedral, the priest announces to K.: "The Court wants nothing from you. It receives you when you come and it dismisses you when you go."[35] One gets the impression that the Court might leave Joseph K. alone if only he could live serenely with himself. K. is driven to seek out the Court and there he ever sees himself as guilty.

Although Joseph K. feels his guilt, he will not declare it. His refusal to declare his guilt is due either to a failure to accept responsibility for himself or to his realization that his guilt is only the guilt of being a member of the race. Therefore, he should not be accused.

"But I am not guilty," said K.; "it's a mistake. And if it comes to that, how can any man be called guilty? We are all simply men here, one as much as the other."[36]

The themes Kafka explores in *The Trial* are familiar to us by now: innocence and justice; frustration and ignorance; guilt and death. Man, forever aware of guilt, is compelled to face the trial of his life in a universe whose pattern and meaning are uncertain and unknowable.

The Castle

In *The Castle* we meet a somewhat different Kafka. The story is a simple one. A man called K. suddenly appears in a strange village, overshadowed by a castle whose residents seem almost divine in the eyes of the villagers. Kafka sets the mood rapidly in the very first lines of the novel.

> It was late in the evening when K. arrived. The village was deep in snow. The Castle hill was hidden, veiled in mist and darkness, nor was there even a glimmer of light to show the castle was there. On the wooden bridge leading from the main road to the village, K. stood for a long time gazing into the illusory emptiness above him.[37]

K. believes he has been called to the village as a land-surveyor. Now that he has arrived, he is not sure if the summons he received came from the Castle or even if there is a job for him to do. He tries desperately to reach the Castle to find out if he is the person he takes himself to be or if he is condemned to insecurity and uselessness in the village. Every attempt to reach the Castle fails. Roads that seem to lead to it, do not; telephone conversations with the Castle are not clear; letters from the Castle prove ambiguous.

> . . . the street he was in, the main street of the village, did not lead up to the Castle hill; it only made toward it and then, as if deliberately, turned aside, and though it did not lead away from the Castle, it led no nearer to it either.[38]

K. cannot gain the security he needs to live. If only he could contact the Castle, all would be solved. But he cannot do this. And so he searches for himself and some relationship with the Castle all his life.

> They . . . inquired if K. could come with them next morning into the Castle. The "No" of the answer was audible even to K. at his table. But the answer went on and was still more explicit; it ran as follows: "Neither tomorrow nor at any other time."[39]

At last, exhausted by his struggle, K. lies on his deathbed. Word comes from the Castle that he can live and work in the village even if he has no right. He has won but it is too late, at least by human standards. He has found acceptability with the Divine Will but his victory, in human terms, is a sad and final defeat.

As one completes a reading of *The Castle*, he is almost bewildered by the multiplicity of themes it develops. The story depicts man as a tragic seeker after truth. Nothing can keep him from pressing on to discovery and knowledge. Unfortunately, he seeks certitude not in a friendly environment but in the twilight zone between salvation and damnation. There are times when it seems everything is opposed to truth and that truth itself resists comprehension.

Kafka's choice of a castle as the object of K.'s search is particularly apt. A castle suggests durability. And one cannot live without a permanent trust in something indestructible. To ignore the castle is to live only in the ever-changing village. It is to live condemned to a formless existence. The castle gives definition and finality to the village.

Man, however, cannot survive only by trust in a silent reality. It is good to know the castle will always be there. But one needs communication before he can be complete. God must speak to us.

Even if God does speak, however, it always remains an unexpected and undue grace.

Kafka makes this evident in a conversation between K. and a landlady. They speak of the chief authority in the castle, named Klamm, and they make reference to Frieda, a girl Klamm once favored but who, since, has given her devotion to K.

> "I must have a talk with Klamm. . . ."
>
> "You're a strange person," said the landlady, . . . "you ask for the impossible. . . . Herr Klamm will never speak . . . can never speak to [you]. . . . You are not from the Castle, you are not from the village, you aren't anything. Or rather, unfortunately, you are something, a stranger, a man who isn't wanted and is in everybody's way. . . . You're not even capable of seeing Klamm as he really is. . . . Klamm is to talk to you and yet Klamm doesn't talk even to people from the village, never yet has he spoken a word himself to anyone in the village . . . that Frieda . . . was admitted without let or hindrance was an act of grace on Klamm's part, but that he deliberately summoned her is more than one can maintain. Of course, that's all over now for good, Klamm may perhaps call 'Frieda' as before, that's possible, but she'll never again be admitted to his presence, a girl who has thrown herself away on you."[40]

Throughout the entire range of K.'s search, what he seeks most fundamentally is an understanding of exactly who he is. He is convinced that the final explanation of himself cannot come from him alone. Something beyond man must tell man who he is and what he must do with life. Man needs a Castle, a Klamm, a God, an answer.

The need for God makes man anxious. For God is demanding, challenging, so different, too silent. He forces us to exercise courage or live in failure. Before God, man is ever shaken with "fear and trembling." He must never be so hopeful of his condition that he finally rests assured.

> K. was often in danger of considering his situation hopeful;
> nevertheless, after such fits of easy confidence, he would hasten
> to tell himself that just there lay his danger. . . . In this life, it
> might easily happen, if he was not always on his guard, that
> some day or other . . . he might . . . conduct himself so im-
> prudently as to get a fall; and the authorities, still ever mild
> and friendly, and as it were against their will, but in the name
> of some public regulation unknown to him, might have to come
> and clear him out of the way.[41]

Sometimes the lack of understanding between God and man is
so great that one thinks not a gentle God but a wild and thought-
less unintelligibility decides our fate. There is a "ludicrous
bungling that in certain circumstances may decide the life of a
human being."[42]

Thomas Mann has given us a series of remarkable observations
on the thought of Kafka as reflected in *The Castle*.[43] Kafka,
Mann comments, felt remote all his life from security in God and
from God's will.

> It is plain that regular life in a community, the ceaseless strug-
> gle to become a "native," is simply the technique for improving
> K.'s relations with the "Castle," or rather to set up relations with
> it: to attain nearer, in other words, to God and to a state of
> grace . . . the village represents life, the community, healthy
> normal existence. . . . The Castle, on the other hand, represents
> the divine dispensation, the state of grace—puzzling, remote,
> incomprehensible. . . .[44]

So needful of grace is K., so passionately and recklessly does
he yearn for grace, that he tries to gain it even by stratagems
and wiles. The central theme of the book is "the grotesque un-
connection between the human being and the transcendental . . .
the remoteness, cruelty, yes, wickedness, by any human standards, of the 'Castle.' "[45]

In concluding our study of Kafka, a reminder of the similarities in his two major novels may prove helpful. Both novels deal with guilt. Joseph K. is arrested and executed for his guilt. K., on the other hand, fails to win the acceptance of the Castle. "Sometimes I feel," Kafka once wrote of himself, "I understand the Fall of Man better than anyone."

Both novels deal with frustration. Both novels ask if man has a place in the scheme of things. Both novels deal with man's final aloneness.

> *The Trial* propounds a problem which *The Castle,* to a certain degree, solves. . . . *The Castle* is perhaps a theology in action . . . the individual adventure of a soul in quest of its grace.[46]

The Trial describes the search for justice; *The Castle* describes the search for salvation. Man needs both. He receives neither without a persistent effort. Yet his persistent efforts do not bring him justice or salvation. In both instances, they can only be given him from above.

ALBERT CAMUS (1913–1960)
Man has value and goodness: he must affirm these in an absurd world by Rebellion

There will be no single thinker in this book whose influence will receive more attention than Albert Camus. The reason for this is because he is the most attractive and popular atheist the twentieth century is likely to produce.

Albert Camus was born in Mondori, Algeria. He married and divorced in 1933 but married permanently in 1940. In the 1934–1935 period, he was a member of the Communist Party. In 1942, he joined the French Resistance and edited the newspaper *Combat.*

Camus' friends know that, between the years 1947 and 1950, he was very close to Catholicism; several   friends anticipated his immediate conversion. . . . Sartre, in his polemic with Camus in 1952, was not far from the mark when he suspected that a certain nostalgia for God was concealed under the very vehemence with which [Camus] proclaimed the absurdity of a world without God.[47]

Camus' literary and philosophical output includes five major works: *The Stranger* (1942); *The Myth of Sisyphus* (1943); *The Plague* (1947); *The Rebel* (1951); and *The Fall* (1956). We shall deal with all of these before our study of Camus is complete.

In 1957, Albert Camus received the Nobel Prize for literature. The Committee cited not only "his important literary production," but acknowledged that he had illuminated "with clear-sighted earnestness . . . the problem of the human conscience of our time."

Camus was a man deeply concerned about his fellow-men. He said frequently that he hoped more than anything else to speak for his time, of the human condition, on behalf of the world's oppressed. He had seen men at their worst during the Nazi occupation, yet remained convinced that "there is more to admire than to despise in man." His statement is reminiscent of Anne Frank's comment: "I still believe that people are really good at heart . . . if I look up into the heavens, I think that it will come · right, and that peace and tranquillity will return again."[48]

Albert Camus had a rare combination in his personality. He united the feelings of the common man with the mind of an intellectual. And, as George Orwell would later do, he spoke for the decency, the integrity, and the independence of man.

On January 4, 1960, he was killed in an auto accident at the age of forty-seven.

Albert Camus, one of France's leading literary figures, was killed today in an automobile accident . . . when the car in which he was riding struck a tree near Sens, seventy-five miles southeast of Paris. The driver, Michel Gallimard, a member of a noted French publishing family, was injured, as were his wife and 18 year-old daughter. . . . The police reported that the crash occurred when the left rear tire blew out as the vehicle was travelling 80 miles an hour. . . . The automobile glanced off one tree and then struck another with tremendous force. . . . News of the death stunned the French literary world. . . . M. Camus . . . had an almost worshipful following among the younger intellectuals and among youth in general, both in France and abroad. . . . François Mauriac . . . said that his death "is one of the greatest losses that could have affected French letters at the present time. A whole generation became aware of itself and of its problems through Camus," said Mauriac.[49]

The death of Camus merited not only this news release but also an editorial comment by the same newspaper.

There is a grim philosophical irony in the fact that Albert Camus should have died in a senseless automobile accident, victim of a chance mishap. . . . It is only superficially that Camus' philosophy seemed to some readers . . . a doctrine of pessimism and despair. Rather it is a creed which calls on men for the most heroic kind of affirmation of life. . . . There can be no surprise that our era responded to Camus' message and a few years ago made him one of the youngest recipients of the Nobel Prize.[50]

This impact that Camus had and still has on the young generation is mentioned also by another commentator.

The majority of youth today . . . think themselves too sophisticated to seek exaltation or transcendence in a hopeless

struggle. . . . Some of these young people . . . identify themselves with the existentialism of Sartre. Many of them, however, find Sartre's negations far too light and think that life
ought to be taken more seriously. . . . In spite of disillusion-
ment and uncertainty about the future, they . . . retain a certain taste for dignity and nobility. These spontaneously recognize their master in Albert Camus.[51]

The total impact of Camus on his time is not something explainable only by the attractiveness of his personality. It is due
to the philosophy he espoused and the literary style in which he
expressed his belief. Before we can ever hope to appreciate his
novels, we must have some basic ideas about his philosophical
positions.

The philosophy of Albert Camus is structured around two
fundamental concepts: the Absurd and Rebellion. Let us examine
these in order.

The Absurd

Camus wrote *The Myth of Sisyphus* to explain his notion of
the Absurd. He wrote *The Rebel* to explore the notion of metaphysical rebellion.

"There is but one truly serious philosophical problem," Camus
wrote in the opening words of *The Myth of Sisyphus*, "and that
is suicide. Judging whether life is or is not worth living amounts
to answering the fundamental question of philosophy."[52]

In the very opening pages of the book, Camus explains his
position clearly and eloquently.

All great deeds and all great thoughts have a ridiculous beginning. Great works are often born on a street-corner or in a
restaurant's revolving door. So it is with absurdity. . . . Rising,
street-car, four hours in the office or the factory, meal, street-
car, four hours of work, meal, sleep, and Monday, Tuesday,

Wednesday, Thursday, Friday and Saturday according to the same rhythm—this path is easily followed most of the time. But one day the "why" arises and everything begins in that weariness tinged with amazement. . . . What follows is the gradual return . . . or it is the definitive awakening. At the end of the awakening comes, in time, the consequence: suicide or recovery . . . [the] density and [the] strangeness of the world is the absurd. . . . A man is talking on the telephone behind a glass partition; you cannot hear him, but you see his incomprehensible dumb show: you wonder why he is alive . . . this "nausea" . . . is also the absurd. . . .

Of whom and of what indeed can I say: "I know that!" This heart within me I can feel, and I judge that it exists. This world I can touch, and I likewise judge that it exists. There ends all my knowledge. . . . For if I try to seize this self of which I feel sure, if I try to define and to summarize it, it is nothing but water slipping through my fingers. I can sketch one by one all the aspects it is able to assume, all those likewise that have been attributed to it, this upbringing, this origin, the ardor or these silences, this nobility or this vileness. But aspects cannot be added up. This very heart which is mine will forever remain indefinable to me. . . . Forever I shall be a stranger to myself. . . .

And here are trees and I know their gnarled surface, water and I feel its taste. These scents of grass and stars at night, certain evenings when the heart relaxes—how shall I negate this world whose power and strength I feel? Yet all the knowledge on earth will give me nothing to assure me that this world is mine. You describe it to me and you teach me to classify it. You enumerate its laws and in my thirst for knowledge I admit that they are true. You take apart its mechanism and my hope increases. At the final stage, you teach me that this wondrous and multi-colored universe can be reduced to the atom and that the atom itself can be reduced to the electron. All this is good and I wait for you to continue. . . . I realize that if through science I can seize phenomena and enumerate them, I cannot, for all that, apprehend the world. Were I to trace its

entire relief with my finger, I should not know any more. And
you give me the choice between a description that is sure but
that teaches me nothing and hypotheses that claim to teach me
but that are not sure. A stranger to myself and to the world . . .
what is this condition in which I can have peace only by refusing to know and to live, in which the appetite for conquest
bumps into walls that defy its assaults? . . . Hence . . . intelligence too tells me in its way that this world is absurd. . . . I
said that the world is absurd, but I was too hasty. This world
in itself is not reasonable, that is all that can be said. But what
is absurd is the confrontation of this irrational and the wild
longing for clarity whose call echoes in the human heart. The
absurd depends as much on man as on the world.[53]

The passage says much to us. It is clear from the beginning
that we are dealing with a thinker who understands our century.
He is, at this point in his development, intrigued with the absurdity of this world and this century. He sounds much like
Sartre. The world is absurd: man is nauseous; reason is helpless.
Camus, however, will progress from this position. His realization that science does not satisfy reminds us of Marcel's insistence
on mystery. Camus' eloquence is not accidental to his contribution. His poetic prose gives us intuition into the mood Camus
describes. It gives us almost an experience of the things he is
trying to analyze.

Absurdity arises not only from the fact that the world is purposeless but from the ability of man to see the lack of harmony
all around him and to grieve over its absence. As man realizes
all is absurd, he must decide immediately whether life is worth
the effort. Before the absurd, we really have only one of two
options. We may run from it in escape. Escape is possible
through many avenues. One may commit suicide or one may
"leap" into transcendence (Jaspers) or into hope (Marcel) or
into Christ (Kierkegaard). If one chooses not to escape, then he
must take the burden of existence upon himself, turn from tran-

scendence, unlearn hope, cling to lucidity, and rebel continuously against this absurd situation. Before one chooses to follow this unrewarding and demanding alternative, he must ask if the whole absurd thing we call life is worth living through.

If we answer the Absurd with suicide, then we say in effect that the Absurd is final and limitless. We surrender to the Absurd, seeing it as inevitable, and as the only possible outcome of everything. Rebellion against the Absurd is an ongoing struggle with it, not hoping for ultimate victory, yet aware that one can always seize some values from life.

In Rebellion, man exercises his freedom against meaninglessness; he fills his life with passion; and he manages to be in spite of all the odds against him.

Camus does not say these consequences make life comfortable, but this is life and this attitude can bring us honesty, lucidity, and dignity.

The concept of the Absurd is only a transitional stage in Camus' thought. Even as he speaks of the Absurd, the need for resistance against it begins to emerge in faint outline. His philosophy leads to Rebellion as its final expression. Absurdity becomes not Camus' final word on life but only the environment for Rebellion or Rebellion's adversary. Rebellion, then, is the second basic concept in Camus' thought.

Rebellion

In *The Rebel,* Camus tries to explain how value can be won from life.

> The purpose of this essay is . . . to face the reality of the present . . . it is an attempt to understand the times in which we live . . . a period which, in a space of fifty years, uproots, enslaves, or kills seventy million human beings . . . [when] slave camps [are erected] under the flag of freedom, massacres

[are] justified by philanthropy . . . on the day when crime dons
the apparel of innocence . . . it is innocence that is called upon
to justify himself.[54]

Camus then argues, we must find a value, we must believe in
something.

> This essay proposes, in the face of murder and rebellion, to
> pursue a train of thought which began with suicide and the
> idea of the absurd. . . . If we believe in nothing, if nothing has
> any meaning and if we can affirm no values whatsoever, then
> everything is possible and nothing has any importance. There is
> no pro or con. . . .We are free to stoke the crematory fires or to
> devote ourselves to the care of lepers. Evil and virtue are mere
> chance or caprice.[55]

In these words, Camus is in agreement with Dostoevsky's position that without some belief or meaning, nothing has importance. At the same time, he takes exception to Sartre's idea that
there can be total freedom and unlimited possibility of choice.
The story is still told, and its accuracy is quite reliable, of the
conversation Camus and Sartre had one morning in a Parisian
coffee shop. The incident took place during the Nazi Occupation.
Sartre was arguing for infinite freedom. Camus refused to accept
this position. If freedom has no limits, Camus said, then you can
turn me over to the Nazi authorities. Sartre agreed that this
should not be done. Freedom, then, Camus concluded, must
have limits.

Perhaps the best way to gain an understanding of Camus' idea
on rebellion is to trace it through a series of propositions.

Rebellion is an affirmation that life is good.
Once I decide not to commit suicide, I do this because I see
that life is good and worth living. But if life is good for me, it
is good for others as well. Therefore, we have a human worth

and a solidarity with each other which we must defend. Let us then stand and fight absurdity. Let there be no running away. Let us become one and explore together what we are going to do about this life we have, this absurd human situation which is good, which we love, but which destroys us. We are strangers in this world and to each other (let us not harm one another); we have plague to combat (let us not die of it but overcome it); we fall (let us learn to stand again). If we live then, it is because we see a good in ourselves. If we rebel, it is because we see a good in human society.

Rebellion is a struggle against life for life.

We must struggle. And we must struggle without hope. There is not the slightest chance we can win. The rebel knows that he will lose and yet he fights. He must never surrender even though defeat is only a matter of time. Resistance gives majesty to human existence. And it gives being to human existence. For man must rebel in order to be.

> What is a rebel? A man who says no, but whose refusal does not imply a renunciation. . . . Rebellion cannot exist without the feeling that somewhere and somehow one is right. . . . [The rebel] demonstrates, with obstinancy, that there is something in him which is worthwhile. . . . With rebellion, awareness is born. . . . As a last resort, [the rebel] is willing to accept the final defeat, which is death, rather than be deprived of . . . freedom. Better to die on one's feet than to live on one's knees. . . . When he rebels a man identifies himself with other men and so surpasses himself . . . the first progressive step for a mind overwhelmed by the strangeness of things is to realize that this feeling of strangeness is shared with all men. . . . The malady experienced by a single man becomes a mass plague . . . this evidence lures the individual from his solitude. It founds its first value on the whole human race. I rebel— therefore we exist.[56]

In a rebel's "no," there is value. In this refusal, there is a stern and stubborn conviction that something is right and that something is good. Rebellion not only leads one to individual survival but brings one to association with others. It creates a community and bestows solidarity upon us. In rebellion, a man becomes aware of himself, the task he is to achieve, and of the freedom which remains his only weapon. In rebellion, a man also becomes aware of others. It is because I rebel that we exist.

There are two types of Rebellion.

Rebellion may be historical or metaphysical. Historical rebellion is a protest against particular conditions in which one lives. Metaphysical rebellion, however, is of more interest to us. It is man's protest against his own condition. He struggles against not just a phase or a form of human life but all creation.

> Metaphysical rebellion is a claim . . . against the suffering of life and death and a protest against the human condition both for its incompleteness, thanks to death, and its wastefulness, thanks to evil. If a mass death sentence defines the human condition . . . the metaphysical rebel is therefore not definitely an atheist . . . he is inevitably a blasphemer. Quite simply, he blasphemes primarily in the name of order, denouncing God as the father of death and as the supreme outrage.[57]

Both types of rebellion, historical and metaphysical, are based on an even more fundamental factor. Both believe in human solidarity and cannot succeed apart from human comradeship.

Rebellion is a search for a new God.

"[The rebel] is seeking, without knowing it, a moral philosophy or a religion. . . . Rebellion . . . is a form of asceticism. Therefore, if the rebel blasphemes, it is in the hope of finding a new god."[58]

Man then needs a new God. This need was recognized by

Dostoevsky in the words of his character, Ivan Karamazov. "Even if God existed, Ivan would never surrender to Him in the face of the injustice done to man."[59] Man needs a God who will give him justice, justice now, and justice for all.

> The rebel does not ask for life, but for reasons for living. He rejects the consequences implied by death. If nothing lasts, then nothing is justified; everything that dies is deprived of meaning. . . . The protest against evil . . . is at the very core of meta-physical revolt. . . . It is not the suffering of a child, which is repugnant in itself, but the fact that the suffering is not justi-fied. . . . In the eyes of the rebel, what is missing from the misery of the world, as well as from its moments of happiness, is some principle by which they can be explained. The insur-rection against evil is, above all, a demand for unity. The rebel obstinately confronts a world condemned to death and the im-penetrable obscurity of the human condition with his demand for life and absolute clarity. He is seeking . . . a new god.[60]

We have already seen how preoccupied atheism is with the problem of evil and existential injustice. Camus is another wit-ness to this central problem of contemporary atheism.

Rebellion is a search for the unity of man.
Rebellion wants all or nothing. All the knowledge in the world is not worth a child's tears. Rebellion includes everyone or no one. Either all must be saved or salvation is undesirable. "The unity of the world, which was not achieved with God, will henceforth be attempted in defiance of God."[61]

> . . . the rebel thus rejects divinity in order to share in the strug-gles and destiny of all men . . . the earth remains our first and our last love. Our brothers are breathing under the same sky as we. . . . With this joy, through long struggle, we shall re-make the soul of our time. . . .[62]

This concern with and for community stands in marked con-
trast to so much of the last century's individualism. It is a characteristic of twentieth-century atheism. This deep sense of solidarity may be due in part to the frequency with which we have
had to form alliances against crises: against Nazism and Communism, against economic exploitation of the worker, against
world anarchy and war itself.

Rebellion is optimistic.

Man . . . on earth . . . is . . . solitary. To the "I rebel, therefore we exist," he adds with prodigious plans in mind which even
include the death of rebellion: "And we are alone."[63]

Yet we must struggle optimistically.

At this moment . . . each of us must fit an arrow to his bow and
enter the list anew. . . . The bow bends; the wood complains.
At the moment of supreme tension, there will leap into flight
an unswerving arrow, a shaft that is inflexible and free.[64]

At the end of this tunnel of darkness . . . there is inevitably a
light which we already perceive and for which we only have to
fight to ensure its coming. All of us among the ruins are pre-
paring a renaissance beyond the limits of nihilism.[65]

With some of these notes on the personality and philosophy of
Albert Camus, we turn our attention to Camus the writer and to
a study of his three key literary works: *The Stranger, The Plague,*
and *The Fall.*[66]
On the occasion of his acceptance of the Nobel Prize for
literature in 1957, Camus delivered an address which gives us
an indication of the objectives his writing sought to achieve.
Some excerpts from this speech may prove a good introduction
to the task now before us.

How could a man still almost young, possessed only of his doubts and of work still in progress, accustomed to living in the isolation of work or the seclusion of friendship—how could he have failed to feel a sort of panic upon learning of a choice that suddenly focused a harsh spotlight on him alone and reduced to himself?

The artist fashions himself in that ceaseless oscillation from himself to others, midway between the beauty he cannot do without and the community from which he cannot tear himself. This is why true artists scorn nothing. They force themselves to understand instead of judging.

. . . most of us . . . rejected . . . nihilism and strove to find some form of legitimacy. We had to fashion for ourselves an art of living in times of catastrophe in order to be reborn. . . . Probably every generation sees itself as charged with remaking the world. Mine, however, knows that it will not remake the world. But its task is perhaps even greater, for it consists in keeping the world from destroying itself. . . . Perhaps it can never accomplish that vast undertaking, but most certainly throughout the world it has already accepted the double challenge of truth and liberty and, on occasion, has shown that it can lay down its life without hatred. That generation deserves to be acclaimed and encouraged whenever it happens to be . . . and to it . . . I should like to transfer the honor you have just done me.

Truth is mysterious, elusive, ever to be won anew. Liberty is dangerous, as hard to get along with, as it is exciting. We must progress toward these two objectives. . . .

The Secondary Writings

In addition to the three major works Camus has written, there are a number of secondary achievements. A word on some of these may help to put *The Stranger, The Plague,* and *The Fall* into clearer perspective.

We choose quite briefly for consideration two plays, *The Misunderstanding* and *Caligula,* and one short story "The Adulterous Woman." *The Misunderstanding* reflects the nihilism of Camus' early years; *Caligula* develops the more sophisticated theme, viz., that rebellion must be exercised with restraint; "The Adulterous Woman" speaks of man's exile and his longing for homecoming.

The Misunderstanding (1944) is the story of a man, Jan, who returns unknown to his mother and sister. He wants to be recognized and to find his home, but he does not make evident to them who he is. He explains to his wife, whom he sends elsewhere in town: "One can't remain a stranger all one's life. It is quite true that a man needs happiness, but he also needs to find his true place in the world."[67]

His mother and sister (Martha) fail to recognize him. They think him to be a wealthy transient and they murder him as he lodges in their Inn. When they discover the identity of their victim, they kill themselves.

In a final scene Martha, Jan's sister and murderer, proclaims: "All I wish is to be left in peace with my anger, my very rightful anger. For I have no intention of . . . pleading for forgiveness before I die. I hate this narrow world. . . . I have not been given my rights and I am smarting from the injustice done me; I will not bend my knee."[68]

Maria, the wife of Jan, on the other hand, kneels and prays as the impact of the tragedy reaches her. An elderly gentleman housekeeper hears her prayer and comes to ask if Maria has called for him. She turns to him pleading for help in the same manner as she prayed to God. He says "No!" and leaves her alone. Maria remains surrounded by the death of husband and in-laws, in a strange town she does not understand, among strange people she has never met before. As the play ends, her arms are raised vainly to the empty heavens.

In *Caligula* (1945) Camus explores a different theme. The message of the play comes across in a key dialogue which

Caligula has with his patrician associates. He has just returned from walking a great deal and tries to explain why he is tired.

CALIGULA: It was hard to find.
HELICON: What was hard to find?
CALIGULA: What I was after.
HELICON: Meaning?
CALIGULA: The moon.
HELICON: What?
CALIGULA: Yes, I wanted the moon.
HELICON: Ah. . . . And why did you want it?
CALIGULA: Well . . . It's one of the things I haven't got.
HELICON: I see. And now—have you fixed it up to your satis-
            faction?
CALIGULA: No. I couldn't get it.
HELICON: Too bad!
CALIGULA: Yes, and that's why I'm tired. (pause) Helicon!
HELICON: Yes, Caius?
CALIGULA: No doubt, you think I'm crazy.
HELICON: As you know well, I never think.
CALIGULA: Ah, yes . . . Now, listen! I'm not mad; in fact I've
            never felt so lucid. What happened to me is quite
            simple; I suddenly felt a desire for the impossible.
            That's all. Things as they are, in my opinion, are
            far from satisfactory.
HELICON: Many people share your opinion.
CALIGULA: That is so. But in the past I didn't realize it. Now I
            know. Really, this world of ours, the scheme of
            things as they call it, is quite intolerable. That's
            why I want the moon, or happiness, or eternal life
            —something, in fact, that may sound crazy, but
            which isn't of this world.

            .   .   .   .

HELICON: May I know what it is, this truth that you've dis-
            covered?
CALIGULA: Men die; and they are not happy.[69]

Caligula begins a wild and unrestrained search for happiness. He rebels against the world in which he lives, a world which will not let him have the moon as his own possession. He executes his subjects indiscriminately, initiates oppressive famines, practices immorality and perversion, decapitates those who do not admire him when he dances, demands to be worshipped when he dresses like Venus. Caligula asserts his freedom and seeks fulfillment in total abandon. It soon becomes clear to all, Caligula included, that liberty must have its limits; rebellion, its restraint.

> CALIGULA: If I had the moon . . . all would be changed. . . . I know that it would be enough if the impossible existed. I sought it in the limits of the world, in the confines of myself. . . . I did not go the way that was necessary. I ended with nothing. My kind of freedom is not good.

"The Adulterous Woman" is a short story in a collection entitled *Exile and the Kingdom* (1957). It is one of the last things Camus wrote. The entire collection deals with the theme of exile and the longing all have to find a country which will give them a home and their rightful kingdom.

"The Adulterous Woman" is a particularly touching description of this search. Janine, the heroine, longs for the lost kingdom, for liberty, for that eternal moment when all is won and nothing lost.

Janine accompanies her husband to North Africa where she is impressed with the primitive life of nomad tribesmen with its dignity and freedom. Looking over the desert visible from the walls of the town, she reminisces:

> Since the beginning of time, on the dry earth of this limitless land scraped to the bone, a few men had been ceaselessly trudging, possessing nothing but serving no one, poverty-stricken but free lords of a strange kingdom. Janine did not know why this idea filled her with so sweet and vast a sadness

that it made her shut her eyes. She knew only that this kingdom had been from all time promised to her, and yet that it would never belong to her, never again except perhaps for that fleeting moment when she opened her eyes once again on the suddenly motionless sky and its waves of coagulated light, while the voices arising from the Arab town grew suddenly silent. It seemed to her that the world had stopped turning and that from now onwards no one would die or grow old. At all places, henceforth, life was suspended, save there in her heart where, at that moment, someone was weeping with pain and wonderment.[70]

The Stranger

The minor works of Albert Camus describe themes which the major works define and develop. The first of Albert Camus' major novels was *The Stranger* (1942). It is the story of a quite ordinary Algerian named Meursault. He is characterized by his complete indifference to everything except immediate physical sensations. He is a man who lives for the moment and sees little value apart from the simple pleasures of daily living. In a fashion, he represents modern man or, at least, many modern men.

Meursault receives the news of his mother's death with faint annoyance at having to ask for a two days' leave from work. After the funeral, he becomes involved in a rather dishonorable agreement with his next-door neighbor. The incident shows his indifference to friendship as the funeral showed his indifference to his mother's life. He is incapable of love and considers truthfulness a mere social convention. Nothing matters and no one really makes a difference.

One day, as a result of a series of accidents, he kills an Arab. He is placed on trial, found guilty, and condemned to death. The experience of murder and impending execution move him

little. The only time in the novel when Meursault becomes
agitated is in argumentation with a prison chaplain who speaks
to him of another life. Meursault violently insists that this life
alone is certain and that the inevitability of death obliterates all
significance human existence might have.

There is something absurd about the fate Meursault suffers.
During the trial, for example, he is condemned to death not
really for the murder as much as for not having wept at his
mother's funeral. This convinces the court of the defendant's
callousness more than the taking of another's life. The murder itself could easily not have happened. A confluence of unintelligible circumstances seem more guilty of murder than Meursault
who merely pulls the trigger. He never really chooses to do what
comes to pass. He simply suffers it.

In passivity and indifference, without anyone's having understood him or he, them, Meursault goes to his meaningless death.

The Stranger is not written only as a literary achievement or
for the aesthetic pleasure it may give. It is written to put Camus'
philosophy of life in another form. It expresses, as Sartre once
pointed out, the *feeling* of the Absurd. *The Myth of Sisyphus*
presented the notion of the Absurd. *The Stranger* brings the absurd to one's emotions and not only to his intellect. The two
works must be read conjointly if one is to understand the message fully.

Absurdity arises from a number of circumstances. It is absurd,
for example, that society should apply absolute moral standards
to the uncertain and chartless course of human life. As a result
of this attempt, Meursault is found guilty not so much for a deed
but for living. His entire life is found guilty and unacceptable,
as any life must be judged if it is subjected to absolute moral
standards.

The absurdity of the entire situation in which man finds himself is highlighted by Camus' plot construction. A man kills without knowing why and is condemned by judges who do not

understand him or his crime. The book thus becomes a bitter satire of man's world of justice, a satire made especially evident in the closing words of the novel:

> For all to be accomplished, for me to feel less lonely, all that remained to hope was that on the day of my execution there should be a huge crowd of spectators and that they should greet me with howls of execration.[71]

Thus Meursault proves to be a stranger to himself, to his fellow-men, and to this world of absolute values. He is an intelligent creature in an absurd situation.

Throughout the novel, the idea that all is indifferent is stressed. Death is the ultimate reason for this indifference. If we must die, what does it matter what we do in life? Thus, the death of his mother or his annoyance in having to request a two-day leave are of equal importance. None of the things which normally give significance to human life reach Meursault: family, affection, love, friendship, ambition.

Nothing moves Meursault. Not marriage:

> Marie came that evening and asked me if I loved her. I replied, much as before, that her question meant nothing or next to nothing—but I supposed I didn't.
>
> "If that's how you feel," she said, "why marry me?"
>
> I explained that it had no importance really, but, if it would give her pleasure, we could get married right away. I pointed out that, anyhow, the suggestion came from her. . . .
>
> Then she remarked that marriage was a serious matter.
>
> To which I answered: "No."
>
> She kept silent after that, staring at me in a curious way. Then she asked:
>
> "Suppose another girl had asked you to marry her—I mean a girl you liked in the same way as you like me—would you have said 'Yes' to her, too?"
>
> "Naturally."

Then she said she wondered if she really loved me or not. I, of course, couldn't enlighten her as to that.[72]

Nor murder:

The sun glinted on Raymond's revolver as he handed it to me . . . the whole world seemed to have come to a standstill on this little strip of sand between the sunlight and the sea . . . and just then it crossed my mind that one might fire, or not fire—and it would come to absolutely the same thing.[73]

Nor the death of others:

I could truthfully say I'd been quite fond of Mother—but really that didn't mean much. . . . I explained that my physical condition at any given moment often influenced my feelings. For instance, on the day I attended Mother's funeral, I was fagged out and only half awake. So, really, I hardly took stock of what was happening. Anyhow I could assure him of one thing: that I'd rather Mother hadn't died.[74]

All is indifference:

It was as if that great rush of anger had washed me clean, emptied me of hope, and gazing up at the dark sky spangled with its signs and stars, for the first time . . . I laid my heart open to the benign indifference of the universe.[75]

If one has to live for something, it must be the present moment.

I have never been able really to regret anything in all my life. I've always been far too much absorbed in the present moment, or the immediate future, to think back.[76]

There are some similarities between Camus' *The Stranger* and Kafka's *Trial*. The judgment against Meursault and against Joseph K. is all wrong. Both Meursault and Joseph K. are modern men who can find no easy answers to save them from their predicament. Both Meursault and Joseph K. go to their deaths because there is something about life they never understand.

The all-pervasive mystery of life is evident in Kafka and Camus. The insolubility of life is responsible for what happens in the novels of both men. Mystery opens Joseph K.'s trial, keeps K. from reaching the castle, shrouds Meursault in strangeness, spreads disease in *The Plague,* and causes disorientation in *The Fall.*

One can see an interesting relationship between *The Trial, The Castle,* and *The Plague.* In *The Trial,* the hero looks back on his life. What did I do? What has happened? In *The Castle,* the hero looks to the elusive future. Where am I going? What must I do today and tomorrow if I would be saved? In *The Plague,* the hero does not look back or forward. There is no running. The past and the future have no answers. Man then stands upright and fights the plague. In the present, he helps, cures, saves, questions, rebels, and perishes.

The Plague

It is evident that by the time Camus writes *The Plague* (1947), his thought has progressed in another direction. It is not absurdity but rebellion which is the message of this novel. And the first discovery the rebel makes is that he shares a common suffering with all men. This realization of solidarity is comforting but still disturbing. For the community in which the individual finds himself resembles a prison more than a free and open city. Camus explains his position in his essay "A Note on Revolt."

In an absurd world, the rebel still has one certainty. It is the solidarity of men in the same adventure, the fact that the

grocer and he are both oppressed . . . the evil which attacked
an isolated man has become a collective plague.

The collective plague that oppresses us is the theme of Camus'
second major novel. Plague suddenly attacks the city of Oran in
Algiers. Thousands of rats come out into the open and die in the
streets as the story begins. The municipal authorities are re-
luctant to take measures against the malady which afflicts the
city until the number of victims reaches the alarming figure of
thirty a day. It is then that a state of siege is declared and Oran
is cut off from the world.

A group of responsible citizens in the town work together to
overcome the plague. These include:

Rieux, a medical doctor, who fights the plague with heroic
dedication.

Cottard, who is happy that the plague has come since it makes
others as apprehensive as he is and it gives him reprieve from
society's pursuit of him for an unknown crime.

Rambert, a journalist who at first selfishly wants to escape from
the city but who finally chooses to stay and fight the plague.

Tarrou, who organizes volunteers to fight the plague. He keeps
a diary of the plague and eventually dies of it. Tarrou expresses
the desire to be a saint without God.

Paneloux, a Jesuit priest, who preaches at first a violent sermon
indicting all sinners as responsible for the divine punishment of
plague. Later, he preaches a less confident but more sympathetic second sermon after he sees a child die. Paneloux is tormented by the suffering of the innocent. He works side by side
with Rieux, an atheist, for the betterment of man. He too
dies of plague, refusing any sedatives which might diminish
his pain.

It is never known whether the organized resistance to the plague is effective. After a six-month siege, the plague begins to leave. And men never know if this is due to a human effort against it or due only to the plague's unintelligible unpredictability. Rieux mentions toward the end of the novel that he is the story's chronicler. He has told this narrative to show how much men suffer in this life and to prove that, in spite of all, there is more to admire in them than to despise. Rieux claims that his story is a protest against the injustice done to man.

As the plague leaves, Oran is joyful. Rieux alone knows what the jubilant crowds do not, that plague never dies and that plague will come again some day.

> . . . Rieux resolved to compile this chronicle so that he should not be one of those who hold their peace but should bear witness in favor of those plague-stricken people; so that some memorial of the injustice and outrage done them might endure; and to state quite simply what we learn in a time of pestilence: that there are more things to admire in man than to despise.
>
> None the less, I knew that the tale he had to tell could not be one of a final victory. It could be only the record of what had had to be done, and what assuredly would have to be done again in the never ending fight against terror and its relentless onslaughts, despite their personal afflictions, by all who, while unable to be saints but refusing to bow down to pestilences, strive their utmost to be healers.[77]

The Plague is filled with meaning. Camus insists that there is a pervasive evil men struggle against but never defeat. This is a theme William Golding will explore in *Lord of the Flies*. In Camus' play, *State of Siege*, the plague is man-made totalitarianism which men can struggle against and do defeat. *The Plague*, however, deals with an even more sinister influence.

Camus artfully shows that even the most incompatible men

can find common cause in fighting plague. In their struggle, they forge a human solidarity and some understanding of each other. In order to achieve these objectives, however, they must enter anew the lists of those who rebel against man's intolerable burden. Thus, Rieux, the unbelieving doctor, Paneloux, a dedicated Christian, and Tarrou, a self-sacrificing humanitarian, all experience comradeship in their need for each other and in their hatred of plague.

Camus' deep love for men comes across strongly in this book. He once wrote: "The world in which I live is repugnant to me but I feel a solidarity with the men who suffer in it." *The Stranger* answered absurdity with indifference; *The Plague* forbids neutrality and demands an impassioned response.

Thus, Rambert declares:

> Until now I always felt a stranger in this town, and that I'd no concern with you people. But now that I've seen what I have seen, I know that I belong here whether I want it or not. This business is everybody's business.[78]

Man's impassioned response, though necessary, must always be a temperate rebellion. He cannot answer absurdity the way Caligula did, in desperate and disorganized revolt. Rieux, in doing what has to be done, in discharging his limited function in society, rebels in a moderate way. He is faithful to Camus' injunction that one must serve man in an incomplete and relative way, without aspiring to the eternal or the absolute solution. Thus Rieux rejects Paneloux's thought that both of them are working for the salvation of man.

> Salvation's much too big a word for me. I don't aim so high. I'm concerned with man's health; and for me his health comes first.[79]

The rebellion this novel summons us to is a rebellion against suffering and against the separation of man from man. It is the plague which leads men to rebel. It is the plague which forces men to become aware of their values and to fight in rebellion for the survival of these. It is the plague which convinces all that they have the ability to love each other.

> They knew now that if there is one thing one can always yearn for and sometimes attain, it is human love.[80]

Rieux is a world apart from Meursault, the indifferent murderer. He is a rebel, revolting against the totality of human suffering.

> . . . a man can't cure and know at the same time. So let's cure as quickly as we can. That's the more urgent job.[81]

There are a number of passages in *The Plague* which give us Camus' thought on a variety of topics. It might be worthwhile to cite these without comment:

Camus seems to be speaking of himself when he describes Rieux as "a man who was sick and tired of the world he lived in —though he had much liking for his fellow men—and had resolved, for his part, to have no truck with injustice and compromises with the truth."[82]

Rieux and Tarrou speak of death and rebellion:

> "Do you believe in God, doctor? . . . "
> "No—but what does that really mean? I'm fumbling in the dark, struggling to make something out. But I've long ceased finding that original. . . . I've never managed to get used to seeing people die . . . since the order of the world is shaped by death, mightn't it be better for God if we refuse to believe in Him and struggle with all our might against death, without

raising our eyes toward the heaven where He sits in silence."

Tarrou nodded.

"Yes. But your victories will never be lasting; that's all."

Rieux's face darkened.

"Yes, I know that. But it's no reason for giving up the struggle."

"No reason, I agree. Only, I now can picture what this plague must mean for you."

"Yes. A never ending defeat. . . ."

"Who taught you all this, doctor?"

The reply came promptly:

"Suffering."[83]

Rebellion frequently enough means doing one's job. Thus Rieux in a conversation with Rambert:

". . . the only means of fighting a plague is—common decency."

"What do you mean by 'common decency'?" Rambert's tone was grave.

"I don't know what it means for other people. But in my case I know that it consists in doing my job."[84]

In rebellion, there is solidarity:

Some, like Rambert, even contrived to fancy they were still behaving as free men and had the power of choice. But actually it would have been truer to say that by this time, mid-August, the plague had swallowed up everything and everyone. No longer were there individual destinies; only a collective destiny, made of plague and the emotions shared by all. Strongest of these emotions was the sense of exile . . . with all the cross-currents of revolt and fear set up by these.[85]

The plague against which we struggle is in all of us and seems to be a universal guilt which we carry in ourselves and forever inflict upon others.

... we can't stir a finger in this world without the risk of bring-
ing death to somebody ... we all have plague and I have lost
my peace ... one must do what one can to cease being plague-
stricken. .... I resolved to have no truck with anything which,
directly or indirectly ... brings death to anyone or justifies
others' putting him to death.

... each of us has the plague within him; no one, no one on
earth is free from it ... we must keep endless watch on ourselves lest in a careless moment we breathe in somebody's
face and fasten the infection on him. .... That's why every-
body in the world today looks so tired; everyone is more or less
sick of the plague. But that is also why some of us, those who
want to get the plague out of their systems, feel such desperate
weariness, a weariness from which nothing remains to set us
free except death.[86]

The depth of Camus' capacity for human compassion comes
across in a conversation between Rieux and Tarrou, and with
Rieux's observation of Tarrou's death. Human sympathy is an
indispensable value.

After a short silence the doctor raised himself a little in his chair
and asked if Tarrou had an idea of the path to follow for at-
taining peace. "Yes," he replied, "The path of sympathy. . . ."[87]

Rieux thought it too: that a loveless world is a dead world,
and always there comes an hour when one is weary of prisons,
of one's work, and of devotion to duty, and all one craves for is
a loved face, the warmth and wonder of a loving heart ... at
this moment he suffered ... and what filled his breast was the
passionate indignation we feel when confronted by the anguish
all men share.[88]

This human form, his friend's, lacerated by the spear-
thrusts of the plague, consumed by searing, superhuman fires,

buffeted by all the raging winds of heaven, was foundering under his eyes in the dark flood of the pestilence, and he could do
nothing to avert the wreck. He could only stand, unavailing, on
the shore, empty-handed and sick at heart, unarmed and helpless yet again under the onset of calamity. And thus, when the
end came, the tears that blinded Rieux's eyes were tears of im-
potence; and he did not see Tarrou roll over, face to the wall,
and die with a short, hollow groan as if somewhere within him
an essential chord had snapped. . . . this defeat was final, the
last disastrous battle that ends a war and makes peace itself an
ill beyond all remedy. The doctor could not tell if Tarrou had
found peace, now that all was over, but for himself he had a
feeling that no peace was possible to him henceforth, any more
than there can be an armistice for a mother bereaved of her son
or for a man who buries his friend.[89]

As one completes *The Plague*, he wonders where Camus'
thought will lead after this. It is many years before Camus writes
another novel. Nine years after *The Plague*, *The Fall* (1956)
was published. And one is surprised. The shift in Camus' thinking at first sight seems unexpected. On closer inspection, however, one can see a connection between this surprising story and
some of the closing thoughts in *The Plague*.

The Fall

The Fall is the story of Jean-Baptiste Clamence, a once-suc-
cessful Parisian attorney, now living as a broken man in Amsterdam. Clamence spends most of his time now in the "Mexico City
Bar." He awaits the occasional tourist who may frequent the bar
and prove not totally uninterested in hearing his tale. *The Fall*
is the account of Jean-Baptiste's life, told in the form of a confession to an unnamed and silent tourist.

Clamence was once a man who had all life could offer. At the height of his phenomenal success, he experienced a terrifying insight into himself. One evening while returning home, he saw a young girl leaning over the railing of a Parisian bridge. As he proceeded on his way, she jumped into the water and cried for help. He made no effort to rescue her. He cannot forget the incident and as he recalls it he is re-convinced over and over again of his cowardice. On an evening after this, he is returning home again across the Pont des Arts when he hears a laugh of derision. He cannot tell where it came from, but he concludes it is the world laughing at him. Clamence's façade of happiness, innocence, and self-contentment crumbles as the days pass.

Soon Clamence is driven to forsake Paris, the scene of his successful but empty life. He goes to Amsterdam, a city he hates, where he becomes both penitent for his crime and judge of others. In this new role of judge-penitent, he regains some self-confidence. He confesses his shortcomings to strangers and then subtly turns the tables and judges his hearers as guilty of the same faults.

The Fall shows us a different Camus, as we have said. It strikes a quiet, almost melancholy note. It has not the flash of the sun or the roar of the pistol that *The Stranger* describes. Nor does it have the groaning terror of a city besieged by plague and struggling against death. It is a work of both enormous restraint and personal intensity.

In its few pages and fewer incidents, *The Fall* manages to give a message of eloquence and durability to all of us. One of the most important moments in the story occurs on the evening when Clamence hears a young girl's cry in the night. Clamence's inability to save the girl convinces him that he has never really had any interest in loving others. His apparent life of virtue was never more than a sham, all show and no substance. The cry of distress comes between and severs forever the Clamence of sham virtue and the true Clamence. It convinces him that he can be something more if he chooses. He can turn toward genuine interest in people, but he decides to remain only as he is.

Freely, Clamence chooses to ignore the cry of distress. Then he finds himself incapable of enduring the personal guilt which that free choice of an artificial self brought with it. That night in Paris, Clamence discovered the true burden of human freedom: ". . . on the bridges of Paris, I too learned that I was afraid of freedom."

> . . . Freedom is not a reward or a decoration that is celebrated with champagne. . . . Oh, no! It's a chore, on the contrary, and a long-distance race, quite solitary and very exhausting. No champagne, no friends raising their glasses as they look at you affectionately. Alone in a forbidding room, alone in the prisoner's box before judges, and alone to decide in face of oneself or in the face of others' judgment. At the end of all freedom is a court sentence; that's why freedom is too heavy to bear, especially when you're down with a fever, or are distressed, or love nobody.[90]

And now what is Clamence to do? He has his freedom and his guilt. He is afraid of the one and distressed by the other. There is no God to assure him of pardon. He seeks a type of forgiveness in the proclamation of his guilt to all who visit the "Mexico City Bar." This does not cure him of guilt. Nor does it give him the freedom he needs to do the things he must do for himself. But it is the most he can do at this point in his life.

A distinct progression then has occurred in the thought of Albert Camus. In *The Stranger* and *The Myth of Sisyphus,* Camus spoke of an individual before a fragmented and absurd universe. In *The Plague* and *The Rebel,* Camus speaks of an individual seeking a value in solidarity before an oppressive metaphysical or historical situation. In *The Fall,* however, Camus speaks of an individual not before a universe or a situation but before himself. *The Fall* shows man as a creature of tension and irony from within himself; a being in exile; a spirit seeking fulfillment, freedom, and an innocence he does not have. The distinctive characteristic of *The Fall* is its insistence that tension, exile, guilt come not from outside but from within a man's heart.

In all of Camus from *The Stranger* to *The Fall*, as in Kafka, there is not a hatred or a contempt for man's predicament. There is only an empty stupor, a total inability to understand, a never-asked but ever-present questioning: What has happened to us and to our world? Whose fault is it? Is there a way out?

In *The Stranger, The Myth of Sisyphus, The Plague* and *The Rebel*, Camus insisted that man was innocent and the world unjust. Man was not criminal but victim. He was sacrificed to a scheme of things which dehumanized him, made a plaything of a fate which always destroyed him.

The Fall is a disquieting book, more disquieting than anything Clamence convinces us that if man suffers, it is entirely his own fault. It seems not too much to see in *The Fall* a movement toward God. It is just possible that this novel expresses a realization of sin and unworthiness which leads to, if it does not come from, grace. Everything about the story is religious: the canals of Amsterdam are there to remind us of the concentric circles of Dante's hell; the title of the book is religious; the concern with man's unworthiness is similar to the themes developed by Graham Greene and François Mauriac; the entire mood in *The Fall* suggests a cry from the depths of human need for a salvation more permanent than any man can give.

The Fall is a disquieting book, more disquieting than anything Camus has written. Until *The Fall*, Camus called men to rebel against all those things which would destroy us. Man was surrounded with evil and had to fight to keep it from him. In *The Fall*, Camus suggests that evil is something man-made. The enemy is not so much the situation in which man is placed but man's freedom. Man can no longer cry, "I, the innocent rebel, protest." In humility and shame, he must pray, "I, the guilty one, need innocence." Clamence is seeking a Christ or a God, though he cannot yet accept either Christ or God. He clings to the truth of himself and to the reality of his self-made guilt, and he almost hopes for another Truth and an assurance of Innocence.

The Fall is a profound statement on the condition of modern man. It deals with man, not yet on the religious level, but on that fundamental level from which religious expression issues. In *The Fall*, Camus has put his finger on the anguish of our age: How can one find innocence again without God? Camus proves himself in the novel a man painfully involved in the contradictions and aspirations of our times.

Before completing our commentary on *The Fall*, a series of passages from the novel may deepen our appreciation of what Camus is trying to achieve.

On vanity and egocentricity: [Clamence indicts himself]

. . . I could live happily only on condition that all the individuals on earth, or the greatest possible number, were turned toward me, eternally in suspense, devoid of independent life, and ready to answer my call at any moment, doomed in short to sterility until the day I should deign to favor them. In short, for me to live happily it was essential for the creatures I chose not to live at all. They must receive their life, sporadically, only at my bidding.[91]

On man's need for a God of forgiveness:

Believe me, religions are on the wrong track the moment they moralize and fulminate commandments. God is not needed to create guilt or to punish. Our fellow men suffice, aided by ourselves. You were speaking of the Last Judgment. Allow me to laugh respectfully. I shall wait for it resolutely, for I have

known what is worse, the judgment of men. . . . God's sole usefulness would be to guarantee innocence, and I am inclined to
see religion rather as a huge laundering venture. . . . I'll tell
you a big secret, *mon cher*. Don't wait for the Last Judgment.
It takes place every day.[92]

On man's need to have a master and on an unnamed atheist
who could be Camus:

Ah, *mon cher*, for anyone who is alone, without God and without
a master, the weight of days is dreadful. Hence one must choose
a master, God being out of style. . . . I knew an atheistic novelist
who used to pray every night. That didn't stop anything: how
he gave it to God in his books.[93]

On Christ:

There was a time when I didn't at any minute have the slightest
idea how I could reach the next one. Yes, one can wage war in
this world, ape love, torture one's fellow man or merely say evil
of one's neighbor while knitting. But, in certain cases, carrying
on, merely continuing, is superhuman. And [Christ] was not
superhuman, you can take my word for it. He cried aloud his
agony and that's why I love him, my friend who died without
knowing.
. . . too many people now climb onto the cross merely to be seen
from a greater distance, even if they have to trample somewhat
on the one who has been there so long. . . . Oh, the injustice,
the rank injustice that has been done him! It wrings my heart!
. . . He, my friend, didn't expect so much. He simply wanted
to be loved, nothing more. Of course, there are those who love
him, even among Christians. But they are not numerous.[94]

The Fall at times is so close to a religious expression or a
Christian conception of things that one might wonder exactly

what Camus thought of Christianity. To complete this rather extensive essay on Camus, a word on his evaluation of Christianity
may prove of especial interest.

Camus and Christianity

In an open letter to Camus, in *Les Temps Modernes* (August,
1952), Sartre wrote of Camus' earlier days and at the same time
broke with him since their respective philosophies now differed
so greatly. Sartre commented:

> You were almost exemplary. For you have within yourself all
> the conflicts of our time and went beyond them because of the
> ardor with which you lived them. You were a real person, the
> most complex and the richest, the last and the most gifted of
> the heirs of Chateaubriand and the scrupulous defender of a
> social cause. You had all the luck and all the merits, bringing to
> a sense of greatness a passionate love of beauty, to the joy of
> living, the sense of death. . . . How we loved you then.

Camus was clearly a man all admired easily. This admiration
led the Dominican monastery at Latour-Maubourg to invite him
to speak to the Catholic clergy there in 1948. It gave Camus the
opportunity to speak out explicitly on his view of Catholicism.[95]

> If there is anyone who can ask anything of the Christian, it is
> the Christian himself. The conclusion is that if I allowed myself
> at the end of this statement to demand of you certain duties,
> these could only be duties that it is essential to ask of any man
> today, whether he is or is not a Christian.

Camus then goes on to admit that in an earlier controversy
with François Mauriac, "François Mauriac got the better of me."

> The other day at the Sorbonne, speaking to a Marxist lecturer,
> a Catholic priest said in public that he too was anticlerical.

Well, I don't like priests who are anticlerical any more than philosophers that are ashamed of themselves. Hence I shall not, as far as I am concerned, try to pass myself off as a Christian in your presence. I share with you the same revulsion from evil. But I do not share your hope, and I continue to struggle against the universe in which children suffer and die. . . . For a long time . . . I have waited for a great voice to speak up in Rome. I, an unbeliever? Precisely. For I knew that the spirit would be lost if it did not utter a cry of condemnation with force. . . . It has been explained to me since that the condemnation was indeed voiced. But that it was in the style of the encyclicals, which is not at all clear. The condemnation was voiced and it was not understood! . . . What the world expects of Christians is that Christians should speak out loud and clear, and that they should voice their condemnation in such a way that never a doubt, never the slightest doubt, could rise in the heart of the simplest man. . . . Perhaps we cannot prevent this world from being a world in which children are tortured. But we can reduce the number of tortured children. And if you don't help us, who else in the world can help us do this? . . . But it may be, and this is even more probable, that Christianity will insist on maintaining a compromise or else on giving its condemnations the obscure form of the encyclical. Possibly it will insist on losing once and for all the virtue of revolt and indignation that belonged to it long ago. In that case, Christians will live and Christianity will die.

Summarizing Camus' difficulties with Christianity is not an easy task. His indictment shifts and changes and, at times, as in the lecture quoted above, he is filled with sympathy for all Christianity is and tries to be. In his more critical moments, Camus regrets a number of attitudes Christianity instills:

1. Christianity preaches an accommodation with a world of injustice founded on the sacrifice of the innocent. It fails to issue a continued and impassioned protest at the death of innocence and the innocent in this life.

2. Christianity thereby creates a climate of indifference to human suffering.

In *The Plague*, Camus insisted that suffering and death cannot be written off as elements in a divine higher purpose. They are horrible and revolting. They must be fought.

As Camus reminded his Dominican audience, "I share with you the same horror of evil. But I do not share your hope and I continue to struggle against this universe where children suffer and die."

3. Christianity too often judges human life by values foreign to it rather than by values man can easily recognize, values one can realize in history and by human action.

In an early work, *Nuptials*, Camus observed: "I love this life with abandon and I want to speak of it freely; it fills me with pride at my human fate."

Or, later, in the same work: "I do not want to believe that death opens onto another life. For me, it is a closed door. I do not say that it is a 'step we must all take' but that it is a horrible and dirty adventure. . . . I have too much youth in me to speak of death."

In an essay, "Summer in Algiers," Camus wrote:

There are words I have never really understood, such as "sin." Yet I believe these men have never sinned against life. For if there is a sin against life, it consists perhaps not so much in despairing of life as in hoping for another life and in eluding the implacable grandeur of this life.[96]

4. Christianity often keeps man from total involvement in his time and from feeling the agony of the human experiment.

I learn that there is no superhuman happiness, no eternity outside the sweep of days. These paltry and essential belongings,
these relative truths are the only ones to stir me. As for the
others, the "ideal" truths, I have not enough soul to understand
them. Not that one must be an animal, but I find no meaning
in the happiness of angels. I know simply that this sky will
last longer than I. And what shall I call eternity except what
will continue after my death? I am not expressing here the creature's satisfaction with his condition. It is quite a different matter. It is not always easy to be a man, still less to be a pure
man. But being pure is recovering the spiritual home where one
can feel the world's relationship, where one's pulsebeats coin-
cide with the violent throbbing of the two-o'clock sun . . . what
negates me in this life is first of all what kills me. Everything
that exalts life at the same time increases its absurdity. In the
Algerian summer I learn that one thing only is more tragic than
suffering, and that is the life of a happy man. But it may be
also the way to a greater life. . . .[97]

One wonders what Camus would have thought of Vatican II-
Christianity: John XXIII, *Mater et Magistra, Pacem In Terris,*
the Council, Ecumenism, Paul VI. Christianity is committed to
mankind so deeply and so explicitly today. This is an age when
we remember none fought evil so relentlessly as Christ. He
never surrendered before it, though it overcame Him in death.
He opposed physical evil with healing, moral evil with forgiveness, prejudice with love, death with resurrection. And the
Church was created to continue this work.

"Let the world know this," Paul VI has exhorted, "the Church
looks at the world with profound understanding, with sincere
admiration, with a sincere intention not of conquering it, but
of serving it; not of destroying it, but of appreciating it; not of
condemning it, but of strengthening and saving it."

In *Ecclesiam Suam,* Paul asked humanity not to plunge "itself into a crude form of pessimism which declares its own vices, weaknesses, and moral ailments to be fatal, incurable, and perhaps even desirable as manifestations of freedom and of authenticity." Yet Paul realized: "The world cannot be saved from the outside. . . . A man must first be understood; and, where he merits it, agreed with. In the very act of trying to make ourselves pastors and teachers of men, we must make ourselves their brothers." One wonders if Camus would still find papal encyclicals unclear or unsympathetic.

> Whether or not [Camus] is an atheistic humanist is a judgment which, it seems to us, cannot be made, despite the strictly nontheistic direction of his thought. When, in his essays, it appears that he is suggesting an atheistic position, Camus has inserted footnote references to caution that he is not making such an inference . . . we will know whether Camus is an atheist only when he writes an essay on God; it is unlikely that this will ever come to pass.[98]

To conclude then: Camus calls not for complete freedom, since he sees this as complete bondage. He writes to discover the restrictions, laws, and values which must limit freedom or, perhaps, preserve it. He is convinced that the world is the only truth we have and that salvation must be achieved in this world. Until we find further answers, we must live in solidarity, struggle, sensitivity to each other, and guilt.

J. D. SALINGER (1919–   )
Man is innocent and sacred in a world of guilt

With J. D. Salinger, we deal once again with an American writer. We intend to consider his thesis in conjunction with that of William Golding, whom we study next and whose view of man is quite different.

Salinger was born in New York, of a Jewish father and a Christian mother. It may be of interest, in view of the plot structure of some of his books, to know that he has no brothers and one sister (Doris, eight years older than he). He graduated from Valley Forge Military Academy in June of 1936. During World War II, Salinger served with the Fourth Infantry Division until the Battle of the Bulge. He landed on Utah Beach, on D-Day, June 6, 1944, some five hours after the first assault forces.

For all practical purposes, Salinger is a recluse. He lives in Cornish, New Hampshire, unavailable to all visitors. While he was writing *Catcher in the Rye,* he did frequent "Nap's Lunch," a teen-age hangout in Windsor, Vermont, across the river from his home. After his book was published, he was no longer seen but retreated behind the protective walls of his own property. Salinger is a painstaking artist. He takes a packed lunch almost every day and writes in a cement-block cell near his home from 8:30 until 5:30.

We shall return to our earlier procedure in studying J. D. Salinger. First, we shall give a summary and some notes on two of his main novels: *The Catcher in the Rye* and *Franny and Zooey.* Later, we shall consider what seem to be typical Salinger themes.

The Catcher in the Rye

The Catcher in the Rye is the story of Holden Caulfield, sixteen, an innocent and painfully sensitive teen-ager. He is in conflict with what he sees to be a depraved, inauthentic, "phony" society. He flees a preparatory school, seeing it as an institution designed to facilitate the passage of youth from innocence to the sophisticated corruption necessary for success. The action continues in various parts of Manhattan and covers some three days of the Christmas season. In New York, it is once again the same story. Hypocrisy is now revealed in a larger perspective. Throughout the novel, Holden feels almost a compulsion to communicate and to love. And throughout the novel, he is thwarted by the phoniness, indifference, and vulgarity which surround him. He comes to resent all the conditions which keep him from meeting others on a genuine level and from loving others as he wishes.

Holden Caulfield is a seeker after the goodness in life, even against oppressive odds. He punches Stradlater, who is twice his weight, because he suspects Stradlater may have seduced Jane Gallagher, without any consideration of the fact that she is the kind of girl who keeps all her kings, at checkers, in the back row. He gives money away to nuns because they never go anywhere "swanky" for lunch. He can read a child's notebook all day and night. He furiously rubs out obscenities scribbled on school walls. And when Phoebe, his young sister, asks him what he would like to be, he explains that he would like to be a catcher in a field of rye, keeping children from falling off the "crazy cliff." He would be the only adult around and he would forever protect the unaware from the hazards before them and from the "crazy cliff."[99]

In his search for goodness, Holden is filled with love and affection for people. He is almost painfully involved at times with certain people: his dead brother Allie whom he loves; James Castle, a schoolmate accidentally killed because he would not retract a statement he believed true; the kettle drummer at Radio City Music Hall; the nuns he meets at a lunch counter; a young boy walking along a curb with one foot in the gutter, humming "If a body meet a body. . . ." Even the ducks in Central Park are an object of his concern as he wonders what they do during the winter. He confesses to Antolini, a former teacher of his, that he can hate people only part of the time.

His love is especially deep for Phoebe. He knows he cannot protect her forever from growing up and this hurts him because he cares so much about her.

Holden quite simply cannot meet society on its own terms. He cannot love as he wishes and as he must. Therefore, he loses his grip on himself and suffers mental disorientation. But he goes on loving to the end. In the closing words of the novel, he confesses that he misses everyone and suggests that if one wants never to miss anyone he ought not tell "anybody anything."

Franny and Zooey

Franny and Zooey is not really a novel but a collection of two short stories. Both together describe the religious and emotional crisis of Franny Glass, the youngest member of the family, and the attempt her brother Zooey makes to help her out of the difficulty.

Franny is first seen being met at the station for a football weekend by a young college student named Lane Coutell. During lunch, her escort proves insufferably boring as he smugly explains his latest "A" paper to her. Gradually, it becomes clear what is troubling Franny. She suffers, like Holden Caulfield, from an intense weariness of all that is phony. She suffers from an oversensitivity to the world.

To escape from her dilemma, Franny tells her escort that she has been reading a religious classic called *The Way of a Pilgrim*. It is the story of an anonymous Russian peasant who roams the land learning and then teaching the Jesus prayer: "Lord Jesus Christ, have mercy on me."

Lane listens in boredom and then dismisses the entire affair. After all, he explains, all religious experience is little more than a psychological problem.

Franny grows ill as the evening continues and eventually faints. When she regains consciousness, she stares at the ceiling, then begins to move her lips soundlessly over and over again in the Jesus prayer.

In *Zooey*, Franny has returned from the weekend and has taken to the couch in the Glass living room, clutching *The Way of a Pilgrim* and petting her cat, Bloomberg. Zooey (Franny's

actor brother) and Bessie (her mother) converse throughout the
story with Franny. There is only one other character who figures
in the story. Though he is dead, Seymour (an elder brother) almost dominates the remaining characters. Seymour killed himself some seven years before. He was, by all accounts, a genius
and near saint.

Zooey tries to bring Franny out of her obsession with the
Jesus prayer mostly by showing her she must not withdraw from
people. (She must not spurn the commonplace, the "cups of
consecrated chicken soup, which is the only kind anybody offers
around this madhouse".) She must not become egocentric. Zooey
fails in his first attempts until, toward the end of the story, he
enters an unused bedroom in the huge apartment. It once belonged to Seymour and it still contains a private phone listed in
Seymour's name. Zooey sits for nearly an hour in a near trance
and then picks up the phone. He finally gets Franny to talk by
speaking of their dead brother Seymour.

Zooey reminds Franny that when they were child prodigies on
a radio quiz program, Seymour always insisted that they shine
their shoes "for the Fat Lady"—that is, for all the lonely, hard-
to-love, unseen but very real people "out there." The Fat Lady,
Zooey explains, is everywhere. One must do everything for her.
The "Fat Lady," Zooey continues, was only Seymour's way of
saying that one must do everything for Christ.[100]

The Need for Innocence

The predominant, if not exclusive, theme Salinger develops in
his writings is the human need for innocence and sincerity.

Holden Caulfield is a creature of innocence. He is sensitive to
beauty and goodness in a world that does not recognize sufficiently the value of these. Because of this, he suffers. His awareness of innocence is something he wants to share with all adults.
They too must be sincere, conscious of their potentialities and

dignity. They must not judge their worth by the standards of our "phony" society.

Adults, however, do not respond easily to Holden's call. He is more receptive, therefore, to children who understand him. Children are themselves; children are innocent; he can love them as he wishes. Yet Holden's association with children is not trouble-free. He worries about them. They have to grow up. And when they grow up, they are going to lose their innocence. Is there anything he can do? If only, he feels, he could be a "catcher in the rye" and save children from the "crazy cliff" of growing up and becoming phony. If only he could spend all his life as a protector of the innocence of men. But things don't work out that way. Innocence and children cannot be perfectly protected. They have to reach for the gold ring the way children always do on a carousel. If they fall off, they fall off. One must not, however, keep them from reaching.

Because Holden suffers so much from the phoniness of the world and because he worries so much about man's loss of goodness, he feels more and more alienated from society. He wants at times to leave it. Eventually, toward the end of the novel, Holden's inability to communicate with society is so final that he dreams of becoming a deaf-mute hermit.[101]

At those moments when Holden feels most alienated, he muses on the ducks at Central Park and wonders where they go for the winter. He feels a strong kinship with their homelessness.

Yet no matter how disappointed Holden becomes, he still dreams of saving or helping his fellow-men.

It would be a bit of an exaggeration to see Holden Caulfield as a Christ-figure in the fullest sense of that word. The theme of innocence, however, is so strong in *The Catcher in the Rye* that some Christ-like elements do show forth. Holden, for example, is not so much a rebel as he is a figure who suffers because of the way things are. He broods over evil, rubs out obscenities scribbled on walls, feels compassion for the youth and lost innocence of prostitutes, and is most himself with children or the child-like. He wants all suffering and still-tender innocence to come to him so that he can save it from the "crazy cliff." Holden, in fact, loves the world more than the world can bear. He has almost too much love to give. The world, as Kierkegaard commented, slaughters love. And the world, not able to absorb all of Holden's love for it, contributes to his breakdown.

Holden's greatest anguish comes from his inability to get all of the love inside himself out. This is a theme Salinger touched upon in the character of Seymour, the eldest brother of Franny Glass, who committed suicide. In a short story describing Seymour's suicide, "A Perfect Day for Bananafish," Salinger shows that Seymour suffers from the same ailment which afflicts Holden.

Seymour speaks of bananafish and banana fever one day on the beach with a little girl named Sybil. Banana fever is what bananafish get when they swallow too many bananas. When they do this, they die.[102] For they want too much from life.

Seymour's problem comes from having "too much sublimity" within him. Life is too rich and love is too deep to go on living. He suffers from banana fever. It is a perfect day for bananafish, a perfect day to die and avoid the poignancy of life. It is the day of Seymour's suicide.

Seymour really had had this problem with "too much sublimity" all his life. At twelve, he threw a stone at a young feminine playmate and did nine stitches worth of damage to her face. Seymour's brother, Buddy, explains the reason for this in one of Salinger's latest books, *Raise High the Roof Beam, Carpenters*. Seymour was compelled to disfigure the girl because she was so beautiful.[103]

The story of Seymour is a strange one. He marries at twenty-five, in 1942, with scars on his wrist from previous suicide attempts. At the time, he is contemplating psychiatric treatment. He has decided to marry a girl of no intelligence or sensitivity.

Seymour leaves her at the altar, then later elopes with her. After six years of marriage and some psychiatric help, he shoots himself in a Florida motel in 1948. It is not until *Raise High the Roof Beam, Carpenters* that we learn of Seymour's reasons for leaving his bride at the altar. His action is explained once again from too much sublimity, love, or sensitivity within him. He does not know how to get it all out and thus suffers as does Holden Caulfield. Seymour has too much joy, he is "too happy" to marry a girl before a crowd of people on the day of his wedding.[104]

Salinger returns to the same theme of saving love and man's inability to express it in another short story, "For Esme—with Love and Squalor." In the story, a soldier at one point sums up its message when he writes that hell is the suffering of those people who are unable to love.[105] The inscription he copies is taken from Dostoevsky. One is reminded over and over again by Salinger of W. H. Auden's warning, "We must love one another or die." It comes across in Holden Caulfield, Seymour Glass, and an unnamed soldier. One can call it banana fever or hell or being too keyed up to be with people, but it comes to the same thing. Man must feel love and express it before man can be saved.

To continue with our analysis of Holden Caulfield and some of his Christ-figure characteristics: Holden hardly does anything wrong. Even his temptation with a prostitute does not possess him, for it was against his principles and, in part, the effect of a feeling of depression.

Holden's entire life is really a pilgrimage seeking the genuine, the sincere, the pure, the beautiful in life. In his search he gives all; he must be thought of as a person who found the "Fat Lady" or Christ in other people. He sacrifices himself in a constant war against evil, even though he realizes that it is an unending task.

Love then, Salinger teaches, is the only salvific value we have. A soldier in "For Esme—with Love and Squalor" gains just enough love from a little girl's attention to live one more day.

Phoebe's love for Holden keeps him sane somewhat longer. Zooey's love for her and for the "Fat Lady," brings Franny back to reality and happiness. Because Seymour cannot express love or find it, he commits suicide. The message is clear: if we can only love, we shall be saved.

Holden's love for others knows no limits, but it is especially reserved for the poor in goods, appearance, and spirit. He gives ten dollars to nuns who never go anywhere "swanky for lunch." He worries about the ducks in Central Park. He realizes how wretched his mother would feel if he died, especially since she is still suffering from the death of his brother Allie. Holden forgives Stradlater and Maurice the bell-boy who betray him and beat him. He is never quite so distressed at what people do to him as he is by what they do to themselves and each other.

Thus Salinger shows that we need salvation, not justice or judgment. We need understanding and love, not an indictment from God or each other nor a threat nor a reminder of guilt. In this regard, he reminds us of Albert Camus.

It is clear that Holden in his innocence does love and loves deeply. His problem is how to communicate, how to reach the other, how to bestow on another one's real self and receive the real other in return. Fifteen times in *Catcher*, he tries to telephone other people. Only four times does he find those available whom he wishes to reach. Every time, he is dissatisfied with the way his attempt at communication has worked out. "I wasn't in the mood," he explains when another telephone experience fails.

As Holden reaches for other people, he searches for himself as well. He feels continually threatened by the world around him which will give him all the free expression he wants only if he shows himself to be what he is not. He is involved in the same search for identity and relief from loneliness which Thomas Wolfe described.

What Holden really needs to be saved is the lost kingdom

Camus speaks of—the lost kingdom Hammarskjold speaks of in *Markings:*

> A sunny day in March. Within the birch tree's slender shadow on the crest of snow, the freezing stillness of the air is crystal-lized. Then—all of a sudden—the first blackbird's piercing note of call, a reality outside yourself, the real world. All of a sud-den—the Earthly Paradise from which we have been excluded by our knowledge.[106]

Holden is in search of the ideal world man has lost forever. He cannot find the ideal present (Jane Gallagher, his ideal girl, never answers the phone); he cannot discover the ideal past (an Egyptian mummy he admires in a museum is defaced); he de-spairs of the ideal future (he cannot always have Phoebe as she is now).

The situation would be helped if only that which was good would remain. But this never happens except in a museum where everything always stays just where it is. This is, in his eyes, an advantage because people are always somehow ruining things.

What Holden then wants most desperately from the world and from other people is some reassurance that his outlook is not futile, some hope that the things he believes in and needs may one day come to pass, some enduring sign that the dream he has dreamed has not been dreamed in vain. Someone must tell him that his view of life is not a fantasy adolescents surrender as they reach maturity, but that it is a vision which can inspire men and a supreme possibility which they can make real if they only try hard enough and will only love enough.

In this search, Holden does not really want to live without God. At times, he gives evidence of his interest in Christ and of his religious feeling. He has moments when he feels "like praying or something." He does not see himself as "religious," but says that he does like Jesus.[107] When he visits his dead brother Allie in the cemetery, he is sure Allie is in heaven, but he is distressed that Allie cannot see the sun and that when it rains, it rains on Allie's grave.[108]

Salinger's interest in religion as a solution to the problem of man occurs in all his writings. In *Franny and Zooey* it is quite explicit; in the short stories, it is a frequent concern; in *Catcher*, religion is more oblique.

In the short story *Teddy*, Teddy's concern with God is constant. Teddy loves God, he explains, but his love for God is not sentimental.[109]

Salinger's rejection of sentimentality occurs again in *Raise High the Roof Beam, Carpenters* when he explains that sentimentality involves giving something more tenderness than God gives to it.[110]

Teddy speaks of God frequently. The trouble with America as Teddy sees it is that it's very difficult to meditate in America. People think you will get sick if you think about God too much.[111]

Holden, to return to *Catcher in the Rye*, represents in many ways our generation of Americans: tough-minded and fragile, humorous and heart-breaking, intelligent, sensitive, affectionate, and generous—fighting grueling battles, leaderless in a world they never made, in agony to authenticity.

Antolini, Holden's former teacher, gives him some of the best advice the boy receives in the novel. He tells Holden he has to find out where he wants to go. Phoebe once told Holden that he never seemed to like anything that was happening. Antolini observes that Holden will find he is not the first person who was ever confused and frightened and heart-broken by the way people act.[112] According to Antolini, while the immature man may want to die nobly for a cause, the mature man wants to live humbly for one.[113]

Holden then typifies many things: man's concern for innocence; man's need to be judged by real and sympathetic standards; man's obligation to protest against the society he lives in and to love it deeply; man's passion to reach his fellow-men; man's yearning for a lost kingdom, an ideal, a good, that lasts, and for reassurance that his deepest hopes are not futile. In Holden, we see something of our need for God, a moral code to fit our problems, and the influence of Christ in our lives.

Salinger is as modern as Wolfe and Camus in his view of man. Holden is in crisis and with him all of us. The sincerity, truth, and innocence he seeks he cannot find in the adult world. He can only recognize these values in immature Phoebe, deceased Allie, the lost ducks in Central Park, or in gentle nuns. He will not compromise and therefore he has nowhere to go. He will not be less than himself. If our Christian vocation means anything, it obliges all of us to find a place in our hearts and in this world for all the Holden Caulfields God has made.

WILLIAM GOLDING (1911–   )
The evil in our lives comes from ourselves

William Golding defends a thesis which is diametrically opposed to that of J. D. Salinger. Man is not a creature of innocence at all; rather he is the source of all the evil in which we live.

William Golding was born in Cornwall, England, on September 19, 1911. He graduated from Bracenose College, Oxford, in 1934 and served with the British navy during the Second World War. *Lord of the Flies*, his first novel, was written in 1954.

The novel opens on an unnamed Pacific Island where a group of English schoolboys, ranging in age from six to twelve, have been castaway. They are the survivors of an unexplained plane crash. The island on which they find themselves has an Eden-like atmosphere about it though there is talk right from the beginning of a "snake-like thing" on the same island.

The first two figures to appear on the scene are Ralph and Piggy. A conch shell is found and Ralph blows it like a trumpet. Tattered boys appear from all directions. Jack Merridew makes the most dramatic appearance, leading a group of choir boys, all wearing black capes. When all are assembled, the boys decide to elect a chief. Jack wants the position very much. The entire choir group votes for him, but all the others vote for Ralph and elect him.

The boys speak fearfully of the "snake-thing" and Ralph tries to calm them.

> "He wants to know what you're going to do about the snake-thing."
> Ralph laughed, and the other boys laughed with him.
> The small boy twisted further into himself.
> "Tell us about the snake-thing."
> "Now he says it was a beastie."
> "Beastie?"
> "A snake-thing. Ever so big. He saw it."
> "Where?"
> "In the woods. . . . He says in the morning it turned into them things like ropes in the trees and hung in the branches. . . ."
> "But there isn't a beastie!" . . .
> "Ralph's right of course. There isn't a snake-thing. But if there was a snake we'd hunt it and kill it. . . ."
> "But there isn't a snake!"
> "We'll make sure when we go hunting."
> Ralph was annoyed and, for the moment, defeated. He felt himself facing something ungraspable. . . . Something he had not known was there rose in him and compelled him to make the point loudly and again.
> ". . . I tell you there isn't a beast!"[114]

Ralph begins to organize the boys into a structure that will assure them of survival. The boys, of course, want more than mere survival, though this itself is a grace. Ralph articulates the desire of the group and of all men when he exclaims:

> we want to be rescued . . . we want to be rescued; and of course we shall be rescued.[115]

A tension which at times expresses itself in open hostility exists between Ralph and Jack Merridew. Jack is made responsible for keeping a signal fire going on top of the mountain in the hope of attracting ships that may pass by. Jack is also chief of a group of boys who become hunters. At one group meeting, Ralph admonishes the group because of a growing breakdown of discipline and authority. Jack takes issue with Ralph's leadership and withdraws from the group with his followers. Piggy advises Ralph that he must take a firmer stand and that Jack would not oppose him if only he would stand up to Jack now.

When a parachute-figure is discovered on the mountain, Jack accuses Ralph of inability to cope with this beast. He tries to take over leadership of the entire island operation. Ralph is supported by the boys and Jack goes off to the forest in anger. Jack and his followers, on a hunt, kill a pig, sever its head, impale it on a stick, and set it in the ground as a sacrifice to the beast of the island.

Another boy, Simon, wanders alone in the forest, comes upon the head of the pig, and converses mystically with it. He returns to tell the group of his discovery. They are all engaged in a frenzied ritual dance as Simon tries to join them. Frightened by his sudden appearance and not knowing who he is, they kill him. As Simon dies, the parachute and its corpse descend on the boys now turned killers of each other.

The next morning Ralph and Piggy accuse the group of guilt for the previous evening's activity. A fight with sharp, wooden spears ensues between Ralph and Jack. But on Piggy's orders, Ralph grounds his spear. Piggy holds up the conch shell, appealing for reason to prevail. As Piggy pleads for sanity, Roger, a henchman of Jack, pushes a huge boulder on Piggy, killing him brutally and shattering the conch shell, the symbol of authority. Ralph runs, comes upon the pig's head, and smashes it. The next day the hunt for Ralph begins. Frantic with fear, Ralph spears one hunter and runs. Jack and his followers set fire to the brush to get Ralph into the open. He runs deeper into the forest. Ralph is doomed and in desperation he flees aimlessly. He comes across a small painted boy and spears him. He wounds another boy and tries to hide. Fire is everywhere. He heads for the beach and begins to cry for mercy. Miraculously, he runs into a naval officer just arrived on the island who ends the hunt.

> Ralph looked at [the naval officer] dumbly. For a moment, he had a fleeting picture of the strange glamour that had once invested the beaches. But the island was scorched up like dead wood—Simon was dead—and Jack had. . . . The tears began to flow and sobs shook him. He gave himself up to them now for the first time on the island; great, shuddering spasms of grief that seemed to wrench his whole body. His voice rose under the black smoke before the burning wreckage of the island; and infected by that emotion, the other little boys began to shake and sob too. And in the middle of them, with filthy body, matted hair, and unwiped nose, Ralph wept for the end of innocence, the darkness of man's heart, and the fall through the air of the true, wise friend called Piggy.[116]

One of the finest commentaries on this story was written by Golding himself for Coward-McCann, his American publisher.

> The theme is an attempt to trace the defects of society back to the defects of human nature. Before the war, most Europeans believed that man could be perfected by perfecting society. We all saw a hell of a lot in the war that can't be accounted for except on the basis of original evil. . . . The officer, having in-

terrupted a man-hunt, prepares to take the children off the island in a cruiser which will presently be hunting its enemy in the same implacable way. And who will rescue the adult and his cruiser?

One of the keys for interpreting the story is the conversation between Simon the mystic and the severed pig's head. The pig is the "lord of the flies" (Beelzebub in Hebrew possibly has this meaning). Simon the mystic and the pig representing original evil meet alone in the forest and the pig is confident of victory.

> What are you doing out here all alone? Aren't you afraid of me? . . . There isn't anyone to help you. Only me. And I'm the beast. . . . Fancy thinking the beast was something you could hunt and kill. . . . You knew, didn't you? I'm part of you. Close, close, close! I'm the reason why it's no go—why things are what they are. . . . I'm warning you . . . You're not wanted. Understand? We are going to have fun on this island.[117]

Holden in *Catcher*, Simon here, Camus in his writings all struggle against the way things are. All are in metaphysical rebellion. Holden sees evil in the society we have made. Simon learns that evil is in each of us. Camus thought of evil as originating in the world outside man until he wrote *The Fall*.

Simon, at one point, moves against the group opinion that there may not be a beast:

> "Maybe," he said hesitantly, "maybe there is a beast. . . . What I mean is . . . maybe it's only us." Simon became inarticulate in his effort to express mankind's essential illness.[118]

At times, there is a realization that original evil pursues us as well as possessing us. Jack explains once to Ralph after a hunting trip:

There's nothing in it of course. Just a feeling. But you can feel
as if you're not hunting but—being hunted; as if something's
behind you all the time in the jungle.[119]

Salinger saw children as good and society as corrupting. Golding sees evil even apart from society, even in children, even on a
forsaken island. For even here men live in fear and without
grace or goodness. A Ralph, a Piggy, a Simon do emerge, but
they never prevail in man's struggle against himself. Man, as
Golding sees him, is born evil and is destined to remain evil.

In the array of characters he assembles, Golding symbolizes
different aspects of human existence. Jack is the symbol of evil;
Piggy, of intellect; Ralph, of reason and authority; Roger, of
sadistic cruelty. The pig's head and the parachute figure fallen
from heaven represent Satan. And Simon is clearly a Christ-
figure. He is a mystic who dies because he delivers a message of
truth that others will not hear. He tries to tell his executioners
that they need not fear the beast. Simon, often alone in the
forest, on the night of his death comes from the forest only to be
mistaken for the "beast." And so he dies, slain by those he
wanted to save.

GEORGE ORWELL (1903–1950)
Man has learned to hate better than to love

With George Orwell, we continue a negative commentary on
modern man. The evil that is in our very bones, as Golding commented, leads us to construct a world of hate in George Orwell's
1984.

George Orwell was born Eric Hugh Blair in Bengal, India.
He lived a difficult childhood, remembering his father's endless
prohibitions and feeling too shy to draw close to his mother
whom he loved. "I do not believe I ever felt love for any mature

person except my mother," he once said of himself, "and even her I did not trust, in the sense that shyness made me conceal most of my real feelings from her."

He grew into maturity hating authority and lived a time, 1927–1932, as a tramp feeling the need to identify with society's rejects. He drifted from dishwashing to tutoring mental patients to bookshop assistant.

When he turned to writing, he coined a pen-name from a river he once lived near and from a common English first name. In 1945, he wrote *Animal Farm* as an indictment not only against Communism but against all authority wrongly used. He wrote *1984* on the island of Jura off the coast of Scotland when recuperating from a lung ailment. "It wouldn't have been so gloomy," Orwell said of his book, "if I hadn't been so ill."

In the last months of his life, he married a second time. His first wife died after a simple operation in 1945. In January of 1950, Orwell suffered a sudden hemorrhage and died.

The viewpoint on man which *1984* offers is depressing. It can be summarized in the words torturer O'Brien addresses to his prisoner Winston Smith: "If you want a picture of the future, imagine a boot stamping on a human face—forever."[120]

The story of *1984* opens on April 4 of the same year. The world at this point in its history is divided into three superstates all at war with each other. By agreement among the superpowers, the war is never to be settled. Constant war keeps the leaders in power.

The action of *1984* occurs in one of the superpowers, Oceania. It is ruled by Big Brother whose image is constantly seen though he himself is not. History is constantly re-written to fit the party line. Language is reduced to a bare minimum called Newspeak. Its vocabulary grows less every year. The end process is to restrict human thought by limiting words necessary to express its concepts. Good party members are expected to think black is white if the Party demands it; they must hate an enemy they never see, Emmanuel Goldstein; children are encouraged to spy on parents; thought police and telescreens that view all are everywhere evident. Four ministries control human life: Minitrue (Educational); Minipax (Peace); Miniluv ((Law and Order); Miniplenty (Economy). The slogans men must live by are constantly repeated: "War is Peace; Freedom is Slavery; Ignorance is Strength."

Winston Smith lives in this world and *1984* is the story of his complete mental, physical, and emotional breakdown. The breakdown is complete when he admits two and two to be five. The "few cubic centimeters" inside his skull, which he dared call his own, have now been invaded.

This novel shows us that hate can corrupt and destroy the human mind and spirit. Hate can create a world where men are no longer human and where human values are crushed. In this world, Winston Smith searches for genuine values. He searches for some permanent truth and human love itself. Yet the world of *1984* offers propaganda in place of truth, human confinement in place of enriching relationships. Men become less and less conscious, less and less able to distinguish truth from falsehood, less and less capable of giving, receiving, or understanding love. In the name of the human spirit, Winston Smith protests against what man is doing to man. In a world he never made and does not want, he strives to hold on to what is left of his personality. Love, not hate, is liberating and creative, he insists. But no one listens or cares.

Winston realizes that what man needs most is human dignity. And only love gives man his human dignity. Hate, falsity, even material advantages destroy man. Orwell seems to be saying that modern man has raised barriers against his fellow-men and has turned to his fellow-men not in understanding but in hate. Orwell is calling for love as effectively as did Wolfe, Camus, and

Salinger. But he is telling us that love does not just happen. We must work together to achieve it.

CONCLUSION: WHAT IS MODERN MAN LIKE?
WHAT DOES HE SEEK FROM LIFE?

We are clearly dealing with a deeply personal and highly subjective preoccupation with modern man. This is surprising since this century of science and technology should have led us, one would think, into objectivity as the only method for interpreting ourselves, each other, and God.

In this section we shall gather together rather than analyze the questions modern man has asked about himself in the literature we have exposed. Man asks about himself, others, and God.

His concern with self leads him to seek many answers:

Guilt: Is there a relief from guilt? Dostoevsky in *Crime and Punishment* claims some relief comes in confession and suffering. Camus in *The Fall* says some relief comes in indicting all men.

Loneliness and Exile: Is there anywhere the type of understanding we need? Wolfe speaks of the bitter briefness of our days in which we are forever strangers to one another.

Freedom: Can we bear the burden of freedom? In a sense, we must. If we are not free, we are nothing or no one.

Self-Knowledge: Who are we? Where are we going?

Innocence: What can we do to regain the innocence we always lose? Salinger asks us to remain sincere. Camus asks us not to hurt each other.

Optimism: We have too much dignity and our world has too much potential for us to be pessimistic.

Solidarity: We must realize we belong to each other. We want the same things. There are no others to understand us or accept us except each other.

Hence, we are led to a concern with each other:

Love: How can we get all the love within us outside? How can we communicate? How can we be authentic with ourselves and accepted by the other, allowing him to be authentic in return?

Suffering: We must stop causing pain. How can we explain to ourselves the suffering of children?

Justice: We want justice now, for all, without delays.

Human Values: We cannot judge men by inhuman standards (Camus). We have a vocation to recognize the grandeur of man, tragic though he be (Wolfe). We must create a world where man can be man even if this can only be done by restrained rebellion.

Our concern with others leads us to a sense of concern about God:

Faith is not easy. Yet without it we fail as persons and we fail each other. Where is our lost kingdom? (Camus). Where is our ideal world? (Salinger). How can we be rescued?

We can accept God if he can take away guilt, give us innocence, help us to love each other, save our human values, end our exile, and lead us to that eternal kingdom where we are rescued and ourselves forever.

We need a God who can give us freedom and fill us with hope. We need perhaps a God who is Christ, a need which has been considered by many of the writers we have studied:

Dostoevsky: "Whom are we to put in Christ's place?"

Wolfe: Christ can be accepted if he can heal our loneliness.

Camus: Christ is the figure of love we never understood (*The Fall*).

Salinger: Holden Caulfield or the "Fat Lady" or someone must do Christ's task for us if there be no Christ.

Golding: There must always be a messenger of hope, a mystic who sees the truth even if we kill him for this and fail to recognize him (Simon).

The most hopeful thing about modern man is the fact that he cares and that he sees himself and his science as not enough. We may not have found the Way and yet we seem to be on the right road.

NOTES

[1] Fyodor Dostoevsky, *The Brothers Karamazov* (New York, Modern Library, 1950), p. 279. Henceforth, *Karamazov*.

[2] *Karamazov*, p. 433.

[3] Fyodor Dostoevsky, *The Possessed* (New York, Dell, 1961), p. 134. © Copyright 1959 by Ernest J. Simmons. © Copyright 1961 by Franklin D. Reeve. These words are spoken by Kirillov.

[4] *Karamazov*, p. 721 (words spoken by Dmitri).

[5] *Ibid.*, p. 278.

[6] *Ibid.*, p. 280.

[7] *Ibid.*, p. 709.

[8] *Ibid.*, p. 262.

[9] *Ibid.*, p. 410.

[10] *Ibid.*, p. 717.

[11] *Ibid.*, p. 721.

[12] *The Possessed*, p. 704.

[13] *Ibid.*, pp. 632–635.

[14] *Ibid.*, p. 689.

[15] *Karamazov*, pp. 384–385.

[16] *The Possessed*, p. 677.

[17] *Karamazov*, p. 301.

[18] Fyodor Dostoevsky, *The Idiot* (New York, Modern Library, 1935), pp. 208–209.

[19] *The Possessed*, pp. 267–268.

[20] *Karamazov*, p. 281.

[21] *Ibid.*, pp. 290–291.

[22] Albert Camus, *The Plague* (New York, Modern Library, 1948), pp. 195–197. Copyright 1948 by Stuart Gilbert.

[23] *Karamazov*, p. 289.

[24] *Ibid.*, p. 300.

25 *Ibid.*, p. 307.

26 The reader is reminded of the comments made in the first pages of this book where we call for an approach to modern man in freedom and love.

27 Thomas Wolfe, *Look Homeward, Angel* (New York, Scribner, 1952), p. xix. Copyright 1929 Charles Scribner's Sons: Renewal Copyright © 1957 Edward C. Aswell, as Administrator, C.T.A. of the Estate of Thomas Wolfe and/or Fred W. Wolfe. Copyright 1952 Charles Scribner's Sons.

28 *Ibid.*, p. 31.

29 Thomas Wolfe, *You Can't Go Home Again* (New York, Dell, 1964), pp. 398–401. Copyright 1934, 1937, 1938, 1939, 1940 by Maxwell Perkins as Executor. Reprinted by permission of Harper & Row, Publishers.

30 Thomas Wolfe, *Of Time and the River* (New York, Scribner, 1935), pp. 410–411. Copyright 1935 by Charles Scribner's Sons.

31 Thomas Wolfe, *The Hills Beyond* (New York, Pyramid Books, 1961), pp. 162–164. © 1935, 1936, 1937, 1939, 1941 by Maxwell Perkins as Executor. Reprinted by permission of Harper & Row, Publishers.

32 *Time* (March 31, 1961), p. 44.

33 *Wie ein Hund! sagte er, es war als sollte die Scham ihn uberleben.*

34 Franz Kafka, *The Trial* (New York, Knopf, 1957), pp. 284–286. Copyright 1937, 1956 by Alfred A. Knopf, Inc.

35 *Ibid.*, p. 278.

36 *Ibid.*, p. 264.

37 Franz Kafka, *The Castle* (New York, Knopf, 1964), p. 3. Copyright 1930, 1941, 1954 by Alfred A. Knopf, Inc.

38 *Ibid.*, p. 15.

39 *Ibid.*, p. 26.

40 *Ibid.*, pp. 62–65.

41 *Ibid.*, pp. 74–75.

42 *Ibid.*, p. 82.

43 These observations precede the text of the novel in the edition we have previously cited.

44 *Ibid.*, p. xiv.

45 *Ibid.*, p. xvi.

46 Albert Camus, *The Myth of Sisyphus*, trans. Justin O'Brien (New York, Vintage Books, 1955), pp. 94, 96. Copyright 1955 by Alfred A. Knopf, Inc. Hereafter, *Sisyphus*.

47 Ignace Lepp, *Atheism in Our Time*, trans. Bernard Murchland, C.S.C. (New York, Macmillan, 1963), pp. 185–186.

48 Anne Frank, *Diary of a Young Girl* (New York, Cardinal Editions, 1960), p. 233. Copyright 1952 by Otto H. Frank. Reprinted by permission of Doubleday & Company, Inc.

49 *New York Times* (January 5, 1960), p. 1.

50 *Ibid.*, Editorial.

51 *Atheism in Our Time, op. cit.*, pp. 183–184.

52 *Sisyphus*, p. 3.

53 *Ibid.*, pp. 10–16.

54 Albert Camus, *The Rebel*, trans. Anthony Bower (New York, Vintage Books, 1956), pp. 3–4. © Copyright 1956 by Alfred A. Knopf, Inc.

55 *Ibid.*, p. 5

56 *Ibid.*, pp. 13–22.

57 *Ibid.*, p. 24.

58 *Ibid.*, p. 101.

59 *Ibid.*, p. 102.

60 *Ibid.*, p. 101.

61 *Ibid.*, p. 61.

62 *Ibid.*, p. 306.

63 *Ibid.*, p. 104.

64 *Ibid.*, p. 306.

65 *Ibid.*, p. 305.

66 In analyzing the literary contributions of Albert Camus, I have found two books especially helpful: Philip Thody, *Albert Camus: A Study of His Work* (New York, Grove Press, 1959) and Thomas Hanna, *The Thought and Art of Albert Camus* (Chicago, Regnery, 1958).

67 Albert Camus, *The Misunderstanding* (New York, Vintage Books, 1958), p. 87.

68 *Ibid.*, p. 125.

69 Albert Camus, *Caligula and Three Other Plays*, trans. Stuart Gilbert (New York, Vintage Books, 1958), pp. 7–8.

70 Albert Camus, *Exile and the Kingdom*, trans. Justin O'Brien (New York, Knopf, 1963), pp. 24–25. Copyright 1957, 1958 by Alfred A. Knopf, Inc. The above translation differs somewhat from the edition we have cited.

71 Albert Camus, *The Stranger*, trans. Stuart Gilbert (New York, Vintage Books, 1946), p. 154. Copyright 1946 by Alfred A. Knopf, Inc.

72 *Ibid.*, pp. 52–53.

73 *Ibid.*, p. 72.

74 *Ibid.*, p. 80.

75 *Ibid.*, p. 154.

76 *Ibid.*, p. 127.

[77] Albert Camus, *The Plague*, trans. Stuart Gilbert (New York, Modern Library, 1948), p. 278.

[78] *Ibid.*, p. 188.

[79] *Ibid.*, p. 197.

[80] *Ibid.*, p. 271.

[81] *Ibid.*, p. 189.

[82] *Ibid.*, pp. 11–12.

[83] *Ibid.*, pp. 116–118.

[84] *Ibid.*, p. 150.

[85] *Ibid.*, p. 151.

[86] *Ibid.*, pp. 228–229.

[87] *Ibid.*, p. 230.

[88] *Ibid.*, p. 237.

[89] *Ibid.*, pp. 260–261.

[90] Albert Camus, *The Fall*, trans. Justin O'Brien (New York, Vintage Books, 1956), pp. 132–133. © Copyright 1956 by Alfred A. Knopf, Inc.

[91] *Ibid.*, p. 68.

[92] *Ibid.*, pp. 110–111.

[93] *Ibid.*, pp. 133–134.

[94] *Ibid.*, pp. 114–115.

[95] Albert Camus, *Resistance, Rebellion, and Death*, trans. Justin O'Brien (New York, Modern Library, 1960), pp. 52–56. © Copyright 1960 by Alfred A. Knopf, Inc.

[96] *Sisyphus*, p. 113.

[97] *Ibid.*, p. 112.

[98] Thomas Hanna, *op. cit.*, p. 67.

[99] J. D. Salinger, *The Catcher in the Rye* (New York, Bantam Books, 1964), p. 173.

[100] J. D. Salinger, *Franny and Zooey* (New York, Bantam Books, 1964), p. 200–202.

[101] *The Catcher in the Rye*, pp. 198–199.

[102] J. D. Salinger, "A Perfect Day for Bananafish," *Nine Stories* (New York, New American Library Signet Books, 1963), p. 16.

[103] J. D. Salinger, *Raise High the Roof Beam, Carpenters* and *Seymour, An Introduction* (New York, Bantam Books, 1965), p. 89.

[104] *Ibid.*, p. 90.

[105] "For Esme—with Love and Squalor," *Nine Stories*, p. 79.

[106] *Markings*, p. 71.

[107] *The Catcher in the Rye*, pp. 99–100.

[108] *Ibid.*, pp. 155–156.

[109] "Teddy," *Nine Stories*, p. 136.

[110] *Raise High the Roof Beam, Carpenters*, p. 67.

[111] *Nine Stories*, p. 138.

[112] *The Catcher in the Rye*, p. 189.

[113] *Ibid.*, p. 188.

[114] William Golding, *Lord of the Flies* (New York, Capricorn Books, 1955), pp. 46–48. Copyright 1955 by Coward-McCann.

[115] *Ibid.*, p. 48.

[116] *Ibid.*, p. 248.

[117] *Ibid.*, pp. 177–178.

[118] *Ibid.*, pp. 110–111.

[119] *Ibid.*, p. 67.

[120] George Orwell, *1984* (New York, New American Library Signet Classics, 1964), p. 220. Copyright 1949 by Harcourt, Brace & Company, Inc. Reprinted by permission of Brandt & Brandt.

3 Modern Man Not Only Seeks But Fears Some Genuine Values

In this section, we shall pause momentarily to consider man's hesitancy before some of the genuine values he needs. The problem of affirming God is not independent of a man's ability to love or to use freedom. Nor is it distinct from the concept of God he forms. To expect a man who does not know how to live to believe, is asking too much. To hope that a man unable to be human might perhaps be Christian, is presumption. Frequently enough it is not God a man is really rejecting but himself. We cannot expect someone who has not recognized his humanity to live in divine sonship built on that humanity.

We shall explore in this chapter, man's fear of love, freedom and God.

Modern man is really afraid of love. He wants desperately to communicate, this is true, but he cannot or will not. One of our difficulties today stems from the fact that we desire the state of being loved rather than the challenge of loving.[1] We want all to come to us. Yet if they do, we remain imprisoned within ourselves. We must burst out of this prison of ourselves, and overcome the separateness from each other which is at the very heart of all human anxiety. If we do not overcome the separateness, we cannot love ourselves or believe in God. Yet how are we to do this? How are we to experience that deeply mysterious phenomenon of love, that experience which can make two beings one while they remain two?

In order to love properly, there are a number of things we must attend to.

We must give of ourselves to another, to share with the other our joy and interest, understanding and knowledge, humor and sadness, weakness and strength. In the process of giving of ourselves to the other, we must develop a sense of concern for the other's life and growth, a sense of care that makes me my brother's keeper—a sense of respect so deep that I never exploit him and so selfless that I never want him to be what I want him to be but rather what he must be. And so I encounter the other and in our effort together we discover ourselves. In love, I discover myself; we discover both of us; and if the love is genuine and deep, I discover all men and God through this experience. If ever we really love one person, we love all persons, the entire world, the experience of life, every man, and God himself. This love is built on our need of each other. Today, I; tomorrow, you. Though we need the other and meet the other, our love or friendship or fraternity serves no utilitarian purpose. In a sense, love must be useless to be genuine.

This is a point that must be stressed insistently in our culture. We must not use the other but rather discover him, respect him, give to him. It is because in a commodity-minded society we have made a commodity of each other that love is difficult for us. We have prized more highly the dead things, the impersonal things of life rather than the dignity and love of each other. Therefore we have become the ever-hopeful and yet the eternally-disappointed ones. We have each other and we have sought less. We have other persons in our world and we have not realized the treasure they are. And so success and prestige, money and power have become the things we strive for. Our society judges a person's worth by how many of the impersonal things of life he has collected.

Our society leads us not only to evaluate others by their impersonal possessions, but also to expect them to act as impersonal things.

> For example, if your automobile starts promptly when you turn the ignition key, you say it is a good car. If it takes a few minutes to get started, you say it is a bad car. . . . According to this system, anything that totally obeys my will, that does in a utilitarian, pragmatic way exactly what I want, is good; anything that is slow to subject itself to my will in a utilitarian way is bad . . . that means, in effect that you are good only if you do exactly what I want as quickly as possible.[2]

Unfortunately then we expect people to be anything but what they should be. We frequently talk about "figuring people out," "getting their number." When I am the object of this kind of relationship, when somebody is cataloguing me, figuring me out as if I were a cross-word puzzle, I resist and become hostile. At times, we feel this need to catalogue, to figure others out in a remote, impersonal, neutral, unrelated, uninvolved way. "Hence for many people the best kind of human relationship is the one furthest from the real human encounter, the real commitment."[3]

The great problem we face in reaching the other is the problem of how to communicate. This was Holden Caulfield's painful difficulty. The basic problem in communicating centers in our lack of faith in ourselves, in the other, in life, in Being. Only a person who has faith in himself can be faithful to others. Everyone needs faith in his love and in its ability to produce love in others. Everyone needs faith in his own reliability in love. But faith involves risk. If we have not the courage to accept the pain and disappointment of being rejected, we shall never love. Too much safety and too much security destroys us, stifles our great schemes, dissipates our noble visions, and imprisons our love. Love is an act of faith—a trust that we can give ourselves and we will be found, that we can offer ourselves and we will be accepted. Love knows it will make mistakes and yet it is not fearful of them.

Love is then an act of faith, but it is also an act of hope. I must be trustful of the other enough to put my meaning and my happiness in his hands. We must see ourselves and our love as a gift to the other. We offer but we do not know if we will be accepted. Whether we are accepted depends not on us but on the other. We must trust him. I must trust you if I am to become a person, if I am to find salvation from impersonalism. "We want to be rescued," Ralph pleaded in *Lord of the Flies*. We must be rescued by each other. It is precisely this hope in the other which enables me to achieve my destiny as a person. It is precisely this trust in the other which enables me to live with significance. If I do not trust the other, I do not influence him or love him. And if I do not influence and love other people, then I have lived without purpose. For if I do not influence and love other people, what am I living for? Only to influence matter or a cold universe or a heartless world? This is not enough for me to live in significance and value. And so I must put my trust in the other if my life is to be worthwhile. This hope, as we have seen, is not the cheap optimism which says, only hope and all things will turn out right. This is false. Many things do not turn out right and life as well as love is filled with tragedy. So my attempts at love may not all succeed. And even if I love, there is no guarantee this love will last forever. For love depends on the freedom of two. Hope then is not a closing of our eyes to the difficulty, the risk, or the failures. But it is a trust that if I fail now, I shall not fail forever—that if I am hurt, I shall be healed —that life is good and love is powerful—that I shall find myself and others and God. This is hope—the only hope that saves, the only hope that permits love and gives life purpose. I hope that as I give myself to another person or to God that the other will not forever reject or always betray. In one simple phrase, I learn to love. And in learning to love, I come to life. I find in myself a capacity and a power I never had before and in reality I see a value I never knew existed. To love and be loved is to encounter not only this person or these friends but Being itself and eternity in time. In the faces of all I love I come to see the faint outline and strangely familiar face of God Himself.

This is why Personalism is so significant a concern in our day. It must lead to God. The reason why God is dead for so many of our contemporaries is because for them love is dead. And if love is dead, so must God be. For God is love.

FREEDOM

It is not only love but also freedom which has become problematic for us.[4]

One of the most pressing tasks our freedom must achieve is the attainment of individuation. As long as we are only a part of the world, unaware of our possibilities and responsibilities, we need not be afraid, but we are not free. When one has become an individual, one stands alone and faces the world and life in all its perilous and overpowering aspects. When man is individualized by his freedom, there is only one productive solution open to him, i.e., a freely-chosen solidarity with other men, uniting him again to the world. But now he is joined to the world as a free and independent individual. If he cannot do this, freedom becomes an unbearable burden.

One of our difficulties today is that we strive for a "freedom from" certain restrictions but we do not move toward a "freedom to" assume certain obligations. If we achieve a freedom from restrictions and do not move toward a freedom to do certain things, we suffer from the burden of freedom and the burden of ourselves. If we have not understood or developed freedom, we do not meet or encounter the other, but we run to the other because we cannot bear to be ourselves and to be free. Thus frequently enough modern man will become masochistic or sadistic. Masochistically, he feels himself inferior, powerless and insignificant. He demeans himself in his own eyes because he cannot bear to face himself or his freedom. He is afraid of himself. Fundamentally, he hates himself. Sadistically, man must dominate someone else if he is going to survive. Owning another keeps him from living with himself, facing himself, creating himself freely. The masochist who sees no worth in himself cannot really believe in God. The sadist who must dominate and own others cannot face even himself, let alone God, as he must. These masochistic or sadistic tendencies in our society are modern man's way of avoiding freedom. To give them popular labels, we may call the masochist a conformist and the sadist a rebel.

The conformist is the individual who has so little use for himself and so little trust in himself that he becomes not what he must but rather what others demand him to be. Thus, he is not alone with his failure or his inferiority. He loses himself in the group. It is true that he is not now alone but he pays the unredeemable price of forfeiting himself and his freedom in the process.

The rebel is the individual who tries to heal his alone-ness by dominating people and destroying things. Thus, the rebel does not feel powerless any more. He destroys everything with which he might have to compare himself and which may make him less in his own eyes. He dominates others lest their independence convince him of his alone-ness and inadequacy.

One thing we must realize about freedom is that men more often avoid it than they seek it. There is an unconscious desire in all of us to want to be weak and helpless. True freedom will not permit helplessness nor will it allow possession of another. The man of true freedom will not surrender his individuality to another even though he may offer his love. Nor will he allow himself to be possessed since he knows another's possession of him destroys both him and the other. The man who submerges his true freedom is filled with shame and forever condemned to bondage and unhappiness. For nothing makes us more ashamed than not being ourselves—and nothing gives us greater happiness than to become what we must be, thinking, feeling and saying what we are.

The meaning of our lives is found in freedom, in the difference your presence and mine will make in the over-all process. If you and I are to make a difference, we must not only love each other but we must also be free and ourselves.

It is when man understands freedom in this responsible way that he finds God. For God is the one who dawns on man in freedom. God is the one who will not let man be neutral or passive. God is the one who tells man he cannot choose this or that forever, but that he must use his freedom to choose himself once and for all, for all eternity. Christianity indeed gives to freedom consequences that atheism never can. For it tells man that a free decision about himself is demanded of him and that this free decision will be irrevocable for all eternity.

Christianity insists that freedom lives only if it finds its proper object and knows what its ultimate choice must be. Otherwise, freedom becomes a wild, restless, futile exercise of action. It becomes a source of anxiety and fear. For one knows not what to choose and whatever one chooses is somehow alien and oppressive. Such a freedom finds harmony with nothing and no one. It is desperation and loneliness.

Christianity asks that man use his freedom to recognize the finite as such and to see God as freedom's ultimate savior. God is not an easy answer, however. For our God is a God who not only gives Himself but withholds Himself. He is a God our freedom never conquers. A God whose Presence and Love are always unexpected, undue, and gracious. God is the one whom we need and yet He is the one who has no need of us. God is the one whom we yearn for, whose glory has taken flesh in time, and whose love has been irretrievably bestowed upon us. Yet He is ever mystery, more hidden than revealed, and so different from us.

Christianity tells us of the dreadful task freedom presses upon us. For man can fail to find himself; he can reject his God, misuse his freedom, offend himself, live purposelessly.

Christianity convinces man not only that he is free but that he is a sinner. Thus his liberty is ever exercised in guilt and in a death-infected world. Christianity tells man his freedom leads to damnation unless it is redeemed, that what man needs most of all is not license or anarchy but an object worth freedom's devotion. Christianity tells us that we cannot give our freedom to the partial or unworthy things in life. Christianity distresses us but educates us when it says that one cannot hope for a utopia here on earth. We must ever be saddened by what we cannot make come to be, tormented by the cries of suffering children, frustrated by the deformation of life around us, injured by the wounded men in our midst whom we never ultimately heal. With patience we must bear with the unintelligibility of our existence. For we are pilgrims and the race of the unfree. Christianity insists we struggle against evil. It tries to keep us, however, from hoping to achieve the impossible and it reminds us that those who see no meaning in existence or who think man can do all things are not deep at all.

Christianity tells us then that human freedom is limited, that it has only so much time, and that it needs redemption. Only God can fully liberate man. He alone can break the bonds of sin, death, and law. For He alone is sinless, deathless, and lawmaker. In the liberty God gives man, man is set free to create himself in grace and for eternal significance.

Christianity assures man that a person is always at issue in freedom, a finite person and the Infinitely Personal. Man is that being where Being and Freedom are at issue. Man is given freedom not to choose this or that perishable good but to accept the only values which never really die, God and one's self. This freedom may be burdensome but it is unconquerable. It may be demanding but it is eminently creative. It is never expendable. It is that limited prerogative with infinite possibilities. It is the only thing man can never deny.

A man who lives with his freedom realizes that he has not in himself all the freedom he needs. And so he surrenders to God that God might redeem his freedom, giving him more liberty and the creative power he needs to be himself. God does not deprive man's freedom of its task or its essential responsibility. He gives it grace to face its greatest challenges with infinite and divine courage. Grace is not exoneration but summons. In it, true freedom is born and challenged and fundamentally victorious.

God's final judgment on us is a judgment of what we have done with our freedom. It is not so much an evaluation of our individual acts or our death-bed attitude, but a judgment as to how we have borne the burden of freedom and of what we have made of ourselves. God alone, who is Freedom itself and who gives man his freedom, can judge what free men have made of themselves in their heart of hearts.

Christianity then is a shelter for freedom in this world, a sacrament of liberty, a preacher of freedom's inviolable and terrifying character. Let all the world know this, that Christians are free men. Let all men hear this, that Christianity can only survive if freedom lives. Christianity is that religion which takes every person seriously and which warns men that in the few moments of freedom they spend in time all eternity is at issue. It is by freedom alone that man can become a recipient of God's endless life and limitless liberty. This is why St. Paul preached to the Galatians (5:13) in pride:

"Brethren, you have been called to freedom."

THE CONCEPT OF GOD

It is not only man's fear of love or misuse of freedom which keep him from God. Sometimes it is his concept of God.

Man today is so often impressed not with the love he has to give or the freedom he must exercise, but rather with the things he has done. God, of course, is neither a thing nor one of the things man has done. Man may easily begin to think that what he has made is more striking than what he was made; he can allow himself to be more intrigued with the things he creates than with himself. In this century man has done so much! We have learned to fly, explored space, unleashed the atom. We have conquered disease, eliminated pain, prolonged life. We have studied the human mind and analyzed the human body in its every member and sinew. We have controlled electricity, created synthetics, measured the universe, reached the moon, and photographed the planets. We have made machines that work infallibly and fashioned them almost in our image and likeness. We cannot be blamed then if we have a practical vision of all things. It is understandable that we are tempted to make of ourselves and of God objects of the very science and technology that has won so much for us.

And so some have dispensed with God and affirmed only man. If man has done so much, there seems to be nothing he cannot do. "Man, save thyself. . . . Come and let us save ourselves." This has become the cry of the optimistic disbelievers in God. The atheist who is so deeply humanistic is afraid that God will halt this prodigious promotion of man. He, at least, cannot see how God can help. Christianity's task is to show such atheism that faith in God can join hand in hand with the noblest aspirations of mankind. It is to show also that without faith in God man's optimism becomes a hollow victory and too often ends in pessimism. Man is not a minder of machines or a creative tinker. He was made for more than making things.

But not all are able to be so optimistic about God's demise. Unable to believe in God, many have likewise become incapable of belief in man. The issues man has to face are so much bigger than man, so destructive of him, so insoluble. How does man face guilt, accept suffering, or endure death? What sends him forever his tortured way searching for permanent truth and unending love? Some have realized that the richness and wonder of life are not made by men but discovered. They are given, not achieved. Man might make things but he does not make freedom or capacity for love. He may one day make a human body but not the human spirit. This was always there, ever with man. It was with man when he first looked in astonishment on the world and it remains now that man has named and catalogued so much of the world.

These things given to man helped make man man. But what is he to do with freedom, love, or the human spirit? How or by whom was man endowed with these? If man has no purpose, not only God but also man are doomed in the twentieth century. We work, we keep running, we were put together rather well. But why? Who are we? What are we for? Without God, these questions could have no final answers. And, of course, there could not be a God. Man has found strangely that it is not God who limits man but man himself is limited. Even without God, man keeps running up against the barrier of himself and of a world too large for him to command in its every aspect and mystery. Man now shivered before the ultimate unpredictabilities of life. He saw clearly the finitude and fragility of existence and he saw it now not with hope but in anguish and anxiety. He saw now that he alone had to bear the entire responsibility for Being. And he knew he was not and could never be adequate to the task. And so he turned in his despair to one of two alternatives and sometimes to both of them.

On the one hand, he entered upon a pitiless critique of everything. Unable to blame God, he now blamed an absurd world and himself for everything. Like a trapped animal that could find no escape, he turned upon himself to destroy himself. There is no God, he insisted. When one saw what man was making of man without God, one could ask if soon there would not be man also.

Sometimes, however, the alternative is not standing in despair and criticism but running. Sometimes man feels he will get by if only he runs hard enough and fast enough. The answer must be somewhere: another job, another woman, another deal, another town. The impression is that if only man can be everywhere, he may find the solution. But sooner or later a man gets tired and grows old and wants to hold on to something rather than to run forever.

If the atheism we are dealing with is pessimistic, we must show that if God is affirmed, freedom and love are not lost but enriched. Is it too much to assume that if man needs God so much, God is there? Man needs love and freedom and they are there. He needs God even more. Is it really a need of God which creates God or is it God who creates the need?

Frequently enough, the God the atheist fears and rejects is the God who should be feared and rejected because he is a God who does not exist. The God who impedes human progress or the God who destroys love and imperils freedom is the only God who is not there. Frequently enough, a rejection of this type of God is an implicit affirmation and a painful yearning for the real God.

Our task in the twentieth century is to present the God modern man needs. God is not a philosophical problem but a personal one. He is not the conclusion of a syllogism but an answer to a searching prayer and a basic need of life. We must destroy all the artificial dichotomies. It is not God or the world but God and the world. It is not God or man but God and man. It is not faith or reason but faith and reason. It is not God or freedom but God and freedom.

God furthermore must not be presented as one who fulfills a utilitarian purpose. Like human love, He is an end in Himself. In a certain sense, God is useless and yet He is the only useful thing we have. We do not affirm God because His existence explains the physical world. We do not affirm God because He contributes to emotional stability (there are emotionally stable atheists). We do not affirm God because He makes one socially respectable or because God is good business.

We affirm God because He is there and because we were made for Him. We affirm Him because without God we cannot fully be ourselves or totally love each other. Aquinas shows well this fact that God is an end in Himself when he says that those who deny God's existence because of evil in the world are given but one reply: "But I am Who am." Beyond all our syllogisms and problems, God exists. And He will not be forever silent or forever still. He is Who is and man cannot declare Him dead. Therefore we must say to our fellow men: Weep not for God but for ourselves if God is dead. To those who say God is dead, we answer that God is living and we say this not really for the sake of God but for the sake of man.

MARKINGS

We can see some of the problems we have been considering in the words of Dag Hammarskjold and Ingmar Bergman. The former grows in belief and devotion as he solves the problem of human love. The latter is tormented rather than set at peace by God because his concept of God is a threatening one.

Markings is a record of Hammarskjold's most intimate thoughts as he lived life. It is as he writes, "the only true profile" of him that can be given. It is "a sort of white book concerning my negotiations with myself—and with God."

Markings then is a history of one man's dealings with himself.[5]

It shows beyond the façade of cool judgment and calm courage, the turmoil of Hammarskjold which went on behind it.

In his first entry, Hammarskjold writes: "I am being driven forward into an unknown land. . . . Shall I ever get there?"[6] *Markings* is the record of this compulsion and that destination. It shows Hammarskjold as a lonely man convinced most of his life of his inability to give or receive love.

> How ridiculous, this need of yours to communicate! Why should it mean so much to you that at least one person has seen the inside of your life?[7]

His need for love is painful:

> We glide past each other. But why? Why—? We reach out towards the other. In vain—because we have never dared to give ourselves.[8]

Uncertain that others can love him, he strives to gain strength from an intense private effort at dedication and sacrifice. He was a man who became exactly what he wanted to be. In the process, however, he missed some of the things his heart longed after: love, emotional warmth, relief from loneliness.

> What I ask for is absurd: that life shall have a meaning. What I strive for is impossible: that my life shall acquire a meaning. I dare not believe, I do not see how I shall ever be able to believe: that I am not alone.[9]

Hammarskjold went on knowing that "what you most need is to feel—or believe you feel—that you are needed." Yet he was convinced he had to be severe with himself.

> . . . you have to be severe with yourself in order to have the right to be gentle to others.[10]

Life, at times, is a struggle stoically sustained for survival.

> The road,
> You shall follow it.
>
> The fun,
> You shall forget it.
>
> The cup,
> You shall empty it.
>
> The pain,
> You shall conceal it.
>
> The truth,
> You shall be told it.
>
> The end,
> You shall endure it.[11]

Hammarskjold, convinced that human sympathy and love cannot be his, substitutes usefulness or sacrifice for these.

> Goodness is something so simple: always to live for others, never to seek one's own advantage.[12]

At moments, he finds himself "longing—among other things, for the Cross."[13]

Soon enough, death will come and Hammarskjold decides he must die dutifully.

> The hardest thing of all—to die rightly—an exam nobody is spared—and how many pass it? . . . You pray for strength to meet the test—but also for leniency on the part of the Examiner.[14]

He speaks of death, at times, in typical existentialist fashion. Heidegger could easily have written the following line:

> In the last analysis, it is our conception of death which decides our answers to all the questions that life puts to us.[15]

Not only death but freedom are existentially evaluated. It was not Sartre but Hammarskjold who wrote:

> To become free and responsible. For this alone was man created.[16]

Since, however, Hammarskjold is a religious man he assigns freedom an object and worries about its misuse.

> Man's freedom is a freedom to betray God. God may love us— yes—but our response is voluntary.[17]

At the age of forty-seven, in 1953, Dag Hammarskjold became Secretary-General of the United Nations. This was a turning point in his personal life. Thus, *Markings* is not only an account of one man's solitary effort to know himself and to love. It is a record also of his discovery of human relationships and God. In his new office, Hammarskjold seemed more certain that love and loyalty could be given him. The mood of the second half of the book, therefore, is quite different.

Now he is thrilled and embarrassed by "the humility which comes from others having faith in you."[18] And failure is ultimately "due to a lack of faith in this harmony between human beings."[19]

As Hammarskjold solves his human problems, his attitude toward God becomes richer, warmer, and more beautiful. Now there is no doubt about his usefulness:

> God has a use for you, even though what He asks doesn't happen to suit you at the moment.[20]

Now the struggle is not so much his own but one in which God is present. "Not I, but God in me."[21]

There are times, of course, when even God becomes strange and distant:

> The night in Gethsemane when the last friends left you have fallen asleep, all the others are seeking your downfall, and God is silent. . . .[22]

Hammarskjold sees now "the wonder: that I exist."[23] Life is not the stern thing he thought it was before. There is a "holiness" in "human life."[24] "In our era," however, "the road to holiness necessarily passes through the world of action."[25]

Now Hammarskjold develops and deepens a spiritual life of devotion to God. He is not unaware of sin's sinister influence:

> Original sin, that dark counter-center of evil in our nature . . . that something within us which rejoices when disaster befalls the very cause we are trying to serve, or misfortune overtakes even those whom we love . . . this something in us which wills disaster, misfortune, defeat to everything outside the sphere of our narrowest self-interest.[26]

Yet the God he serves is a God of gracious forgiveness.

> Forgiveness is the answer to the child's dream of a miracle by which what is broken is made whole again. . . . In the presence of God . . . we are forgiven.[27]

Therefore we live in faith. And this is somehow an ultimate answer.

> Faith is, faith creates, faith carries. It is not derived from, nor created, nor carried by anything except its own reality.[28]

Now life has meaning and purpose:

. . . at some moment I did answer *Yes* to Someone—or Something—and from that hour I was certain that existence is meaningful and that, therefore, my life, in self-surrender, had a goal.[29]

The response of faith is not easy. It is made in personal courage and from human solidarity, in grace and before God. It leads one to worship, not comprehension:

> Thou,
> Whom I do not know
> But Whose I am.[30]

Thus, Hammarskjold can pray in an entirely new way:

> Before Thee, Father,
>   In righteousness and humility,
>
> With Thee, Brother,
>   In faith and courage,
>
> In Thee, Spirit,
>   In stillness.[31]

Hammarskjold wrote in the beginning of "being driven . . . into an unknown land." He wondered, "Shall I ever get there?" In the last entry, just days before his death, he seems to have found his destination. The final words of the book read:

> Is it a new country . . .
> Or did I live there
> Before Day was? . . .
> The seasons have changed
> And the light
> And the weather
> And the hour.

> But it is the same land.
> And I begin to know the map
> And to get my bearings.

It is difficult to appreciate the mysterious and important value of Hammarskjold's life. Every attempt to do this sounds like cheap analysis or sentimental admiration. For this reason, we have tried to make the author speak in his own words. Once again he demonstrates the irrefutable proposition that love is the only way to Love.

INGMAR BERGMAN

The existential preoccupations of our day which we have seen our philosophers puzzle over, our writers describe, and even our statesmen, as Hammarskjold, mark down, are not absent from the world of the motion picture. This is how it should be. For the film as an art-form is a distinctively twentieth-century artistic medium. All the other artistic media we use to reflect and transform our century are borrowed from other centuries. Film-making is indigenous to this century in which we live. One could, of course, interpret modern themes and a search for God in a thousand different motion pictures. Since we are limited, however, let us choose a typical, and it seems not extravagant to say this, the best example we have.

To date, Swedish-director and screenplay-writer Ernst Ingmar Bergman has made more than two dozen films. From these, seven emerge with uncommon power. And together they seem to form one vast masterpiece of literary and religious significance. Four of these films stand apart: *The Seventh Seal* (1956), *Wild Strawberries* (1957), *The Magician* (1958), and *The Virgin Spring* (1959). The three remaining works form a trilogy: *Through a Glass Darkly* (1961), *Winter Light* (1963), and *The Silence* (1963). The trilogy is concerned with the problem of

human communication. The four films previous to it are concerned with death, human feeling, faith, and miracle respectively.
Bergman himself has described his reasons for writing the trilogy:

> *Through a Glass Darkly, Winter Light,* and *The Silence* stand together. My basic concern in making them was to dramatize the all-importance of communication, of the capacity for feeling. What matters most of all in life, is being able to make contact with another human. If you can take the first step toward communication, toward understanding, toward love, then no matter how difficult the future may be—you are saved. This is all that really matters.

In *Through a Glass Darkly,* a family learns finally how to speak to each other and the picture ends on a hopeful and serene note. In *Winter Light,* a minister, tormented by immorality, human silence, and estrangement from God, remains in his ministry because he sees a light even though it be winter, a brittle but real chance that God and men will speak to each other again. In *The Silence,* the inability of sex to substitute for genuine love or compassionate speech is made frighteningly clear. Sex must always be a symbol or sign of a love at least initially present before it takes on significance. If it issues from love, then it says what it must and it leads to a growth in love.

Through a Glass Darkly is one of, perhaps, the two finest achievements of Ingmar Bergman (*The Virgin Spring* being the other). Some of the best lines Bergman has written occur toward the end of the film. Minus, a teen-age boy, asks his father if God exists. When the father answers affirmatively, the boy asks for a proof. There is a proof, his father explains, but one must listen carefully. The proof is the reality of love. It is not clear if love proves God exists or if love is God Himself. But for one who loves, there is God.

Minus then reflects that if God is love, his sister, just taken mentally ill from the house, must be surrounded by God. For Minus loves her; her father loves her; if God is with her then, she will be saved. The father answers that there is hope that this will come to pass.

For the first time, Minus and his father communicate. It is in accepting the reality of love and God together, that they reach an understanding with each other in communication. The final words in the picture sum up a critical need for man today. Minus, alone, says to himself in wonder and happiness: "Papa *talked* to me." Man's search for genuine Fatherhood in the universe and for a God who speaks to him in revelation is expressed in those few words. God speaks to us only if we speak to each other. The Word of God was spoken in the midst of human words.

The Seventh Seal is a religious allegory in which a knight and Death play chess for a few days more of life. Mia (Mary) and Jof (Joseph) together with their son are saved by the knight who delays death long enough for "one meaningful deed." This is important. For the son of Mia and Jof "will grow up to be a great acrobat—or a juggler who can do the one impossible trick," i.e., making a ball stand absolutely still in the air.

One is confident that the son of Mia and Jof will make a ball stand absolutely still in the air, i.e., that he will transcend nature itself.

Bergman's concern with death finds its fullest expression in this screenplay. "Bear this in mind, you fool. Your life hangs by a thread. Your time is short," Skat declares. One is made to feel as the action progresses that death must not touch the family of Mia and Jof yet. It claims all the other characters of the story, but it does not reach these three. Death at times appears quite terrible. It explains to Skat who is about to die that there is no way out, no loophole, no exception. Yet at the end of the story as Death leads all away in a weird dance, Jof observes them against the horizon and somehow death seems a little less tragic. In

language reminiscent of the *Apocalypse,* Jof describes the scene
for Mia: "They dance away from the dawn and it's a solemn
dance toward the dark lands, while the rain washes their faces
and cleans the salt of the tears from their cheeks."

Bergman expresses modern man's problems with life and God
in a dramatic dialogue between the Knight and Death.

> KNIGHT: Through my indifference to my fellow men, I have iso-
> lated myself from their company . . . Is it so cruelly inconceiv-
> able to grasp God with the senses? Why should he hide himself
> in a mist of half-spoken promises and unseen miracles? . . .
> What is going to happen to those of us who want to believe but
> aren't able to? And what is to become of those who neither
> want to nor are capable of believing? . . . Why can't I kill God
> within me? Why does He live on in this painful and humiliating
> way even though I curse Him and want to tear Him out of
> my heart . . . I want knowledge, not faith, not suppositions, but
> knowledge. I want God to stretch out his hand toward me, re-
> veal Himself, and speak to me.
> DEATH: But He remains silent.
> KNIGHT: I call out to Him in the dark but no one seems to be
> there.
> DEATH: Perhaps no one is there.
> KNIGHT: Then life is an outrageous horror . . .
> DEATH: Most people never reflect about either death or the fu-
> tility of life.
> KNIGHT: But one day they will have to stand at that last mo-
> ment of life and look toward the darkness.[32]

The fear of death and the fear of a faith which does not give
complete knowledge beset modern man as they beset the Knight.
Yet there is a persistence about man's feeling that life has to have
a meaning, that death is not without purpose, that perhaps there
is Someone in the dark, and that maybe after all it is faith which
we need most and the courage to accept it. Bergman's God, however, is so silent. He is at times the spider-God of *Through A*

Glass Darkly. The God who will appear to us but whose eyes are cold and whose face is stony and horrible. The imagery of a spider-God is expressed also in *Winter Light.* Because Bergman's concept of God is of One mute and threatening, Bergman is tormented rather than fulfilled by his need for God. Faith seems not to be something he accepts in generosity and courageous love, but something which is forced upon him relentlessly in suffering, something he does not want but cannot live without.

Thus, the Knight confesses to Mia:

> Faith is a torment, did you know that? It is like loving some-one who is out there in the darkness but never appears, no matter how loudly you call.[33]

The Knight is less tortured by God's strangeness while he is with this family. Thus he continues: "Everything I've said seems meaningless and unreal while I sit here with you and your husband."

> I shall remember this moment. The silence, the twilight, the bowls of strawberries and milk, your faces in the evening light. Mikael sleeping, Jof with his lyre . . . I'll carry this memory between my hands as carefully as if it were a bowl filled to the brim with fresh milk . . . And it will be an adequate sign—it will be enough for me.[34]

The Knight in *The Seventh Seal,* as does Minus in *Through a Glass Darkly,* expresses man's need for a God of Revelation and Incarnation, for a God who is a light in the winter darkness, who is seen at least darkly. For such men as Bergman, the search is not for God alone but for God who speaks a Word that humans can see and hear and touch.

As Death comes for the Knight he is at long last able for prayer. It is not a perfect or a tranquil prayer. It is, however, all he can do. And it is enough.

From our darkness, we call out to Thee, Lord. Have mercy on
us because we are small and frightened and ignorant . . . God,
You who are somewhere, who *must* be somewhere, have mercy
upon us.[35]

In *Wild Strawberries* and *The Magician,* the scene shifts from
man's direct relationship with God to his problems with himself.
It is almost as if Bergman were saying, God will be there and
He will appear more clearly if we can only do what we must.
Wild Strawberries is the story of an old physician who has lived
his life with his mind alone. Because there is no human warmth
or love, his life is successful but empty. He reminds us of Jean-
Baptiste Clemance in *The Fall.* Thus Marianne tells Isak, the
aged physician:

You are an old egoist . . . You are completely inconsiderate and
you have never listened to anyone but yourself. All this is well
hidden behind your mask of old-fashioned charm and your
friendliness. But you are hard as nails, even though everyone
depicts you as a great humanitarian. We who have seen you at
close range, we know what you really are. You can't fool
us . . . It would be terrible to have to depend on you in any
way.[36]

The Magician is the story of Albert Emanuel Vogler, who is
apparently a charlatan, although one is never quite certain. He
is disguised to resemble Christ and he comes into conflict with
Vergerus, a scientist who seeks to expose him and who is certain
that all in life is empirically explainable. In Vogler and Vergerus,
the lines are drawn in an ancient battle. It is faith and reason
which are at war.

It is when Vogler doubts himself and listens to rational ob-
jections that he is least effective. At that moment, he loses his
powers:

I am . . . afraid. Then I become powerless . . . The time when we really believed that we healed people. Then there was some meaning in it.[37]

Vergerus is quite clear in presenting the attitude of the faithless scientist. At times, he sounds like Rakitin in Dostoevsky's *Karamazov*.

Mr. Vogler, I would like to make an autopsy of you. . . . Weigh your brain, open your heart, explore a little of your nerve circuits, lift out your eyes. . . . Science today is better equipped than ever to penetrate all the obvious mysteries. . . . Everything can be explained.[38]

Yet Vergerus is not fully content with his position. He reminds us of Dostoevsky's contention that the atheist still yearns for God. Vergerus must combat and expose Vogler not, one suspects, for society's benefit but for his own peace of mind. To Manda, a member of Vogler's troupe, he explains himself.

MANDA: . . . you should leave us in peace.
VERGERUS: I can't do that.
MANDA: Why?
VERGERUS: Because you represent something which I most abhor.
(Manda looks questioningly at him.)
VERGERUS: The unexplainable.[39]

Vergerus sounds disappointed when Vogler cannot mesmerize him or conjure up visions for him. "Perhaps I regret that I was incapable of experiencing anything."[40]

While man tries to decide if he must live by faith or by reason, God seems a distant and uninterested party. "God is silent and people chatter."[41]

One is never quite certain as the action moves back and forth if it is faith or reason which is winning the day. When faith seems to gain the upper hand, Vogler's triumph is exposed as trickery. When reason prevails, Vergerus' discoveries seem insufficient and unsatisfying. One is never quite certain if Vogler himself is a man genuinely in command of supernatural power or only a magician and a sorcerer. Yet one tends to favor Vogler even if there be something of deceit in him. As Cardinal Newman once commented, perhaps superstition, though an evil, is a lesser evil than rationalism. For superstition at least recognizes something more than man in life. It is, at best, a perverted form of faith, but it is more humble and more searching than rationalism.

When one is ready to despair of Vogler, when all his trickery seems exposed, he is, in the final scene, summoned to the king's court to perform. As his coach drives off, Vergerus is left behind with his commonplace, matter-of-fact world. And Bergman writes into the script:

> In this way the mesmerizer, Albert Emanuel Vogler, makes his triumphant entrance into the Royal Palace.[42]

In *The Virgin Spring*, perhaps Bergman's finest film, the action shifts from man's concern with himself and his fellow-man back to God. In this film, God makes his first miraculous intervention into man's world. On the spot where the beautiful virgin is brutally slain, a spring bubbles forth from the dry land.

In *The Virgin Spring*, man's universal guilt is recognized as every member of the household, even the most innocent, expresses a feeling of guilt for the girl's death. Bergman is less tormented in this story. It is in this film that God is described as "more merciful than you think." Here death is seen not as fearful but as liberating. Just as smoke cringes and curls back from an opening into the air outside, so we fear to enter a greater reality than the one we know. But once the smoke reaches the outside air, it is at last uncrowded, finally free, and it inherits all of heaven for its domain. With this description, a little boy in the story is asked not to fear death.

As Bergman reaches this plateau, as his concept of God is purified, he is less anxious to deny Him and made more serene by His Presence.

"To me," Bergman once wrote, "religious problems are continuously alive. I never cease to concern myself with them; it goes on every hour of every day."[43]

"Man's essence," Sartre wrote, "is his existence." Man's essence, says Bergman, is God's existence. It is as man discovers human harmony and a God of grace and speech that he is set at rest and finally begins to understand himself. "I believe in life," Bergman writes, "in this life, a life after death, all kinds of life." And art is most effective, he argues, when man recognizes and reverences God. "Art lost its basic creative drive the moment it was separated from worship."[44]

It is not art only but man who needs worship. Thus in *The Virgin Spring* as the girl's father slays her killers, he embraces his daughter's battered body, and stares in wonder at the miraculous spring. He falls to his knees. Begging God for forgiveness, he prays:

Here I will build unto Thee a church . . . I know no other way to be reconciled with my own hands. I know no other way to live.

NOTES

[1] I have found Erich Fromm's *The Art of Loving* (New York, Bantam Books, 1963), helpful in this section on man's fear of love.

[2] "Personal Communication and the Missions": An address by Charles A. Curran to the Annual Mission Secretariat Meeting, Washington, D.C., September 1962.

[3] *Ibid.*

[4] I have found the following helpful in this section on man's fear of freedom:

Erich Fromm, *Escape from Freedom* (New York, Holt, Rinehart & Winston, 1941);

Karl Rahner, "Freedom in the Church" and "The Dignity and Freedom of Man," in *Theological Investigations* (Baltimore, Helicon Press, 1963), vol. II;

Karl Rahner, "The Christian Teacher: Freedom and Constraint," in *Theology for Renewal* (New York, Sheed and Ward, 1964); and finally

Karl Rahner, "On the Theology of Freedom," in *Freedom and Man*, ed. John Courtney Murray (New York, P. J. Kenedy and Sons, 1965).

[5] Quotations are from Dag Hammarskjold, *Markings*, trans. Leif Sjoberg and W. H. Auden (New York, Knopf, 1964).

[6] *Markings*, p. 5.

[7] *Ibid.*, p. 87.

[8] *Ibid.*, p. 40.

[9] *Ibid.*, p. 86.

[10] *Ibid.*, p. 111.

[11] *Ibid.*, p. 201.

[12] *Ibid.*, p. 89.

[13] *Ibid.*, p. 55.

[14] *Ibid.*, p. 86.

[15] *Ibid.*, p. 160.

[16] *Ibid.*, p. 53.

[17] *Ibid.*, p. 97.

[18] *Ibid.*, p. 93.

[19] *Ibid.*, p. 95.

[20] *Ibid.*, p. 89.

[21] *Ibid.*, p. 90.

[22] *Ibid.*, p. 97.

[23] *Ibid.*, p. 113.

[24] *Ibid.*, p. 99.

[25] *Ibid.*, p. 122.

[26] *Ibid.*, p. 149.

[27] *Ibid.*, p. 124.

[28] *Ibid.*, p. 145.

[29] *Ibid.*, p. 205.

[30] *Ibid.*, p. 214.

[31] *Ibid.*, p. 123.

32 *Four Screenplays of Ingmar Bergman*, trans. Lars Malmstrom and David Kushner (New York, Simon and Schuster, 1960), pp. 111–112.

33 *Ibid.*, p. 137.

34 *Ibid.*, p. 138.

35 *Ibid.*, p. 162.

36 *Ibid.*, pp. 179–180.

37 *Ibid.*, pp. 297–298.

38 *Ibid.*, pp. 263, 266.

39 *Ibid.*, p. 293.

40 *Ibid.*, p. 264.

41 *Ibid.*, p. 294.

42 *Ibid.*, p. 325.

43 *Ibid.*, p. xxi.

44 *Ibid.*, p. xxii.

II

GOD AS THE CATHOLIC
CHURCH UNDERSTANDS HIM

4 Catholic Theology and the Problem of God

There is something misleading about the title of this fourth chapter. For we shall not really give the Church's full statement on God. The Catholic Church does not understand God only in the terms we shall here explore. She sees Him as a Trinity and in Christ. We do not here, however, speak of Trinity or Christology. This is too much at the moment for our contemporaries who seek God. We give instead the Church's simplest statement on God. We treat of what traditional seminary manuals call *De Deo Uno*. Of the God who is one, not yet seen as three, and prescinding from the Incarnation, the Church has spoken officially on very few occasions. Instead of the multiplicity of statements one might expect, she has in reality made but four: there is a knowable God; He possesses some attributes which we can realize; He is a God able to know; a God of concern, choice, and love.

If theology is the science which deals with God, then what theology says of God is one of its most significant concerns. Theology, though it is a science of God, is essentially bound up with a human viewpoint on God. What theology says of God, then, in terms men can understand is the criterion of its relevance. If theology is relevant, then it must speak meaningfully of God. There is no denying this equation. What theology says of God should be of interest to all men. We have seen the breadth and depth of modern man's concern with the problem of God. God is clearly one of those fateful human questions which Pascal tells us "takes us by the throat."

The God of whom we speak here is the God all religions accept and all atheists deny. This is the God no different from the three-person God Christianity confesses, no different from the God-in-Christ of whom the New Testament speaks, not alien from the God of supernatural revelation who speaks both to Jew and Christian. This is God in his simplest and most basic consideration. To deny God on this level is to make impossible any further discussion between Christian and non-Christian or non-believer. The theology of God we here discuss, *De Deo Uno* if you will, is that aspect of theology which says least about God. Yet it is also that aspect of theology which demands much in spite of the little it requires. We are asked to accept the existence of God, recognize some of His characteristics, and predicate of Him the ability to know what He is about, and to love that which He is and makes. From this vantage point, the Church will preach of God in all the richness and fullness that man's mind and God's grace permit. Even if at times these problems seem too basic and somewhat lifeless for a man who contemplates God in human flesh, upon a cross, and in His Risen Body, yet they contain in themselves some of the vitality and dynamism which makes Christianity what it is. It is never without value that a man who accepts himself as complete reflects upon the least and most fundamental factors which make him what he is.

Since we cannot say everything about God all at once, we prescind from certain considerations. What we speak of here is the broadest possible basis for a discussion of God. We speak only of God as God, with no further qualifications.

The first statement we seek to establish is this: *God is and He can be known by man from the things He has made.*

In dealing with this problem we shall explore four sources of data on the question: the testimony of the Scriptures, the testimony of the Church, the testimony of man, and the testimony of our fellow Christians.

In treating the Scriptures, we shall consider the God before and beyond Scripture, the God of the Hebrew Scriptures, the God of the Christian Scriptures, and the knowability of God from the Scriptures.

THE TESTIMONY OF THE SCRIPTURES

First, a word on the God before and beyond Scripture. It is well for us to realize that the world in which we live is in fact supernatural. This means that we live in a world ordered to a personal, Trinitarian God beyond the world and in the world. God does not call man except supernaturally. No man is called by God only to natural finality or natural fulfillment. The whole world is touched with grace and the whole world is redeemed. God and Christ, St. John tells us, enlightens every man who comes into the world. No man can live without a God-encounter. No man ever lives without a supernatural call from God. God is everywhere and for everyone. Or, as Catholic theology more technically states it, every man is given sufficient grace. The God who is for everyone, we must remember, is the God of grace. There is no other God.

We shall see later that the Church insists that God can be known with certainty by human reason. The Church defines this possibility for human nature. Even independently of explicit Revelation from God, man is so constituted that he can know there is a God. When one thinks of it, the alternative would be a cruel one indeed. It would be saying that God creates man to find Him but makes it quite impossible that man find Him. Few men, when one considers the whole range of human history, are given the grace of appreciating God's explicit Revelation. This is due, one suspects, not only to man's failure in witnessing his God as he ought but also to God's own inscrutable designs.

The Church then would find it difficult to accept any man's definitive judgment that God's existence is unknowable. We say definitive judgment because sometimes agnosticism is only a passing phase of a man's journey to belief. Sometimes agnosticism is not really agnosticism but belief under another name and in different words. The Church then could not accept as a definitive statement on God and man Sartre's contention that there is no God. Nor could she be content with Heidegger or Jaspers when they pause intellectually powerless before a Transcendence that may or may not be God. A more comprehensive judgment on Heidegger or Jaspers would have to await, however, an analysis of all the values they predicate of Transcendence.

The Church speaks of the possibility that man can know God apart from Revelation. It also indicates that the possibility would remain even if man were without grace. It is the *possibility* of all these things, we must remember, of which the Church speaks. She does not say that things ever happen this way, that is, she does not say that any man ever recognizes God's existence without grace. One might ask why she should bother at all making a statement on man's theoretical possibility before God in a hypothetical state where man is denied grace. It is a legitimate question and one we must answer before this survey on God's existence is complete.

Granted the definition of the Church then, God must be met with in some form or other in the non-Christian and non-Biblical world of man's religion and philosophy simply because man is man. Grace is not reserved for the Christian or for the man who believes the Scriptures. It is given in graciousness and generosity by God to all. For man, though he is an act of God's freedom, is not made free from God. He could not be. God could only give man what God had to give. So God made man in freedom and by means of His freedom alone. Apart from God's sovereign freedom there was no other reason to make man. Making man freely, God gave man God's own freedom. Making man in love and from love, God gave man God's own love. This is the endless wonder of that mighty deed we call creation.

Every time man expresses love and acts in freedom, he touches God. For love and freedom are not man's invention. They are man's discovery and God's gift. There is no other source for them.

Man then could not be made free from God. He had to be made in God's image and likeness. God had no other image or likeness to use except His own. The only alternative then to making man in God's image was to make man nothing and no one. It was God's decision to make man someone that compelled Him to make man like Himself. For God was the only One and the only Someone there was. So man and God are simply inseparable from each other. As long as man is and will be, he has something of God in him. Therefore man is always reaching and dealing with God. For he always reaches and deals with man. This is a truth theology must recognize if it is going to express itself fully. Man's failure before God is not only a failure in turning from God but also in turning from man's true self.

Man sins and fails when he will not allow God to be God, when he tries to make God into man's image and likeness. Being man, he necessarily is involved with God but with a God he will not allow to be God. Being in the world, he is in contact with God but he gives his devotion to the world of God forgetting the God of the world for whom man must reserve his deepest dedication.

God then stirs to life in man and in the world even outside the history of Revelation. He does not do this as gloriously as He does it in His words and in His Son, but He does do it. If man will allow this God to be Himself, then man finds salvation. Simply stated, man's task is in learning to deify the proper value. He must deify God, not himself or the world. When God stirs within man, man's salvation depends upon his allowing this God to be what God must be. Man then never ignores or misses God —but he does mistake God and he does misuse God. God is always there, but too often we refuse to recognize Him in His there-ness. We try instead to make Him in the image of our here-ness. God then is inescapable but not inconfusable. God is inevitable but not unmistakable. God is always found but not on His own terms. Man is always in contact with God but not always with the right God. God always speaks to man as man, but since man is not always man God is not always God to him. God and man could entirely miss each other only if God would become nothing while man remained something (which is impossible) or if God remained something while man became nothing (which never happens). God will become an irrelevant concern when man becomes an irrelevant concern. But man never becomes an irrelevant concern since no one is ever irrelevant to himself.

The God before and beyond Scripture is a God who expresses Himself in Scripture. He does not express Himself in Scripture as fully as He does in His Son, but He does verbalize or incarnationalize Himself in Scripture. It is not His final Word nor His last Communication, but there is something distinctively divine about God's scripturalization of Himself. This leads us to our second question: the God of the Old Testament.

The Jewish Scriptures assume that God is. Since it is unthinkable that God does not exist, the problem of man's search for his God takes on a different tonality. The approach to God in the Old Testament is so distinctive and so challenging that a study of it somehow manages always to be refreshing.

Since God exists, no man can afford to be ignorant of Him. But how does man learn of God? He does this by listening to God who always speaks to the man who is attentive. This listening to God is of indispensable significance. Only God knows who and what God is. He is utterly Other. Man knows of God as God speaks of Himself. And so the Old Testament is a book about

God, about the utterly Other One, about the One who is not only the Source of man and his world but rather that Different Being whose life is self-sufficient and whose existence is independent of our existence. Though the Old Testament is a book about God, it is not really a book about the utterly Otherness of God. It is not a metaphysical or a philosophical or even a scientific study of God. More properly, it is a book about God and Israel, about God in His Emmanuel dimension, about God as He meets His people, and as He does things. The things God will do will reveal what He is, but their primary object seems to be God's expression of love and involvement with man rather than an expression of His nature.

And so, although the God of Israel is a hidden God, although He speaks at times of His absolute dominion ("I am the Lord"), He presents Himself more often as a doer of things ("I form the light"—"I have made the earth") and as a dealer with men. In fact, God is described in the Old Testament in the language man uses to describe his fellow-men. He is then a God who speaks and reveals but always in human terms.

In the Old Testament, man learns of God quite differently from what Western man might expect. It is not man's reasoning but God's revelation which ultimately is instructive. Man learns of God not as he speaks of God with his fellow-men, but as he listens to God speaking. It is not as though man learned so much of God on his own and then God filled in the picture. Rather, it is more a question of faith and Revelation working side-by-side with man's reason which teaches man most and best.

One of the first things the God of the Old Testament does is to tell man His name. To know the name of another, for the ancient Semite, was to know who and what the other was: his identity, qualities, character, potential. To be nameless is to be worthless (Job 30,8). If one has a name, then his nature is equivalent to it. "As his name is, so is he; 'Fool' is his name" (1 Samuel 25:25).

And so God speaks His name to Israel, and God's name becomes Israel's proud and awesome possession. Yahweh is God's name. The meaning of His name tells us something of God's role in our history. Yahweh might best be translated: "I shall be there as Who I am shall I be there."[1]

Once God tells men His name, He is involved with men. Israel understood this: "You are in our midst, Yahweh; and we bear your name. Abandon us not" (Jeremias 14,9). In the name of God, the Jews understood something of God's role and purpose in their history. He would be immanent in their history ("I shall be there"), yet mysteriously transcendent to their history ("I shall be there as Who I am"). God is not made by history, for before history and without man He is still Yahweh. "I am Yahweh; I do not change" (Exodus 3,6). After creation God becomes not God but God-with-His-people. God is not only immanent in and transcendent to history, He is also transparent through history (in history and among men He is known "as Who I am shall I be there").

Israel's approach to God is unique. The Old Testament gives us a concept of God which could never have been derived from surrounding cultures. Everything else in Israel's culture may have been borrowed but not her concept of God. Not only was Israel's concept of God independent, but it was in direct opposition to neighboring cultures. The Old Testament concept of God was Israel's and God's passionate protest against what man had made of God, against every polytheistic, pantheistic, humanistic conception of God. The gods of the Canaanites, the Mesopotamians, the Assyrians were all too human. In their fighting, stealing, cruelty, adultery, they suffered the same afflictions and moral problems as man. But Israel's God is sinless, unspeakably holy, involved with man. He might be described in human terms but somehow He remains totally different from man. Israel's God was sovereign; His concern with man was unexpected; His love for man was a grace. Magic and human stratagem could not control Yahweh as it controlled the gods of Israel's neighbors. Though magic might be practiced in Israel, it was never part of her official religion. Man simply had no means of controlling the free God who cared for man in his own way.

Israel's concept of God is the starting point for an Old Testament understanding of man. Life and man are not analyzed in themselves but only in respect to the will and purpose of Yahweh. Israel does not proceed from man to God as we do. For Israel, God is—and then man is. What man is depends on what God is and what He says of man. God is the Lord of universal history and of man. Man is weak but God is strong. Man lives a short span but God lives always. Hence, for Israel there is no such thing as secular existence. Every object, person, place, or deed has a religious significance and can only be understood after God has been understood.

When we approach God it is generally by way of a cosmological metaphysics. From the world, one proceeds to a first cause, then to an intellectual first cause, then to a personal Intelligence, finally to Transcendence. The Old Testament deals in exactly the reverse order. God is first seen as Transcendence and last of all as Maker of the world. This free, personal, active, loving Being has made a world. What the world is or the men who live in it, only He really knows. It is His Lordship that one must recognize first before he can evaluate the creatures (history, time, people, nature) over which that Lordship has dominion.

The Old Testament view of man then proceeds from a constant relationship with the Will of God. The enigma of man is hidden in the depths of Yahweh's mystery. Of this much, Old Testament man is made certain. He is a responsible being, one whose historical task must be approached with complete seriousness. For his destiny is to be a bearer of God's Will in the world of creation. He is a being who proceeds from God as do the natural surroundings in which he lives. There is to be no hostility then between man and nature. Nature is not filled with terror but it is an indication of the glory and the power of the Creator. Nor is there to be hostility between man and man. All peoples form one great family. And the list of nations in Genesis 10, which is unique in Eastern literature, includes Israel in the general context of humanity even though she knew she was special. Israel's difference comes not from natural capacity nor inherited nobility, but from a free election by God who might have chosen any nation since all are equally His.

It is only when one understands the Old Testament concept of Yahweh's Lordship that one can understand how dearly the Jews prized earthly possessions, children, long life, friendship, love, beauty, political freedom. All come from Yahweh; all had to be used in submission to His Will; He was indifferent to none of these things. God's demand and dominion is laid upon man in his spiritual and physical entirety. It is the whole man who lives for God, not just a spiritual side of him. The physical and material cannot be unimportant or inferior or even undesirable in the service of Yahweh.

Is there then a problem of God at all in the Old Testament? There is but it is different from what we might expect. The problem is not whether or not God is but whether or not we can accept the God who is. He is free and different. He comes only on His own terms, when He wishes, at His time. This problem with God tormented Israel and tempted her into magic and idolatry. She wanted in her weak hours the God she wanted and not the God who is. Thus at times Yahweh was an embarrassment for Israel and she felt keenly the pagan challenge: "Where is your God?" It disappointed Israel that she had to wait.

The problem that Israel had with God then was in accepting Him properly, not in affirming His existence. The atheist in the Old Testament is not one who denies God but one who wishes his own type of God. This reminds us of Dostoevsky's comment that men are not basically unbelievers but idolaters. The problem then for the Jew is not cognition but recognition. God is not a problem to understand but a Person one must accept as He wishes. God creates His own problem, so to speak. He comes in freedom, confronts man in human terms and demands an acceptance of Himself. The Old Testament then does not present the problem of God in abstract or philosophical terms. Men do not debate whether He exists or what He is like. The Old Testament presentation of the problem is concrete and urgent. God is there. What are you going to do? The fool refuses to recognize Him. What are you going to do? The problem of God in the Old Testament is a problem of man. Are you willing to wait for God to come to you as He is and when He wishes? For God is Yahweh, the One who shall be there as He is or not at all.

It should not surprise us if we find that the New Testament accepts the existence of God with the same assurance which characterized the older Scriptures. It never occurs to the men who write and preach, who build churches and believe that there is any value in questioning whether or not God exists. For man in the New Testament, as in the Old, God is simply there. He is there in spite of all His incomprehensibility and He is there for man in spite of all His sublimity. This fact needs not proof nor explanation in the New Testament and it receives neither. The only real difference in the New Testament is its transformation of the ancient problem of Yahweh into the new problem of Jesus.

To delay too long on the New Testament approach to the problem of God is to become involved in Christology which is not the purpose of this present study. The reality of Christ does make some differences, of course, in the total comprehension of what man calls his concept of God. Christ enriches the idea that God is Father, His and ours, and that God is not only Father for the community, Israel, or for the few, Israel's kings or prophets, but for each and every individual. One might pray "Our Father" or "My Father" with equal effectiveness. Christ also brings out more clearly the relationship between man's love for his brethren and for his God. The one is so much a part of the other and the

two are so closely united that, as St. John comments, to claim
one without the other is to show oneself a "liar." As Christ clari-
fies our concept of God, He emphasizes and embodies the love
and freedom which must characterize man's approach to God. In
doing this, He gives us the correct attitude toward the problems
in belief which we considered in the last chapter. Love of self,
neighbor, and God are artfully united in His teaching so that one
loves neighbor as self and discovers that this is only the second
commandment. The first is love of God. Christ assigns love as the
ultimate human and divine value. God is necessitated to give to
Other in love. This self-giving and self-communication, this sharing of love, is at the basis of Trinitarian doctrine. God must give
Himself to Other in order to be. Father must give of Himself to
Son else Father is not paternal and Son does not exist. Fatherhood and Sonship demand communication. And apart from
Fatherhood and Sonship there is no God. Made in the image of
God, man is necessitated to love, to give of self in order to be.

Christ's concept of God is of a God before whom man need
not fear. A God gentle enough to clothe the lilies of the field or
paternal enough to send the only Son He has, is a God one never
does justice to when he sees Him as forever wrathful or without
compassion. As the New Testament follows Christ in His every
deed and word, it creates a Figure of enormous love and warmth
and light. And it is at that point when the reader is most cap-
tured by Christ and inspired by His love that Christ assures us:
"He who has seen me, has seen the Father." To have seen Christ
is to have seen God. And who could think that Christ could not
understand or could not love?

The end result of Christ's offer of love and of His concept of
God is a promise of freedom. It is not just a freedom from political servitude or Egyptian bondage or the painful oppression of
disease or the debilitating effects of hunger. It is more. It is a
freedom from sin, from the Law, from life that has no meaning,

from final death. It is the freedom that sets man free from his narrow self and from his fundamental fears. But it is not a cheap or easy freedom. It is purchased only with effort, in love, and by the painful death of Christ Himself. The question Christ poses is not whether or not man is made for freedom, but whether or not he is equal to the task.

Christ then centers the problem of God in the problem of love. This should not surprise us since the New Testament tells us that God is Love.

There is then a close relationship between the Old Testament and the New. The Word of God written in the Old Testament possesses an inner orientation to the Word of God not only written but made human in the New. The first Word of the Old Testament looks to the final Word of the New, which is Christ. As Karl Rahner asserts, the inner nature of the Old Testament Word is such that anyone who abandons himself to its hidden dynamism and allows himself to be carried beyond the limits of his personal interpretation and the letter of the text, will mysteriously and secretly partake of the benediction really contained in the New.[2]

What relation then should we expect to find between the idea of God in the Old Testament and in the New? It is not as though there emerge two ideas which one then puts side by side. There is rather an inner consistency and unity between both so that they fuse into one. The New Testament idea of God must already be active in the Old Testament or else Christianity is all wrong. God is the same in the Old Testament and in the New not only because He is the same, unchanging God, but because the entirety of salvation history is a progressive revelation, begun in the Old Testament. The God of Israel and of the New Testament Community is the same God who reveals in both Testaments with the same purpose in mind, namely Christ Himself.

There are two passages in the Bible which are of especial interest to us now. One is taken from the Book of Wisdom, the other from Paul's letter to the Church at Rome. The common theme which both explore is man's ability to know God even apart from explicit Revelation. It seems not too much to assume that the passages in question presuppose the reliability of human intelligence in this endeavor. One suspects that even if there were no grace, a situation which probably never obtains, man yet would not be powerless before a problem of such significance for his human welfare and eternal salvation.

Both passages take it for granted that God is the Author of nature, and, as we have seen before, that there should not be hostility but a certain harmony between nature and man and God. It seems incorrect to view nature as unable to aid in the discovery of God. If our fellow-men are of crucial importance for the discovery of God, nature, made by God, should also help. Man may be God's image but nature cannot be without His traces and His influence.

The Old Testament speaks frequently of God's authorship of nature. The very first chapter of Scripture makes this very clear.

God said: "Let there be light!" And there was light. (Genesis 1,3)

God made the firmament . . . and God called the firmament sky. (Genesis 1, 7–8)

Then God said: "Let the waters below the sky be gathered into one place so that the dry land may appear!" (Genesis 1,9)

And so it was. God made the two great luminaries, the greater luminary to rule the day and the smaller one to rule the night—and the stars also. (Genesis 1,16)

Nature, which is the work of God, ought to speak of God, the Old Testament reasoned.

When I see the heavens, the work of your fingers, the moon and the stars which you have formed; What is man . . . ? (Psalm 8,3)

O Lord, our Lord, how glorious is your name in all the earth. (Psalm 8,9)

The heavens are telling the glory of God. And the sky shows forth the work of his hands. (Psalm 19)

How many are your works, O Lord! In wisdom have you made them all: The earth is filled with your creations. (Psalm 104,24)

Where were you when I laid the foundations of the earth? . . . Have you ever in your life commanded the morning? Or assigned its place to the dawn? . . . Have you ever gone to the sources of the sea? (Job 38: 4,12,16)

It is in the context of this thinking that the passage we are interested in from the Book of Wisdom (13, 1–9) had been written.

For all men are foolish by nature and had no perception of God,

And from the good things that were visible they had not the power to know him who is,

Nor through paying attention to his works did they recognize the workman,

But either fire, or wind, or swift air,

Or the circle of the stars, or rushing water,

Or the heavenly luminaries, the rulers of the world, they considered gods.

And if through delight in their beauty they supposed that these were gods,

Let them know how far superior is the Lord of these,

For the originator of beauty created them;

But if it was through awe at their power and operation,

Let them conclude from them how much mightier he who formed them is.

For from the greatness and beauty of what is created,

The originator of them is correspondingly perceived.

But yet little blame attaches to these men,

For perhaps they just go astray

In their search for God and their desire to find him;

For living among his works they search

And believe the testimony of their sight, that what they see is beautiful.

But again, even they are not to be excused;

For if they had power to know so much

That they could try to make out the world,

Why did they not sooner find the Lord of all this?

The passage from Wisdom is so convinced of God's know-ability from the splendor of nature and the power of man's reason that it holds accountable all, pagans included, who do not proceed to a knowledge of God from the things God made.

There is a failure about this: "Nor through paying attention to his work did they recognize the workman" (13,1). It is a failure which need never have happened since there was a way out of it: "Let them conclude from them how much mightier he who formed them is. For from the greatness and beauty of what is created, the originator of them is correspondingly perceived" (13,4–5). The end result of failure when one might easily not have failed is accusation: ". . . they are not to be excused: For if they had power to know so much that they could try to make out the world, why did they not sooner find the Lord of all this?" (13, 8–9).

Wisdom here makes an act of faith in the reliability of human intelligence, nature's finality, and the knowability of God. There are some qualifications in the passage which must not be overlooked. The pagans who are accountable for now knowing God in this way are not any pagans but those educated enough "to know so much." Pagans are not indicted in each and every situation, but only as a group of educated men. The implication seems to be that at least for these men the step from what God has made to God is a rather easy process. "From the greatness and beauty of what is created, the originator of them is correspondingly perceived."

One can proceed to a knowledge of God's existence and some of His attributes then even apart from explicit Revelation. It is man as man and not as believer or Jew who is assigned this radical potential. *Wisdom* assures its readers that men *can* have a natural knowledge of God from the things God has made. The passage is a strange mixture of Biblical faith with philosophical overtones, it is true. But it is a passage the Church accepts as genuinely Scriptural and therefore unmistakably inspired.

In Paul's letter to the Church of Rome we confront a somewhat similar theme. Paul goes further than *Wisdom*, though in-

fluenced, it seems, by the Old Testament passage. In Romans
(1,18–23), we read:

> . . . God's anger is breaking forth from heaven against all the
> impiety and wickedness of the men who in their wickedness are
> suppressing the truth. For all that can be known of God is
> clearly before them; God has shown it to them. Ever since the
> creation of the world, his invisible nature—his eternal power
> and divine character—have been clearly perceptible through
> what he has made. So they have no excuse, for though they
> knew God, they have not honored him as God or given thanks
> to him, but they have indulged in futile speculations, until
> they have become dark. They called themselves wise, but they
> have turned into fools, and for the splendor of the immortal
> God they have substituted images in the form of mortal man,
> birds, animals, and reptiles.

Paul then speaks not so much of an unbeliever's ability to know
God but of the fact that pagans or gentiles know God (v.21).
The accusation that Paul levels is not against a failure to affirm
God but against a refusal to honor God. Once again, man's ac-
countability for his failure is cited. *Wisdom* wondered why men
did not know God when they could have known Him so easily.
Paul says that these knew God in actual fact. He wonders why
they did not honor God as they should have.

God, Paul makes clear, used nature not as a demonstration of
His power, as a mighty feat, but as a means of revealing Him-
self. "For all that can be known of God is clearly before them;
God has shown it to them" (v.19). God is revealed; man sees
Him; and then looks away. This is the dreadful and baffling
aspect of the problem as Paul sees it. Why does man look away?

Paul's insistence that nature bespeaks God reflects his Old
Testament and Jewish background. He goes on to say, more
boldly than *Wisdom*, that not only God's existence but some
clearly specified characteristics of God are knowable to man from

creation alone. These include the invisibility, eternal power, and divine character of the God who is above nature and yet is perceived through it. "Ever since the creation of the world, his invisible nature—his eternal power and divine character—have been clearly perceptible through what he has made" (v.20).

Paul then holds these men accountable for not worshipping the God they saw. He uses the term "anger of God" to show God's displeasure and therefore man's culpability. The "anger of God" is a classic Old Testament metaphor indicating strong opposition between God and sin.

The harsh indictment of paganism and of the world of unbelief by Paul must be balanced by what Paul says later in the same letter about the atheist and his conscience.

> When the heathen who have no Law instinctively obey what the Law demands, even though they have no law they are a law to themselves, for they show that what the Law demands is written on their hearts, and their conscience will testify for them . . . if people who are uncircumcised observe the requirements of the Law, will they not be treated as though they were circumcised? . . . if . . . they obey the Law, they will condemn you, who break the Law, although you have it in writing, and are circumcised. . . . For the real Jew is not the man who is one outwardly. . . . The real Jew is the man who is one inwardly, and real circumcision is a matter of the heart, a spiritual, not a literal, thing. Such a man receives his praise not from man, but from God. (2,14–16; and 26–29)

Paul then indicates that God calls the man without explicit Revelation to Himself in two ways: through the world He made, a world which speaks of God and reveals Him as invisible, powerful, and divine; and through conscience where "what the Law demands is written on their hearts." Paul's treatment of this complex question has at one and the same time a disarming simplicity and a refined sophistication about it.

Pagans are not in total darkness. God is with them in nature and conscience. Paul's insistence that they are not in total darkness harmonizes with St. John's observation that a "true light . . . sheds light upon everyone."

One might pursue Paul's thought on this question in his sermons at Lystra (Acts 14,15–17) and in Athens (Acts 17,24–27), but the line of reasoning is not fundamentally different.

We might then draw two broad conclusions from the teaching of *Wisdom* and *Romans* about the knowability of God or the problem of atheism.

First, men should proceed and can proceed (therefore, they are guilty if they do not) from God's world to God. Nature tells all who do not refuse instruction that God is originator of the world and that He is a Reality of beauty, might, and power (*Wisdom*). Explicit Revelation is not necessary for man to discover this much.

Furthermore and secondly, men already know of God and some of His characteristics (invisibility, power, nature) from creation, yet strangely refuse Him homage. God's anger then bursts forth from heaven against them and accuses them of negligence. These are men who have "no excuse, for . . . they knew God [and] have not honored him as God or given thanks to him. . . . They called themselves wise but they have turned into fools."

These then are some basic insights from Scripture into the problem we have been considering throughout this book. Scripture, as we have seen, postulates God and then, in the light of this postulation, it considers the enigma of man and the whole range of human problems and experience. Urgently, it asks over and over again what will man decide about God. Without embarrassment, it warns over and over again that a total inability to find God is sinful and will be punished. Scripture does not view the problem of unbelief from a twentieth-century perspective. It does not explore the possibility of man's serving God under a different title or another name. It does not decide what one is to think of the man whose denial of God is a denial of a false concept and not of the true God. It does, however, speak of a problem which is ageless and with inspired insight it says something valid for every century.

THE TESTIMONY OF THE CHURCH

As we began a study of this central question, we said that after the data of Scripture had been explored, we would consider the testimony of the Church on this problem. The Church's clearest statement, though not her only pronouncement, on the knowability of God by all men comes from the first Vatican Council. It should not surprise us that its foundation is set in Scripture.

What we shall do in giving a full statement of the Church's testimony is to deal with two documents from the Magisterium, or official teaching of the Church. The first is, as we have said, a statement from first Vatican; the second is an official document from the pontificate of Pius X.

The statement from Vatican I is a definition, whose import is roughly the same as the phrasing we used in first exposing this problem. Vatican I contends that God can be known with certainty from the things God made. Since this decision is definition, it binds the Church to its acceptance absolutely. One does not, however, accept a definition uncritically or without exegesis. This is a norm for the proper interpretation of a Scriptural statement. It is also a criterion for correct magisterial exegesis. As with Scripture, we must explore the background, intention, and actual wording of the definition before we know what the Church teaches. The Church's teaching is not a matter of indifference for the Catholic intrigued with the problem of a man's unbelief and the God whose acceptance means belief.

There were a number of influences which preceded Vatican I.

These help to explain in part the position taken by the Council. The intellectual climate of the second half of the nineteenth century was such that the assembled episcopate sought to avoid two difficulties. Either of these alternatives would be destructive of ecclesiastical teaching or of a true evaluation of man's intellectual capability before the problem of God. Neither alternative was desirable.

The Bishops did not want, on the one hand, to cede to rationalism the idea that God could be known so easily and so completely that grace was unnecessary and Revelation superfluous. Nor did they, on the other hand, want to give the impression that man's intelligence was so enfeebled by sin that it could do nothing relative to God without supernatural assistance from grace and Revelation. Either alternative was problematic and avoiding both was not an easy task. In the proper statement of this problem lay a key to the true problem of God and belief, the Fathers of the Council reasoned. But how were they to proceed? The realization that their statement would take the form of a definition added gravity and solemnity to the deliberations and discussions which ensued.

The Council was particularly plagued by a system of thought which preached the latter of the two alternatives we explained above. Traditionalism, as it was called, found man helpless without supernatural assistance. Understanding Traditionalism was not an easy accomplishment. For it is practically impossible to consider what man would be like without Revelation and grace. Since man, as we know him, has always had both, we are somewhat restricted in trying to see what he would be like without either or with neither.

In its purest expression, Traditionalism (especially as proposed by Bautain, Lamennais, and De Bonald) said that no knowledge of God is even possible for man without a primitive revelation. If this primitive revelation from God did not teach man that God existed, man would never suspect that God existed, at least in his natural and unaided situation. We come to know of God's existence, the Traditionalists argued, because this revelation has been preserved and passed on to generation after generation.[3] It is this position, Traditionalism in its pure form, which is excluded by Vatican I as unacceptable to Catholic teaching on the nature of man and the knowability of God. It is this form of Traditionalism that we shall be speaking of when we refer to it subsequently.

There is, it might be helpful to know, a more mitigated form of Traditionalism which Vatican I does not consider. This mitigated Traditionalism maintains that man has the physical capacity to form a judgment of God's existence. Yet man never achieves the intellectual refinement for this type of thinking apart from human society and its traditions.

In addition to these influences from the intellectual climate of the day, Vatican I had before it two further factors which had to be taken into consideration.

Scripture, first of all, seemed to speak of man's *being able* to find God from nature without Revelation. Traditionalism made light of this, but the Council felt it could not. Scripture furthermore made it clear that man learns precious little about God without Revelation. To discover what God was really like, man needed God. Rationalism made light of this, but the Council once again felt it could not.

In addition to Scriptural teaching, the Council Fathers were aware of the Church's Tradition, especially expressed in the Patristic period, that God could be known by man from created reality. Theophilus of Antioch was not untypical of this Patristic Tradition when he wrote:

God has called everything into existence from nothing, so that his greatness might be known and understood through his works. Just as the soul of man is not seen, as it is invisible, but is known through the movement of the body, so God cannot be seen with human eyes; but he is observed and known through providence and his works. Just as one, at the sight of a well-equipped ship which sweeps over the sea and steers toward a harbor, becomes aware that there is a helmsman on her who directs her, so also one must be aware that God is the director of everything, even though he is not seen with bodily eyes. . . . (To Autolycus, 1,4–5)

Although rationalism bothered the Fathers of the Council, it was really Traditionalism's depreciation of human reason relative to God's existence which was a primary fear. The Fathers worried over agnosticism outside the Church (which claimed man never really knows if there is a God or not) and Traditionalism within the Church (which maintained that unless God aids man with Revelation, he never knows of God's existence). At the heart of this difficulty there was at issue a real but unspoken difference between Protestant and Catholic Christianity on the nature of man after the fact of original sin. The Catholic tendency is to leave man in possession of all his natural powers even though these are seen as weakened. The Protestant tendency is to see man as totally in need of supernatural help whenever God is discussed on any level.

And so Vatican I with all this in mind reached two decisions:

1. A natural knowledge of God is *possible*.

2. This knowledge is achieved through an intellectual process.

The Council document expresses this decision in two ways, first by a statement of the Church's position, secondly by a prohibition of false teaching.

In setting forth the Church's position, Vatican I issued the following document:

The same and holy Mother Church holds and teaches that God, the origin and end of all things, can be known with certainty by the natural light of human reason from the things that he created; "for since the creation of the world his invisible

attributes are clearly seen, being understood through the things
that are made" (*Romans* 1:20) . . .[4]

In prohibiting false teaching, the Church spoke in this fashion:

If anyone says that the one and true God, our creator and lord,
cannot be known with certainty with the natural light of human
reason by means of the things that have been made: let him be
anathema.[5]

A proper understanding of these statements depends on an
analysis of four key elements.

The Church, first of all, describes the God of whom it here
speaks as "the origin and end of all things" (*rerum omnium
principium et finem*). To say this much is essential. For a knowledge of God's existence requires at least a minimally descriptive
notion of what we mean by God. Otherwise we become so lost
in ambiguity that we say nothing. The Council takes it for
granted that "God" means at least this much: a supreme Being,
who is distinct from the world, and who in some very undefined
way is the initiator and final point of creation. The Council is
careful to say the least possible about God. It does not even,
technically speaking, refer to God as Creator but rather as
"origin and end of all things." To say less than this is to have no
God. For one who is not supreme Being is a creature; and one
not distinct from the world is only the world; and one neither
initiator nor terminal point of creation is little more than creation itself. One is not to adore a creature, the world, or creation.
Therefore the God whom men must worship must be at least
what Vatican I describes Him to be.

The second element in the Church's statement refers not to
the object but to the means of man's knowledge. Man can know
God "by the natural light of human reason" (*naturali humanae
rationis lumine*). Earlier drafts of this statement were worded

somewhat differently. They referred not to man as man but to man after original sin (*ab homine lapso* or *uti nunc est*). This was changed because the Council wanted to speak of man as man and not man in a particular state. The Council wanted to affirm that man as such, with or without sin, has the intrinsic capacity to conclude God exists.

Bishop Gasser who wrote the official record of Vatican I comments that "the statement as to whether man can know God with certainty by the natural light of reason in the condition in which he now lives is not at issue; the document is concerned rather with the condition of human nature as such."[6]

The third element in the statement makes reference to the starting point of man's natural knowledge of God. Man proceeds "from the things [God] created" (*e rebus creatis*). The Council's statement here is assertive, not exclusive: i.e., it says something is so without saying that other things are not true. Vatican I makes it clear that man can come to a knowledge of God mediately and indirectly through creatures. It does not, however, exclude other ways of knowing God naturally, i.e., ontologism or direct intuitive apprehension. The Church calls the cosmological approach to God valid. Man can come to God by perceiving the world around him. There is, however, no intention of excluding metaphysical or moral arguments, Bishop Gasser cautions. "If we assert," the Bishop writes, "that God is known by the natural light of reason through creatures . . . , we have no intention of excluding reference to God by means of His image which is impressed upon man's immortal spirit; one cannot therefore maintain that a metaphysical argument is not valid."[7]

The final element the Council writes into its decree concerns the quality and the reality of this knowledge of God which is natural and from creatures. The quality of the knowledge is "certain"; the reality is but a "possibility." As the document expresses it, "God . . . *can* be known with certainty" (*certo cognosci posse*). The Council made a point of avoiding a word that one might have expected. When it refers to knowledge, by reason, from creation, one expects a word like "demonstration" to follow rather than "certain knowledge." Yet the Council says that God can be known, not demonstrated, by reason. One wonders why. The answer to the question lay in the desire of the Fathers to avoid any phraseology which might seem too much like philosophical reasoning or at least sound too scientific. "Demonstration" was simply more specific than the Council wanted to be.

Gasser admits that "in a sense 'certain knowledge' and 'demonstration' are identical, yet the weaker expression was preferred."[8]

In the earliest drafts of this document, the phrase "can be known" (*cognosci posse*) appeared but without the qualification "with certainty" (*certo*). Some bishops feared that the additional phrase "with certainty" might achieve not only the desirable effect of excluding Traditionalism, but that it might also overextend the role of reason and thus aid rationalism. A majority, however, did not share this fear. It is not only knowledge but a sense of security or certitude in that knowledge which man needs if his awareness of God's existence is to mean anything for him. Suspicions or surmises are not enough.

It is well to note also that the Council speaks only of the possibility that man may affirm God's existence without grace. It does not speak of the fact. In reality, it may be that man is always given grace to achieve this vital decision of God's existence.

It is well also to note that the Council says nothing of "proofs" concerning the existence of God.

It is some two generations before the Church officially turns again to this problem of God's existence and man's knowledge. During the pontificate of Pius X, an oath against Modernism (*Sacrorum Antistitum*) was issued on September 1, 1910. The document takes up the same questions we have seen discussed in Vatican I. It repeats Vatican I to some extent and then adds changes which are first found here. The document reads:

I profess that God, the origin and end of all things, can be known with certainty by the natural light of reason from the created world, that is, from the visible works of creation, as a cause from its effects, and that therefore his existence can also be demonstrated.[9]

Three changes from Vatican I are immediately evident:

1. "From the things he created" (*e rebus creatis*) now becomes "from the visible works of creation" (*per visibilia creationis opera*).

2. The progression from creation to God is determined more accurately by this present document than by Vatican I's statement. The progression is "as a cause from its effects" (*tamquam causam per effectus*).

3. Vatican I stated that God "can be known with certainty." The present document adds "therefore, his existence can also be demonstrated" (*adeoque demonstrari etiam posse*).

A brief explanation of these new terms may aid our understanding of the Church's official position. When the text mentions "from the visible works of creation," one need not conclude that this refers only to things which fall under external experience. When the text adds "as a cause from its effects," some use of the principle of causality is certainly indicated, but one need not conclude that any particular way of causality in finding God is indicated (e.g., efficient causality). By far, however, the most important addition is the use of the word "demonstration." It is a word, as we have seen, that the Vatican Council assiduously avoided. Exactly what does the position of this statement add to the Church's official teaching?

The document seems to take the certain and unscientific knowledge of God, stipulated in Vatican I, and to express a wider possibility for human reason without grace. *Sacrorum Antistitum* mentions a scientific knowledge of God as a distinct possibility for unaided reason. This would seem to necessitate two things. First, man is capable not only of reaching a conclusion but of reflecting on the process of reasoning which led him to God so that he is now conscious as to how he took the step he did. Second, there is a process of reasoning valid not only for this individual personally in finding God, but valid and convincing for man's intellect as such. This is not to say there is such a thing as one proof which proves all to everyone. What is said here is this much, that man can not only be sure of God's existence from creation, as Vatican I said, but that he can arrive at this judgment through some use of the principle of causality (taken in its widest possible understanding) and that he can reflect so clearly on the process leading him to the judgment that this process may be convincing for others. *Sacrorum Antistitum* gives to Vatican I's statement an objective and scientific dimension it did not have. Boldly, it says more than Vatican I; cautiously, it does not go too far, leaving open a multitude of possible approaches to God. To say one way is valid, to assume that perhaps it is best, is not to say all other ways are invalid. It does assure us, however, that there is such a thing as at least one valid way. And it takes man's possibility of knowing God's existence out of the realm of the deeply subjective and thoroughly ambiguous so that for all practical purposes man is left only with agnosticism. The document before us may have been influenced by the Modernism it sought to counteract, but it says something valid for the Church universal in any age or under any influence. It is a deadly serious business to know whether or not man can come to a knowledge of God's existence. Agnosticism's inadequacy and atheism's culpability depend on this. To say that man's reason is reliable, that human nature is essentially sound even after the Fall, that man even without grace retains a possibility for God, to say this much is to establish the fundamentals of man's problem with God. If man without grace *can* reach God, how much more might man do in grace? In neither of the two statements of the Church we have considered is the question raised as to whether there is such a thing as a man who lives without grace or who ever searches for God without divine assistance.

It is well to realize also that *Sacrorum Antistitum* does not canonize any Aristotelian syllogistic process in the use of causality or in the conclusion one's reason reaches. It seems only to say that there is a *possibility* that the common and unspecified knowledge of which Vatican I speaks *can* evolve into a scientific, reflexive, convincing demonstration of God's existence. This demonstration involves some appeal to the principle of causality but not necessarily in any Thomistic sense of the word.

One wonders why *Sacrorum Antistitum* went further than Vatican I. Actually, this was conditioned, as we said before, by the difficulties of the age. Vatican I said "God . . . *can* be known with certainty." This was sufficient to exclude Traditionalism. Such was not enough for *Sacrorum Antistitum*. Pius X had to add the concepts of "demonstration" and "causality" because Modernism could accept Vatican I's statement with ease and turn it into total subjectivism. The Church does not, of course, *create* positions to exclude unacceptable doctrine. It does, however, enunciate what is already present in its Tradition in a way clear enough to fend off an influence it sees as threatening the Catholic community.

It may help us to conclude this section on the testimony of the Church with a number of observations on both documents viewed jointly. One can, for example, still maintain that an internal approach to God is more convincing if one wishes. He cannot, however, exclude the validity of the approach the Church has declared sufficient.

As one views both documents, it becomes evident that some use of analogy in the conception of God is indicated in all the Church says of the problem. A total estrangement of creation from God, either in grace or sin or pure nature is not considered a possibility. The Church seems to assume that there is a sense in which God and creation are inseparable. As long as creation is, there is something of God's Being and Image in it. Finding one, man need never be far from the other.

It is important to realize that *Sacrorum Antistitum* does not use "demonstration" of God's existence in a mathematical or logical sense. It is not a question here of only cognition but recognition. This demands some personal involvement. As we well know, in things not empirically probative, a man's intellect can resist and refuse. It takes an effort for man to totally exclude the idea of God from his mind as he looks out upon creation. Yet if one so chooses, he may so choose. Whenever we deal with persons, and God is personal, intellect is not enough.

The testimony of the Church is a witness, as we have indicated before, to a non-historical situation. It is just possible that no one ever did come or ever will come to a knowledge of God in the way the Church describes. The alternative to this position, however, seems to be skepticism. It is not so much a question here of the Church's being interested in a philosophical problem. It is rather an attempt by the Church to consider man as man. This is never without theological significance. Even if grace is always given to the man searching for God, one ought to know if reason has any value in this problem. If it does not, then man finds God only from grace and in total subjectivity. The human contribution is dispensable. And man might just as well be a creature without reason. God and Christ are certainly found subjectively. The Church merely indicates that the subjectivity is not total, that reason is not useless, and that objectivity has its own values and reasons.

In Vatican I, we have a defined position of the Church. In *Sacrorum Antistitum*, the theological qualification is weaker though considerable. Because of its connection with Vatican I's statement and with the whole range of Catholic Tradition, the latter document may be termed a theologically certain position.

Both documents we have examined come to us from the late

nineteenth and early twentieth century. They counteract the influence of Traditionalism and Modernism. We have no document
of sufficient magnitude for the second half of the twentieth
century. The problem of God has taken a new turn since the
Second World War. The Church is now formulating a response
to this challenge. It will be a response, of course, taking into account what the Church said before, yet pledging her to new
goals. Her involvement in social concerns (*Mater et Magistra*),
her passion for peace (*Pacem in Terris;* Paul VI at the United
Nations), her eagerness for a dialogue with the world (*Ecclesiam Suam*), her internal renewal (Vatican Council II), her
unfeigned, sincere, proven love for the world and the men she
serves, all this must move the men of good will the Church
reaches for. Paul VI has spoken on atheism so frequently. His
first Easter message and his first Encyclical expressed knowledge
of and love for the contemporary atheist. His creation of a
special commission to study twentieth-century atheism is unique
in ecclesiastical history. The Church today is speaking clearly
and concretely on the very questions that drive some men to unbelief or at least aloofness. It is difficult to see how she can do
more. She is in agony at the moment for all men, especially for
those in agony for God. The Church, after all, is also in search of
God. The fact that she knows the road and sees His light does
not keep her from being a pilgrim for God.

THE TESTIMONY OF MAN

We now turn our attention to the third major source of data
before us. Having examined the testimony of Scripture and of
the Church, we are concerned now with what we call the testimony of man, namely the proofs for God's existence. Before we
say anything specifically about the proofs, there are a few observations we should make in general.

If anything should be clear to us by now, it is the realization that the whole problem of God is not an unreal or an irrelevant problem. Men have thought of God since the dawn of history and they still think of Him. Therefore, thinking of God is a constant human concern. Thinking is a serious endeavor for man. Its greatest promise comes to fruition only if man's thinking illuminates man's life and enriches it. Thinking of God is no different. It is a serious and satisfying concern only if it is meaningful and only if it illuminates and enriches human life.

As Scot philosopher Macmurray commented: "All meaningful thought is for action; all meaningful action is for friendship." Therefore, if God does not deepen my love or friendship, thinking about Him is not truly significant for me.

Ultimately my thinking will help my belief only if I consider what I think about capable of making me more a person. If I believe, it is because I feel faith is contributive. Belief and thinking about God must have something to do with my life as a man. None of us seeks what he does not want or need. Proofs of God's existence cannot prove anything to me if I do not seek or want God. To a man attuned to a need for God almost anything can "prove" God to him. For God speaks to man in all being and in creation's every need for something more to give it permanence and meaning. The man attuned to God may turn to anything for his "proof": a metaphysical argument, a human experience, a clear night, a tranquil sea, a sleeping child. Even a flower can prove God and there is a sense in which even a flower contains all the splendor and richness and basic theology of life. There is beauty and "proof" of God everywhere. It may be the wonder of my mind or this flower or that human heart. All have the mystery of life and the image of God about them. Thus Christ Himself could see God everywhere: in the lilies of the field, the pearl of great price, a fish net hurled into the sea, a hen gathering her young, children playing in the market place.

In a sense, a man must have a touch of the mystic or the poet, of the martyr and the lover about him before God can really be "proven" to him. And so frequently enough proofs for God's existence are nothing more than explicit formulations of things we have accepted already. More often than not, they are ways of saying more coherently what we have already said to ourselves spontaneously.

In evaluating what we mean by "proofs" of God's existence, Cardinal Newman's idea of the illative sense in belief is a noteworthy insight for modern man. The convincing character of God's existence is really the conclusion of a convergence of probabilities. Sometimes probabilities converge on one point with so much force that it would be unreasonable for me not to assign it certitude and existence. The probabilities are sometimes more effective than scientific facts since they remain personal and mysterious in spite of their objectivity and clarity. There is so much probability of God's existence that one is not unreasonable when he makes this judgment. As a man's intellect judges, his will, God's grace, and all his emotional power converge and are transformed into this brilliant thing we call faith.

Specifically, we can divide the "proofs" for God's existence into psychological and metaphysical approaches.

Psychologically, there are a number of things which reach me:

LIFE. I am living. Life must have meaning, I feel. Who or what makes me live and why? I did not ask for life and yet I see it as a gift, as something I must never lose once I have it. I spend all my days reflecting on life, experiencing myself and yet I still remain with an intellect that never solves the mystery of life or of self. What has been given me is so rich and deep that I live on the surface of life and this is sufficient for me to love it and to want it and never to let it go. If this is the surface, where are the depths and what are they like? The adventure of life lies in the "something more" one always senses, sometimes grasps, but never exhausts. At moments, I almost see the heart of the matter, the veil parts, and something unspeakable touches me. I return to my ordinary tasks but I never forget those moments and I await them in the future. The wonder of this ordinary thing we call life is the conviction it leaves with us that it is extraordinary, irreplaceable, and just possibly imperishable. Who put life on this planet and in my heart? What forever turns my eyes to the darkness where the Source of my life is present and keeps me begging for the help I need to live and for more of life than I have now?

HAPPINESS. Why are we not enough for ourselves? Why do I not learn contentment here on earth when I learn so many other lessons well? Why has not someone in all the course of human history learned the secret, found the key, discovered the thread which will teach all men perfect happiness here? We have, it seems, all we need. It is almost impossible to think of what we need that we have not invented or purchased or possessed. Yet there is a need that remains which we never articulate, a yearning so deep that we are speechless when we try to express it. Who put the need in our hearts? What does it require for satisfaction? Sooner or later I tire of myself and others and life as I know it. Disappointment always comes. No one keeps it away forever. When we have done all we can for each other, even when we give all the love and energy and time we have, still it is not enough. We stand baffled and ask others what more we can do and we ask ourselves, how much do we need? We learn happiness here but it is a searching happiness looking for more, an uncertain happiness eager for guarantees it never receives, a brittle happiness fearful that the wrong moment or the unthinking person may destroy it. And then what are we to do? Is there no one wise enough to understand, strong enough to defend my happiness forever, loving enough to give me all the love I need in the way I need it?

CONSCIENCE. Why do I struggle against myself to achieve goodness? Why do I never set my own norms for goodness and rest content with them? No one knows me better than I know myself. Why should I not be able to decide the goodness I need and the way in which I must become good? What forces me outside myself in my search for goodness and approval? What is it in me or outside me that makes me feel guilty or virtuous? Who or what dares to tell me I am evil or that I must struggle against my very self?

DESIRE. Why do we always demand a different order of things, a justice we never achieve, a love we never reach, a truth we cannot have, a world different from ours? What was it really we hoped to find on the summit of Mt. Everest? What do we really hope to find on the planets? Could it be a new God or another self or at least someone who can say you are this and this is the answer to your every question? In all our solar system, there is no other planet which has so much as earth, probably no other planet with the precious gift of life. Earth has all we need, it seems. Yet this is not enough. And we look to the lesser and lifeless planets and wonder why we did not stay here or what they have to teach us. The planets are little more than another object for a search that will go on as long as there is man. We never despair of finding the total answer and yet we know that in any man's lifetime we never shall.

PERSONALITY. Even if we explain a man's body or mind, we never explain personality. I should never doubt whether I am a person or whether there are other persons. Any philosophy or theology which tells me to do this cannot enrich my life or give meaning to it. Yet as I accept the uniqueness of personality, I wonder what its Source is. I lose so much in life: pencils and books, money and position, youth, wife, children, family, friends, and love. I lose everything. I keep nothing. Eventually, I die. Yet we suspect that as long as there is personality, we can survive any loss. Personality is the ultimate value in the universe. Christianity tells us Love is Personal and this unites into one Reality the two things man needs most.

The psychological arguments should come first in any "scientific" demonstration of God's existence. These appeal to all men whereas the metaphysical arguments may not be personally suitable. Acceptance of the Unmoved Mover sometimes leaves the inquirer unmoved. We presuppose the reader's basic understanding of the famous "five ways" of St. Thomas and only list them here as a reminder:

1. From moved to Unmoved Mover;
2. From things caused to a first efficient Cause of all;
3. From non-necessary things to Necessary Being;
4. From degrees of perfection to Perfect Being;
5. From order in the world to Supreme Orderer. (This seems to be the most effective metaphysical argument for our contemporaries.)

Since this is not a book of philosophy, we shall not analyze these "ways," but only comment on their general import.

There are a few things to make clear first of all about Thomas himself and his intention in giving us these metaphysical arguments.[10]

It still surprises some to hear that Thomas was a most unconventional, quite revolutionary, and dangerously liberal thinker for his contemporaries. In fact, his thought and writings were condemned for a time by ecclesiastical authority.

Aquinas . . . was not the typical medieval figure. He was a man of the university, a man of the city . . . the innovator, not the

traditionalist. Not surprisingly, the view applies to his treatment
of the problem of God. The more typical medieval figure was the
man of the monastery, the man of the countryside, and within
monastic tradition the problem of God was not the understanding but the taste of him . . . the achievement of Aquinas was
that for the first time in history he effected the transposition
of the problem of God into a state of systematic theological understanding. His instruments were a developed metaphysic of
causality, an articulated gnoseology and psychology and, above
all, an adequately elaborated doctrine of the analogy of being.
The achievement represented the culmination of centuries of
collective thought, patristic and Scholastic. It was also the
personal triumph of a uniquely penetrating intelligence. . . .
Aquinas was the Christian theologian. His thought was directed
by a sense of the awesome biblical truth that God is the Holy
One whose Name is ineffable. . . . Aquinas . . . exploited all
the rational resources of a sophisticated ontology and an
elaborate theory of knowledge to enforce the conclusion that
all human knowledge of God ends in ignorance.[11]

Yet though Aquinas was quite aware when speaking of God
that "to Him we are united as to one unknown," still he was certain that human intelligence by its own native power could
make and demonstrate the highest of metaphysical affirmations,
that God is. Aquinas kept a balance between our ignorance and
our knowledge of God.

The important thing to appreciate, however, is Thomas' idea
on the "ways." Aquinas' five ways are no more than this: "ways."
And they are only convincing in the light of the Insight into
reality Thomas was trying to convey. The "proofs" presuppose
an acceptance of Being as Thomas understood it: the acceptance
of order in the world, the reliability of the human mind, the possibility of Transcendence, an analogy between God and creation. Seen in this light, the "proofs" are convincing.

Too much apologetic in the use of these "proofs" or too much of an assumption that the Five Ways can function apart from any context, that they have a sort of *"ex opere operato"* dynamic about them, that they convince all except the ignorant or the evil, this is to employ the "ways" of Thomas in a manner he never intended.

It is well to realize also that valid and helpful though Thomas' approach is for any century, it is a matter of fact that he was writing for thirteenth-century readers. It is unfair to assume that Thomas would have presented his thought in exactly the same way if he were writing after Kant or in an age of Existentialism or for the twentieth century. The problem of God for the Middle Ages was not whether God existed or whether reason could know Him, but rather: What is God like?

This meant more for Thomas than reason's reflection on the reality of God's existence. For Thomas was not a philosopher groping for a metaphysical judgment but a theologian, eager to understand God from Revelation, and certain that the mind could know God exists if it worked within the framework he took for granted.

For a man who doubts Being or significance in life or analogy or human knowing, Thomas' "proofs" prove nothing. It is well to realize also that even if they do prove God to the right person who accepts Thomas' basic Insight (and it is a valid one) they never prove God the way a scientific hypothesis is proved. They are not true because they work every time but because they have a certain validity about them for some. To expect Thomas' "proofs" to be infallible arguments when they do not encounter ignorance or evil, is to claim for them more than Vatican I claimed for a knowledge of God from creation and more than *Sacrorum Antistitum* claimed for a demonstration of God from causality. The Church never defined only one valid way to God nor even one way which is effective every time with everyone. The Thomist would not want to do more with the

Five Ways of Aquinas. Nor, for that matter, would Thomas. It is in overextending the "proofs" that one misuses them. It is in assuming that the "proofs" are quite adequate in the proper context that one gains maximum effectiveness from them.

We mentioned above that Thomas would have written his "ways" somewhat differently had he been writing for our century. Of all his "proofs" the argument most convincing for our contemporaries is the argument from the order around us to the Supreme Intelligence which so ordered what we find. A proper presentation of this today requires that the argument be presented with a proper metaphysics of man. When all is said and done, the argument for God should not be based on questions of the universe, in a sort of cosmological search for God, but the argument ought to be based on the human way of life in this universe. Ultimately, the earth was designed for us. And the idea of God comes to man not really from the universe but from man's situation in the universe. For man to assume that he and the universe in which he lives is all chance is to ask too much. It is to assign to chance more intelligence than any intelligence we know. Ultimately, man's situation in the universe is produced by God, Thomas would argue. And the God who created man and situated him is the God who has the final answer on man.

These then are some thoughts on man's testimony to God's existence. This section demonstrates once again the intriguing character and perennial interest of the problem of God. Cardinal Newman mentioned in his *Idea of a University* that if man never had any other religious idea except that of God, with this idea alone

> . . . you have enough to fill the mind; you have at once a whole dogmatic system. The word "God" is a theology in itself, indivisibly one, inexhaustibly various. . . . Admit a God, and you introduce among the subjects of your knowledge, a fact encompassing, closing in upon, absorbing every fact conceivable.

This idea of God can fill the mind as Newman says and yet remain a mystery. For as Augustine once commented: "If you have comprehended, what you have comprehended is not God."

This idea of God can capture man's interest on every level. As we have seen, it raises questions for the philosopher, forms the subject matter of our literature, reaches our statesmen and film-makers, influences our psychology, and challenges the emotions, will, and intellect of modern man. This idea of God pursues the authors of Scripture, gives substance to the Church's teaching, and endless labor to the theologian. No other idea we know has done so much *to* man and *for* man. If God is dead, as Nietzsche claimed, the idea of Him survives with frightening power. Next to the idea of God, every other of man's ideas seems weak and transitory. No other idea stays with man so long or disturbs him so much. Christianity tries to make clear that it is in serving the right idea of God that man reigns.

THE TESTIMONY OF FELLOW-CHRISTIANS

The final source of data on the problem before us is the testimony of our fellow Christians. Under this heading, we shall survey the thought of Paul Tillich, Karl Barth, and John Robinson.

Paul Tillich—God is the Ground of Being: Radically Immanent

We will deal here with three concerns of Tillich: Faith, Courage, and God.

Faith, Tillich asserts, is the state of being ultimately concerned. It means that a man is concerned about life ultimately, unconditionally, infinitely. It means that he refuses to be ultimately concerned about any created thing. In a sense, it is even wrong to have faith in the Bible. It is the God beyond the Bible to whom man must look. In an act of faith, a created being is grasped by and turned to the Infinite. Faith is that existential encounter in which man becomes concerned not about *a* being but about Being itself. Thus faith is the state of being grasped by the power of Being itself. Faith is an unconditional and infinite concern about the meaning of life.

Why does man need faith? Man exists in a state of finitude. He does not know who he is or where he is going. He feels estranged from some great, unknown thing that is demanded of him.

> The state of our whole life is estrangement from others and ourselves because we are estranged from the Ground of our being, because we are estranged from the origin and aim of our life. And we do not know where we have come from or where we are going. We are separated from the mystery, the depth, and the greatness of our existence. We hear the voice of that depth; but our ears are closed. We feel that something radical, total and unconditional is demanded of us; but we rebel against it, try to escape its urgency, and will not accept its promise. . . . Sin in its most profound sense, sin as despair abounds amongst us.[12]

Faith brings about the healing of this estrangement.

> It is as though a voice were saying: "You are accepted. You are accepted, accepted by that which is greater than you and the name of which you do not know. Do not ask for the name now; perhaps you will find it later. Do not try to do anything now; perhaps later you will do much. Do not seek anything. Simply accept the fact that you are accepted." If that happens to us we experience grace.[13]

Faith then for Tillich is a concern over the ultimate significance of our existence. It is a passion for total solutions, total Being, ultimate value. It is a refusal to belong to the world only or to finite problems only. It is a dedication to the fundamentals of existence and it is a healing experience giving us wholeness again and acceptance. But faith never occurs without courage.

Tillich's idea of courage begins with the proposition that man is a being who is able to ask questions. He is in fact the only being who asks questions. The Infinite does not ask questions nor do beings below man. This questioning being, man, is filled with wonder and curiosity about the phenomenon of being. He is simply astonished that things are. But this wonder over being is not unaware of a darker realization that things might not be. Being is thus everywhere and always threatened by non-being. The man who seriously asks the question, "Why is there something, why not nothing?", has experienced the shock of non-being. He becomes anxious about this. Man's very existence is involved in the problem of being and his most fundamental fears come from the realization that things might not be. The only way man can cope with his existential anxiety is by having "the courage to be," which Tillich defines as self-affirmation in spite of the possibility of non-being.

Man then in courage, "the courage to be," makes an act of faith. But there is doubt in his every act of faith just as there is the threat of non-being in man's every act of being. He makes an act of faith infinitely, ultimately, courageously concerned about Being. Faith says "Yes" in spite of the anxious "No" which man feels. The "Yes" of faith does not *take away* the "No" of doubt, but it takes doubt and anxiety into itself. The "No" of doubt is taken into the "Yes" of courage and faith.

Man's act of faith, like man himself, is not free from threat. This is necessary. For it means that the man of faith is not divorced from concern, not a stranger to the need of struggling over the meaning of life, not unburdened of the responsibilities of human existence. The man of faith feels at times the loneliness of the ultimate situation. There are moments when the religious man feels deserted by man, by God, even by himself. He realizes only his task and is baffled by the unreality and non-being all around him. He experiences the loneliness of having to die and the emptiness of personal guilt.

Filled with ultimate concern, man turns to God as the only object worthy of his every care. God is the only One of whom man can legitimately be ultimately concerned. God is so unique and so final that one cannot really say He exists or does not exist. For even the category of existence limits the Unlimitable and conditions the Unconditional.

God is the only Infinite Power of Being capable of resisting non-being. If God is not, then non-being is. There is either Something or nothing. We never really then formulate an argument for the existence of God. Every argument for His existence presupposes that *being*, hence God, already is. All that man can do is make an act of courage in which he affirms the power of being against non-being. God is thus the Infinite Ground of courage.

The human heart seeks the Infinite because there it wants to rest. Nothing less than God satisfies our expenditure of ultimate concern. For nothing else reaches the very center of our personalities where ultimate concern is demanded. God alone speaks to that mysterious reality in man which makes man the person he is. No one else, even ourselves, gets quite that far. God alone touches man's rational, responsible, deciding center. Hence He alone invites, demands, and can legitimately accept our ultimate concern. It is when we decide for what we are and ought to be that we are in grace, with God, and ultimately concerned about life. If we decide against what we are, we choose non-being, are without the courage to be, and hence in sin.

God then is not *a* being or *a* person. He is not subject or object. Our belief must be placed in that God beyond God (that is, beyond our concepts and affirmations or denials), in that "Thou" who is closer to the "I" of myself than even my very "I" is to me. God is the Ground of Being. One does not argue, prove, demonstrate, conclude, conceptualize, or categorize God. God simply is and man either has or he does not have the courage to accept What and Who is.

Karl Barth—God is Wholly Other: Radically Transcendent

Karl Barth is not pleased with Tillich's Immanent God nor with Tillich's concern with addressing himself to man's anxiety and existential situation. The Biblical message of God is "thrown like a stone" at man and not accommodated to him, Barth argues. For Tillich, reason and philosophy have something to say about God. For Barth, they do not.

We shall deal with Barth under four broad titles: the abyss, his critique of Vatican I, a series of general conclusions, and a corollary on the manner in which God reveals Himself.[14]

It is true that in the Christian Church people speak about God. Therefore, there is knowledge about God in Christianity. But this knowledge comes exclusively from the Word of God and Revelation. This must be so because there is an abyss between God and man, an abyss so deep that it makes God and man totally different from each other, an abyss so unbridgeable that only grace, Revelation, or something supernatural can bring God and man once more in contact with each other. What is the nature of this abyss and what has caused it? Actually, two things led to this situation: creation and sin.

When God created, He produced something outside of and opposite to Himself. In creating, God projected outside of Himself a completely different existence. Creation then is radically different from God. It cannot help us find God at all.

Sin has widened the abyss between God and man. We are not only different from God ontologically but even morally. For God is by essence good while man is by nature evil.

God then is an absolutely different Being. Man is no-nature (*Unnatur*); he is no-knowledge (*Unerkenntis*); he is nothing (*das Nichtige*). Man cannot come to a knowledge of God because something in man is inseparable from God nor because man's nature cries out for God. Man only knows God when God permits it. For man is not a vestige of God. He is so different from God because of creation and sin that nothing of man bespeaks God. God and man do not reflect each other, but they are over against each other (*gegenüber*).

Barth then takes exception to any natural knowledge of God or even to its possibility.

It does not surprise us then that Karl Barth would have a problem with the Catholic tendency on this question. Aquinas, for example, defends forcefully the knowability of God by human reason alone. He does this with a delicacy that Barth does not always appreciate. For Thomas, man does not know much about God by reason alone without grace; in fact, few men know God this way; and no one is saved by this natural knowledge of God.

Barth, understandably, cannot accept Vatican I's position on the knowability of God. The Council, Barth argues, has created a God of reason distinct from the God of the Bible. We simply cannot know God by the light of human reason or by any natural power. Reason, philosophy, proofs, natural theology—nothing helps. Human logic and human thought on God only produce demons and dead gods, idols which take the place of the true God of the Bible. This false God of a false reason is a God of doubt, incertitude, and emptiness. Furthermore, the Scriptural passages from *Wisdom* and *Romans,* usually cited by Catholics in support of a natural knowledge of God, speak only of man already in a state of faith.

Barth, as a Catholic reads him, performs a meaningful service for Christianity in calling us again to a realization of the Otherness of God, but his call is so radical that it overstates the case. Even Emil Brunner, a former disciple of Barth, realized this and reminded Barth that sin may corrupt man's nature but not to the point where he is not even able to use his reason to know God again.

Barth's extreme position makes dialogue with him difficult. What Vatican I, for example, is trying to say and what Barth seems not fully to appreciate, is that an incomplete knowledge of God need not be false. When Vatican I cites *Wisdom* or *Romans*, its exegesis is not arbitrary and not easily disregarded. Scripture speaks in those passages not of men of faith but of unbelievers who apart from Revelation maintain a natural intellectual capacity for God. An emphasis is placed on the ability to reason to God from creation and not necessarily from grace.

Barth, of course, in his approach to the problem of God's knowability remains consistently fideistic. His fideism influences also his approach to apologetics, ecclesiology, and sacramentality. For Barth, man must fully sacrifice his intellect in his search for God. And man's reason which is reliable in so many other areas is powerless before man's most urgent question: Is there or is there not a God?

Barth identifies knowledge of God with justification and salvation. To be able to know God is to be already justified, therefore in a state of grace and faith. The Catholic position differs. It agrees with Barth that there is a vast difference, from man's viewpoint, between the God man reaches with his reason and the God of grace. Yet it sees them both as the same God and not as two entirely different beings.

As a corollary, it may be well to consider how Barth understands God's revelation of Himself granted his position on the great difference between God and man. God reveals Himself, Barth insists, apart from man's idea of God. The Crucifixion, in fact, is God's "No" to human life, thought, and judgment. God must be known not through man but only through God (*Gott wird durch Gott erkannt*). How does man know this God? Only in Revelation. What does Revelation say about this God who stands before man? What does God say about God to us? Actually, many things:

God is the One we must love most of all. To love is to want to exist in terms of another. God is the One on whose terms we must live more than on any other's.

God is the One we must fear most of all. There is no escape from God. Man must meet Him. And God wants to be feared. But this fear of God is not like the fear we have for creatures. This fear of God is the only fear we experience which is understood only in terms of Infinite Love.

God is the One who is Master. He is the only one who has the right and power to master man. He is Master but He is merciful to man. He is the One from whom man must expect everything. He demands that we not interpret life only on our terms (sin) but in terms of Him whom we feel a need for (grace) and whom we ought not to resist.

God is the One who clearly reveals Himself, clearly enough for faith not to be ignored nor insecure. The man of faith who accepts His God's clear Revelation does not forever question his faith or his God. He accepts, learns, grows certain, and believes with serenity.

Yet the God who clearly reveals Himself makes it quite evident that He is Mystery. He is Other, different. He is God. "I am God and not man" (Hosea 11:9).

John Robinson—"Honest to God"

John A. T. Robinson, the Anglican Bishop of Woolwich, borrows heavily from Rudolf Bultmann, Dietrich Bonhoeffer, and Paul Tillich in constructing his thesis. From Bultmann, he borrows his sympathy for a Christianity without mythology, a Christianity which de-mythologizes our images of a God "out there" or "up there," of a God circumscribed by spatial limits. From Bonhoeffer, he borrows his eagerness for a Christianity that is not "religious" nor even "theistic." The influence of Bonhoeffer on Robinson is strongest in Christology and morality. From Tillich, Robinson borrows his expression of God as ultimate reality, a God whose existence one does not question but a God over whose nature man ponders. Seeking to understand ultimate reality, man sees God as the Ground of Being. He is not "out" anywhere but deep in the heart of all reality. God is what we take seriously without any reservation. He is the *Thou* that cannot be limited by another. Robinson quotes Tillich frequently and the passages he chooses are worth repeating here in part. Tillich in *The Shaking of the Foundations* writes and Robinson requotes:

> Our period has decided for a secular world. That was a great and much-needed decision. . . . It gave consecration and holiness to our daily life and work. Yet it excluded those deep things for which religion stands: the feeling for the inexhaustible mystery of life, the grip of an ultimate meaning of existence, and the invincible power of an unconditional devotion.[15]

In the same book the Bishop quotes, Tillich observes:

> There is no ultimate privacy or final isolation. We are always held and comprehended by something that is greater than we are, that has a claim upon us, and that demands response from us. The most intimate motions within the depths of our souls are not completely our own. For they belong also to our friends, to mankind, to the universe, and to the Ground of all being, the aim of our life. Does anybody really believe that he can escape from the responsibility for what he has done and thought in secret? . . . The centre of our whole being is involved in the centre of all being; and the centre of all being rests in the centre of our being. I do not believe that any serious man can deny that experience, no matter how he may express it.[16]

On the concept of grace, Tillich writes and the Bishop agrees:

> Grace strikes us when we are in great pain and restlessness. It
> strikes us when we walk through the dark valley of a meaning-
> less and empty life. It strikes us when we feel that our separa-
> tion is deeper than usual, because we have violated another life,
> a life which we loved, or from which we were estranged. It
> strikes us when our disgust for our own being, our indifference,
> our weakness, our hostility, and our lack of direction and com-
> posure have become intolerable to us. It strikes us when, year
> after year, the longed-for perfection of life does not appear,
> when the old compulsions reign within us as they have for
> decades, when despair destroys all joy and courage. Sometimes
> at that moment a wave of light breaks into our darkness, and it
> is as though a voice were saying "You are accepted."[17]

It is not difficult to be in sympathy with what Bishop Robinson
is trying to do in his book. He is unmistakably right in saying
that mystical and poetic expressions about God are not adequate,
that our former images of God did not capture God. But he
seems not to realize that his new concepts are also imperfect
and the concepts beyond the new concepts will be imperfect.
There is just no simple, perfect, final way for man to speak of
God or think about God. And so our new concepts are good as
long as they serve and help. But they, like our former concepts,
are only symbols that man reaches for in his effort to express
the mystery of God who is deeper than man's thought and larger
than man's words.

Robinson seems at times unaware of the fact that most people
never really believed God sat on a seat of majesty "up there." It
was merely a way of trying to say that God was majestic and beyond our ability to contain Him. If this concept once helped
and meant something, it is difficult to think it was all wrong. It
served to convey the idea that God is transcendent, beyond us,
more meaningful than we. Perhaps Robinson, and Tillich on

whom he relies, are correct in saying that we need new images of God, images that are more immanent. If we do, then their effort is praiseworthy. For God is immanent as well as transcendent. Therefore if we think of God as Someone "in here," we must still be concerned about the God who is "out there." Saying God is "in here" must never be so total an improvement on saying that God is "out there" that the one fully excludes the other.

In recovering one biblical truth about God, the Bishop should not make progress at the expense of other truths about God. There is simply no one human truth about the true God. And so phrases like "immanent," "depth," "ground of being," ought to take their place beside symbols such as "transcendent," "beyond," "out there." There is no absolute way to the absolute God. Robinson may have written an either/or book when a both/and book would have been more accurate.

With Robinson, we complete the first major point in our theological section on the problem of God. We have seen how Scripture, the Church, philosophy, and our fellow Christians view the power of man's reason before the question of God's existence. Scripture takes that existence for granted, but seems to indicate man's intellect, unaided, can make the judgment that God is. The Church defines that man can, unaided, conclude God exists from an observation of creation. It teaches that that existence can be demonstrated by some reference to the principle of causality. Psychologically and metaphysically, we considered arguments men offer in support of the thesis that God exists and we tried to evaluate these in terms of our over-all considerations. Finally, we saw how Tillich and Barth differed from each other in approaching the question of God's existence and how Robinson attempts to transmit and apply Tillich's theory.

What the theologian is trying to say to our contemporaries in this position, is that God is not impossible to find. Not only grace and Revelation but reason and creation aid man in the task. The problem is with man, his effort to be human, his misuse of his talents. God has not set man upon a dark and hostile ocean with no harbor of light nor any favorable wind. To Sartre, the theologian says that God is avoided only after an enormous effort and at a terrible price. In the thought of Heidegger, Jaspers, Kierkegaard, and Marcel, the theologian feels he is working with either an affirmation of God's existence or philosophies that need not essentially exclude this affirmation. The theologian is trying to say to Kafka and Wolfe, to Camus and Orwell, that God is not nearly so aloof and that man must not mistake the tragedy of his existence for its lack of significance. The theologian wants the Holden Caulfields and the stranded humans in *Lord of the Flies* to look about them and to ponder and perhaps even to pray. We do not want to say that God's existence is something man finds easily or always in a predictable fashion, but only that the God who is there does not hide Himself forever, rather He calls us in a thousand different ways. Though we may have to suffer and struggle in trying to affirm God's existence, we must never despair. Not only grace but even reason will not let us rest content with denial.

As man reaches the judgement that God exists, a multitude of questions press in upon him. Scripture and the Church do not only say that God is there, but they locate the affirmation of His existence in a context of fuller description. Reason is not satisfied with the fact that there is a God. It wants and needs more. Grace makes man restless for a deeper relationship and a clearer intelligibility. Our emphasis now is not on the subjective dispositions man experiences as he learns of God. This requires an analysis of the act of faith which is not our present concern. What we are trying to establish now is an understanding of what Revelation tells us of God seen in His simplest and most basic reality.

Our second major theological question then is this: *The Nature of this God Who Is.*

Frequently enough, it is from this point forward that a theology of God becomes little more than natural theology with a few Scriptural quotes and Patristic references. It becomes a supernatural metaphysics rather than an inquiring into the Nature of God derived from Revelation.

Theology is not faithful to its own potentialities when it describes God as *Ipsum Esse Subsistens.* It is not that this is not true, but it is not the way theology ought to describe God. It says too little and misses too much. When some seminary manuals continue, that from the central truth of God as *Ipsum Esse Subsistens* one can ascertain positive and negative, communicable and incommunicable, absolute and relative, quiescent and active attributes, one suspects that distinctions are being multiplied without growth in intelligibility or relevance. Sometimes the attributes assigned God are so philosophical that one wonders why all this cannot be presupposed from natural theology. If a theologian sees his task only as a re-statement of philosophy, he has not discovered theology's proper province nor even its vocabulary. So many theological studies of the nature of God seek to solve questions such as whether or not there is a formal Scotistic distinction in God, or whether or not there is only a virtual minor distinction between the essence of God and His attributes.

Another difficulty with a statement on God's Nature comes not so much from the use of non-theological language but from an uncritical evaluation of what Revelation is trying to say of God. At times, we have a listing from Scripture of God's attributes compiled so indiscriminately and unsynthetically that one is bewildered. Thus, God is called good, merciful, kind, loving, forgiving, a God of hope, a God of speech, Lord of history, powerful, angry, active, just, and so on. Once again all this is true but what does it say? One is almost tempted to add or invent another two dozen attributes. Theology is not a listing or a collection of things Revelation says, but a synthetic perception of Revelation's basic message, internal unity, and contemporary relevance. Theology is not multiplicity of fact or plethora of data but Insight and Intelligibility. A theologian is not a computer. He is a man who hears God and the Church and tries to speak relevantly to his fellow-men of what he has heard or learned from this experience. He is a man attuned to Revelation's perennial validity and to his age's passing but very real concerns. He is a man who is most effective when his love for God is deep, when his care for his brethren is sympathetic, and when his writing is something the Christian community can assimilate and pray over.

If we limit our discussion to the unifying elements in God's revelation of Himself, we shall manage to proceed least philosophically and most theologically. We shall consider God only under the aspects of His singularity, personality, and love. To say this much of God is to say all we know of Him. One might add as many attributes as he wishes after these three. They all derive from these. To lessen the number of these is to say too little of God. He must be seen as one, personal, and loving before we can even hope to give modern man a basic concept of Him.

We proceed in this fashion because it seems to be a more meaningful, pastoral, and ecumenical approach to the Nature of God.

THE SINGULARITY OF GOD

Let us first consider God insofar as He reveals Himself to us as unique, singular, and one.

In Scripture, God reveals Himself as the only God there is:

Hear, O Israel, the Lord is our God, the Lord alone: so you must love the Lord your God with all your mind and heart and strength. (Deuteronomy 6:4)

I, the Lord, am your God . . . you must have no other gods beside me. (Exodus 20:2)

This theme, that there is only one God, is repeated by Christ
in the New Testament. When one of the Scribes "saw . . . Jesus
. . . he asked him:

Which is the first of all the commandments?
Jesus answered, "The first one is. Hear Israel! The Lord our
God is one Lord and you must love the Lord your God with
your . . . whole strength." (Mark 12, 28–30)

So conscious is the New Testament of the one-ness of God
and of His uniqueness that even when it confesses Christ as
divine, it does not thereby say there are two gods. There is only
one God. The marvel is that He is Father and Son, not that there
are two gods. The marvel is that love can achieve such a singularity. Separate personalities need not necessitate separate gods.
The wonder of Christ is not that He has divine power but that
He is so much like the Father. In the Sonship of the Word,
Fatherhood finds a complete and eternal expression. Because of
the Son, God is forever a Father and ever self-giving. Had God
not a Son, we would never have existed. It is in God's ability to
surrender Himself totally to another and lose nothing of Himself
that the faint traces of creation are seen. We become possible
only because God is a self-giving, yet self-possessed Reality. The
secret of the universe, of life, and of love is hidden in that
mystery we call the Trinity.

The New Testament appeal for the unity of man is built on
the premise that God is already one and that we can be one
with Him and one with each other. When we were made, we
were made in the image and likeness of the only God there is.

Scripture's witness to the fact that there is only one God and
that He is not divided, is repeated by the Christian consensus or

Tradition of the Church. The one-ness of God and His singularity is stated in almost every creed, profession of faith, and conciliar decision from early Christianity.

For example:

> *The Nicene Creed* (a.325): "We believe in one God . . . and in one Lord . . . of the substance of the Father, God of God. . . ."[18]

> *The Constantinople Creed* (a.381): "I believe in one God, the Father almighty . . . and in one Lord Jesus Christ . . . of one substance with the Father . . . and in the Holy Spirit . . . who is adored equally with the Father and the Son."[19]

> *Council of Florence* (a.1442): "The holy Roman Church, founded by the decree of our Lord and Savior firmly believes, professes, and teaches: There is one true God, all-powerful, unchangeable, and eternal, Father, Son, and Holy Spirit, one in essence but three in persons. . . . These three persons are one God, not three gods; for the three persons have one substance, one essence, one nature, one divinity, one immensity, one eternity."[20]

> *Creed of the Council of Trent* (a.1564): "With firm faith I believe and profess each and every article contained in the Symbol of faith which the holy Roman Church uses; namely, I believe in one God. . . ."[21]

> *Vatican I* (a.1870): "The holy, Catholic, apostolic, Roman Church believes and professes that there is one true and living God. . . ."[22]

The uniqueness and singularity of God are not referred to here in the same way as they were in natural theology. We do not refer to a unified, ultimate cause of the world which is *known* and therefore not believed. This is not the God who is a conclusion to a syllogism, Someone necessitated by reason's exigencies, a Force required to explain contingency or intelligibility or order or finality. In faith, it is not a Cause but a Father who caused the world which becomes the object of our concern. It is not anyone but this God whom we accept, Someone who exceeds reason's demands and expectations, Someone who strikes us with wonder more than with necessity. It is not a Force but the God of Abraham, Isaac, and Jacob, the God of grace and speech, the Triune, creating and saving Lover of men who captures our attention. We believe what this God says of Himself, that He alone is God, that there is no other God, that He is the only God we have. This one God is not only sufficient for us but superabundant. As the God of Revelation addresses us, we become aware of the fact that there could be no other god like unto Him. Nor would we want there to be.

GOD IS PERSON

Our next endeavor is to consider God's revelation of Himself as "Person." We are not here concerned with a metaphysics of personality. This is more the province of a study in Trinity or Christology. Our present purpose is more concrete. It is to show that the God of whom we read and hear in Revelation is described in terms that are personal. We would say of anyone we met that he was a person if he could act freely, dialogue and reach other persons on the level of their personhood, and if he could assume attitudes toward us or reality sufficient for us to see him as distinct and differentiated. The God of Revelation comes across in precisely this manner. He is One who acts freely, dialogues, and assumes attitudes. It is not too much to conclude then that He is personal. The personal dimension of God will become even clearer when we take up the final point of this section of God's nature, namely His revelation of Himself as Love. For the moment, let us stay with the problem at hand.

God acts freely.[23] The God of whom Scripture speaks and whom the Church preaches reveals Himself as doing the things only persons do. He acts freely. He acts within our world and yet He never fully identifies Himself with it. Because God never identifies Himself fully with the world, the Church has never deified the world. The world is seen by the Church as a thing of glory but also as a thing which withers. It is the fact that God made the world and acts freely in it and reveals Himself through it which impresses the Church far more than the world itself. It is only by seeing how God uses the world that we come to understand His freedom.

God is evidently the master of the world He uses. He is not just another name for a world-process or an evolutionary force. Hence, the Church always condemns Deism, on the one hand, where God loses mastery of the world, and Pantheism, on the other, where God is imprisoned by His world. The God of Revelation is a free agent who masters what He makes and who is mastered by nothing made. He is a Person, so to speak, and the only Person who has no need of created persons. He needs neither history nor men. He intervenes freely and transcendently in creation. Yet this free personal God is never controlable nor predictable by human calculations. He acts when He chooses, for the purposes He chooses, with the creatures He chooses, at the moment He chooses. Thus, Revelation proclaims ever and anew the remarkable freedom and unparalleled sovereignty of God.

God dialogues. We have not yet been able to provide a satisfactory philosophical or scientific answer to the problem of how God does all and yet man is free and independent. We shall discuss this in some greater depth later. For the moment, let us say a word about God and dialogue with man, without making reference to the "how" of this.

God is so transcendent that He works in the world in His own categories. Man in the world and before God depends on God for all and yet it seems that he is independent of God enough to determine his own destiny. God it seems has set man free of God so that man might engage in a real dialogue with Him. God is a God who wishes to speak and to be answered. This is the source of the Father-Son relationship in the Trinity. God made us in the image of Himself, in the image of one who wishes to speak and to be answered. Just as the Son is the Father's Word and Answer, so we, if we would be God's sons, must hear the Father's Word and give answer.

Thus, man can harden his heart:

> . . . encourage one another every day . . . so that none of you may have his heart hardened. . . . For we are true partners with Christ . . . if you hear him speak, do not harden your hearts. . . . (Hebrews 3, 13–15)

The author of *Hebrews* goes on to indict the Old Testament people of the desert for not answering when they could have.

> For we have had good news preached to us, just as they did, but the message they heard did them no good because they did not agree through faith with what they heard. (Hebrews 4, 2)

The New Testament presents man's relationship with God as a perilous and responsible association. It has an urgency about it, a somber warning of failure, a challenge to decision and action. It is vital, dynamic, alive and uncertain, hopeful and serene.

> For the message of God is a living and active force, sharper than any double-edged sword, piercing through soul and spirit. . . . No being created can escape God's sight, but everything is base and helpless before the eyes of him with whom we have to reckon. Since then we have in Jesus, the Son of God, a great

high priest who has gone up into heaven, let us keep firm hold
of our religion. For our high priest is not one who is incapable
of sympathy with our weaknesses, but he has been tempted in
every way just as we have without committing any sin. So let
us come with courage to God's throne of grace. . . . (Hebrews 4,
12–16)

Man may harden his heart, as we have seen, or he may resist
the Spirit:

You stubborn people, with heathen hearts and ears, you are
always opposing the holy Spirit, just as your forefathers did!
Which of the prophets did your forefathers not persecute?
(Acts 7, 51–52)

Thus man can obey or not obey God's will. He can indeed
contradict God:

. . . of Israel he said, "All day long I have held out my hands to
a disobedient and obstinate people." (Romans 10, 21)

There is a real dialogue between God and man because both
are free. In real dialogue with God, man sees that His God is
personal. In an eminent way, he comes to understand the dignity
of his own person-hood. Even God addresses man as free, independent, able to refuse, a creature He made and yet respects,
a creation of His whom He fills with being, grace, and dignity.
It is because of this very real dialogue that God can demand of
man and receive from him a genuine answer. In a way we shall
never fully appreciate, man's genuine answer to God is not a
matter of indifference to God.

If God and man dialogue, then man is a real co-partner and
co-performer with God. This dialogue gives man personality,
reveals God as Person, and makes man's life real, serious, and

decisive. In a way we do not fully understand, God will have the final word in the dialogue and in history. At the end of time, God will speak a word that man can no longer withstand or refuse. And when this is done, the full meaning of history, man, and God will be made known to us.

God assumes attitudes. What man must discover about God is not what God *is*, but *as whom* God has revealed Himself. Of course, *as whom* God reveals Himself has a reference to who and what God is. But we must be content with knowing God in the way God wants us to know of Him, rather than in knowing God as God.

Therefore, as Rahner suggests, it seems better to speak of God's attitudes toward us rather than of His attributes. Attributes belong to a fixed nature which one understands. A person is better described as one who assumes attitudes than as one who possesses attributes. In the final analysis, it is more important for man to know how God behaves toward man than for him to know how God is in Himself. The "attributes" of God then, as given in the Scriptures, do not form an abstract, metaphysical doctrine of God as much as they announce His personal character and His relationship with man. Scripture tells us *as whom* man has experienced God in history. This God is good, personal, merciful, loving, forgiving, dear to us, compassionate for our salvation. That God is such a God is not a philosophical intuition but a marvel. That God should be such a God is not a fact but an insight which astonishes. This God who is in all things as the Ground of Being, this God who is Other than we in His transcendent splendor, this God who is the heart of all reality, this God who makes reality real, this God loves—and He loves me. That the God who has made us and to whom we must one day return is such a God, this is the great message of Christianity.

The Scriptures then do not provide us with an analysis of the ontology of God but with a history—the history of the experiences in which man has come to know God. The Scripture tells us that God spoke with us, that He saved us, that He lived and died with us, broke bread with us, and loves us.

When Vatican I spoke of God, it listed some of what we can conveniently call God's attributes. In an effort to describe God somewhat, the Council singled out some fifteen characteristics of God's nature. God is one, true, living, creator, lord, all-powerful, eternal, unmeasurable, incomprehensible, limitless in perfection, spiritual, simple, unchangeable, distinct from the world, and perfectly happy.[24] We have worked with three characteristics which we think synthesize the description of God given in the Scriptures and by the Church. One might be scientifically more complete if he would add to the three characteristics we have listed two others: God can do what God must do; and, God is forever. To do this adds little to our understanding of God as personal though it aids our appreciation of God's intrinsic nature. The one-ness, personality, and loving character of God arrest man's attention more than any other considerations.

GOD IS LOVE

The third and final point in our discussion of God's nature concerns God's revelation of Himself as Love. We have already explored the one-ness and personal dimension of God. In trying to understand God's revelation of Himself as Love, we are more interested in the New Testament than in any other document.

Love, let us clarify this first of all, is not a thing a person does. It is not an attribute of our nature. Rather, it is the free bestowal of one person upon another. It can only be accomplished by someone who possesses himself. One who possesses himself can deny himself and so give himself to another. Thus it is that God, supremely possessive of self, is the most self-denying and self-giving, hence most loving Being we know. Love is a gift of self and a surrender to the other which is always a wonder and a grace. God loves God in this way. The Father is the Father's gift to the Son and the surrender of Himself to the Son. But God loves us in this way too. God is God's gift to us.

Love, it must be emphasized, is always in terms of an I-Thou or a "two" relationship: It is in terms of another person and not in terms of a third element, a common cause, or a task to be done. God does not love us for something else but in ourselves. We must not love God for something else but for Himself.

The New Testament tells us something the Old Testament only intimates. The New Testament tells us that God has taken a position with regard to man that He will never go beyond and never withdraw from. God has revealed Himself in the New Testament as love and binds Himself forever to be that "Person" who loves man and saves man. In the Old Testament, God appears frequently enough as a solicitous, just, lenient ruler. The Old Testament brings us as servants of God to a deep love for this Master of Majesty and unapproachable light. But the Old Testament does nothing which gives man an insight into God's own life, into the mystery of God's self. With the coming of Christ, God reveals Himself clearly as love. Christ is an Event of God, an epiphany of God, a coming of God. He is not an attribute of God. In Christ, God is seen and known. And He is seen and known to be love. Christ is the Event in which God comes in love fully and without restraint. God has bestowed Himself upon us as a wonder and a grace in Christ Jesus. God has shown Himself as Love in Christ Jesus. And Christ declares that we are not servants of a benign Master, but that we share a community of life with this God whom no one has seen or can see. We are the friends and sons and partners of this God whom only the Son knows. And so the New Testament looking at God says in wonder, "God is love." When the New Testament says this, it does not give us a statement on God's nature, but it speaks of an undeniable, unsurpassable experience. God is felt as love. In reaching God, we know that we are loved and we feel the full power of love itself. God experiences God as love and we experience God as love. Such must be our condition before God, Christ declares. A once-for-all experience is ours in coming to know God in Christ. We experience in Christ God's bestowal of His entire self upon us. And we have seen in this that God is good and that God therefore is love.

These then are some insights on this second major theological problem, namely the nature of this God who is. The concept of God we have now presented is the type of concept which frees man for belief. It does not hold him in fear and unbelief as Bergman's terrifying concept of God might. This is not the spider-God of *Through a Glass Darkly*, but the unique, personal, loving God of the New Testament. Thus the things we have said of God here are of importance to modern man in his search for God.

The one-ness of God is a reminder to man not only of the fact that there are no other gods and that therefore man must have no idols, but it is also a challenge to him that he serve God single-mindedly. This is not a God man can serve in distraction. He must be served in devotion. God is that One whose one-ness is not just man's discovery, but that One whose one-ness is demanding. God is the One for whom there are no alternatives. Since He is irreplaceable and unrepeatable, He cannot be served as an after-thought. There is no other god not only because there cannot be, but because man has only one ultimate love to give. God's one-ness is a guarantee that man will not give his love to the wrong god, as he might if he had a choice, and that he need not divide his love, as he cannot in its most radical expression, between two gods.

Likewise, the fact that God is personal says much to modern

man. It tells us that personality has an explanation and a finality, that God is personality's Redeemer from nothingness or confusion. It says that our personality need only say in part what must be said. We need not be the final answer to all things or even to ourselves. We need not bear the entire burden of Being. God's personality proclaims to the existentialists we studied earlier that Transcendence has a face and a heart, that Being is not mute and without understanding, that hope has an object and that the anguish of our lives is noticed and not without purpose. Because God is personal, the authenticity Holden Caulfield sought is not a senseless search, and the end of loneliness Thomas Wolfe dreamed of is a distinct possibility. Because God is personal, the homecoming Camus wanted can happen. Because God is personal, Kafka's castle will be reached and after the trial the verdict shall be in our favor. Because God is personal, we know that we shall be rescued by a Person from the island of our sin and death, and with a sigh of relief we recognize the fact that the human spirit shall not be tyrannized forever.

The fact that God is love, finally, says much to our fellow-men. It tells us that love is never wasted, always returned, and forever indestructible. I am sure not only that there will always be Someone worthy of my love, but that I shall always be loved. At the center of all reality is a Being, responsible for everything, who loves me and who died for me. I know too that this loving ultimate Reality is safe and secure forever since death and non-being do not undo Him. The Risen Body of Christ is a human sign for us that even death does not destroy. Christ's Risen Life is a guarantee that nothing, not even our hate or our sin or our death-dealing hands, can end love. For Christ returned from the grave still loving us. Christ is Christianity's good news that God loves not with a strange love but that He was able to love with a human heart the men He met and meets.

GOD KNOWS: HE HAS INTELLIGENCE

If God exists, it is important for us to know whether or not He is aware of Himself and of us. If God is one, personal, and love, we must know how intellectual His personality is and how conscious His love manages to be. Is He aware of what He does as He surrenders His Personality to another Person of the Trinity? Does He love, as we love, knowing some things but taking a risk and accepting the mystery of another in love? Or does God love with total clarity and unthreatened security? If God acts freely, dialogues, and assumes attitudes, does He do this in an organized intellectual fashion or is His free action sometimes arbitrary and possibly unaware of its consequences? Does He dialogue with man unaware of the drift or the outcome of the engagement? Does He assume attitudes toward us as they strike His fancy or does He do what He must and what we need? It is of inestimable importance for knowing men to know if God knows and how He knows. Man does not deserve solution, but He does deserve some assurance that the God to whom he entrusts his intellect, personality, and destiny knows what He and man are all about.

The Scriptures assure us that God knows. On almost every page of Scripture the fact that God is a knowing "Person," that He is not a dumb or un-understanding Force, is emphasized. God knows what He has created. He knows creation is good. He knows the sin of Adam. He knows the heart of man.

Theology usually describes the knowledge of God as a thing without limit. God alone is all-knowing. Yet the omniscience of God as Scripture presents it, is not so much a knowing of all things actual and possible, as though God were an immense and measureless reservoir of knowledge. This is true, but the Scriptures see the knowledge of God in less abstract and more personal terms. God's all-knowing-ness means that a personal

God sees totally into the person of man. God knows man better than man knows man. And the man who knows God knows he is fully known by God.

> Thou hast searched me and known me, O Lord;
> Thou knowest when I sit down and when I stand up;
> Thou discernest my thought from afar.
> Thou . . . art intimately acquainted with all my ways.
> For there is not a word on my tongue,
> But Lord, thou knowest it all.
> Thou . . . dost put thy hand upon me;
> Such knowledge is too wonderful for me;
> It is too lofty; I am not equal to it.
> Whither shall I go from thy spirit?
> And whither shall I flee from thy presence?
> If I ascend to the heavens, thou art there! . . .
> If I take the wings of the dawn . . .
> Even there thy hand will guide me,
> And thy right hand will hold me.
> If I say, "Darkness will surely cover me,"
> Then the night becomes light about me.
> Darkness makes it not too dark for thee. . . .
>
> (Psalm 139, 1–12)

This idea that God sees even in secret is mentioned by Christ:

. . . your Father who is unseen and your Father who sees in secret will reward you. (Matthew 6, 18)

What matters most, is not that God know all that would or could be, but that He know all that is. What matters most, is that God know us. Thus we can be reassured that someone understands us fully and infinitely. Somehow we always feel that if only someone would really understand us we would be loved. Frequently, when we say in desperation, "You don't understand me," we imply that if the other person did, all would go well. But the other person cannot always do this. God is the only one before whom the statement, "You don't understand me," is never true. God knowing us fully, loves us most effectively. Only a God who understands us fully and loves us effectively can judge us perfectly. And judging us perfectly, we are sure that God will save us from all that will destroy us. God, because He knows us so well, is the only one before whom we can be fully ourselves. God is the only one before whom explanations are not needed and before whom words are superfluous.

Thus, the knowledge of God is different from ours. His knowledge is always personal. He never knows indifferently or as a spectator. Because His knowledge is personal, Scripture describes it as a knowledge filled with concern and solicitude. Philosophy can tell us that God is omniscient; only God can tell us what this knowledge means. To be known by God, in Scripture, is to be considered, to be loved, cared for, chosen.

I know my sheep and my sheep know me, just as the Father knows me and I know the Father, and I am giving my life for my sheep. (John 10, 14)

. . . if one loves God, one is known by him. (1 Cor. 8, 3)

Now my knowledge is imperfect but then I shall know as fully as God knows me. (1 Cor. 13, 12)

Thus, the knowledge of God is without limit. This is a defined position of the Church.[25] The marvel of God's knowing is not in His greater command of data but in the manner of His knowing. God knows all in perfect lucidity. He is the only one for whom there is no mystery. God knows with limitless understanding and in total security. His knowledge is creative: when He knows me, I am. His knowledge is salvific: when He understands me, I am rescued. God's knowledge, like God Himself, is love to uttermost—a deep, unconquerable, knowing concern for all He made.

A THEOLOGICAL DISPUTE

The knowledge of God poses a philosophical problem which theologians have debated for centuries. Simply stated, the terms of the debate are basically these. God knowing Himself, knows all things. What exists, He knows as real. What can exist, He knows as possible. God, it is clear, must be sovereign over all He has made. Yet men are free:

> If anyone says that the free will of man . . . in no way co-operates with the awakening call of God by an assent by which man disposes and prepares himself to get the grace of justification; and that man cannot dissent, if he wishes, but, like an object without life, he does nothing at all and is merely passive: let him be anathema.[26]

> If anyone says that after Adam's sin man's free will was destroyed and lost . . . let him be anathema.[27]

> If anyone says that it is not in man's power to make his ways evil, but that God performs the evil works just as he performs the good . . . so that Judas's betrayal no less than Paul's vocation was God's own work: let him be anathema.[28]

The problem then is this: How can God be sovereign and men be free?

In attempting a solution to this problem, two traditional schools of thought have grown up in theology. One, called Banezianism, reasons in this way. God's sovereignty is preserved by reference to a theory called physical predetermination. According to this principle, a created element moves our freedom to act and does this infallibly. It predestines us before our act to act in this way, but it does this freely. No act of will can be made without this physical pre-motion and no act of will can ever be made against it. What this created element is, we do not know but it achieves all it must: it leads us to act as God wishes, yet so influences man that he remains free. He freely does what he must. The theory of physical predetermination preserves God's sovereignty, but one can rightly ask if it really leaves man free.

The other school, called Molinism, reasons in this way. God knows not only what exists (the real) and what can exist (the possible), but even what would exist if He had chosen another order of circumstances than those which are real (futurible). *Scientia Media* is the technical name given to this knowledge by which God knows what might have been had He chosen differently. Man is free, Molinism argues, because God chooses one order of circumstances only after He considers how man would freely act in it. Therefore, man is free. Whereas Banezianism emphasized God's sovereignty, Molinism emphasizes man's freedom. Each is an attempt to solve the problem. Both fail. Molinism preserves man's freedom, sacrificed in Banezianism. But it does this by creating a number of theories such as *scientia media* and futuribles which have no foundation in reality. It is difficult to know what the object of knowledge such as *scientia media* really is. The futurible, it seems, ought to be either real if actualized or a possibility if not. To predicate a reality between real and possible existence is asking too much. Even if there were such things as futuribles and *scientia media*, Molinism would still not have provided theology with a satisfactory solution. For it would make God a spectator of man, not acting creatively until He observed carefully what men would do if He so acted.

Both theologies fail theology, as we have said. Banezianism is too mechanical in its theory of physical predetermination, and it destroys human freedom, except in name only. Molinism is too anthropomorphic in its theory of God's dependence on man's action for His own action, too artificial in its insistence on *scientia media* and futuribles. And it destroys God's sovereignty, especially His sovereign freedom. Banezianism and Molinism set about their task of explaining God's sovereignty and man's freedom by denying one of the terms of the problem. They each explain one reality but only at the expense of another reality which is just as real as the reality they defend.

There may be no total solution to the problem. It would be wrong for us to be too harsh with Banezianism and Molinism since at least these theologies tried, and tried mightily, to expand the frontiers of man's knowledge. Yet a better approach might be possible. The crux of the problem lies in the concept of created freedom we employ. There is no reason why we must conceive of created freedom as distinct from or opposed to divine freedom. Is it not possible for us to see created freedom as a sharing in divine freedom, just as we see created being as a participation in divine being? We do not say created being is unreal or not different from God because it is participated. Must we say created freedom is unreal or not different from God because it is participated? Granted this, there is no great problem in defending God's sovereignty or our freedom. On the one hand, God knows and controls the free acts of His creatures for it is His freedom they use when they are free, just as He remains Lord of His creatures since it is His being by which they live. On the other hand, we can fail by choosing un-freedom and non-being. It is in accepting God's dawning upon us in freedom which makes us free men. If we choose freedom or intelligibility, we choose God. Yet we are able to choose slavery or absurdity. Thus, man's responsibility is awesome. Being itself is at issue in his choice.

To state the absolutes of this problem as simply as possible, this much we know and must ever maintain: We are free and God is Lord.

Conclusion

Scripture discovers a great truth for us when it tells us that the knowledge of God is personal and filled with love. It is really because God loves without limit that He knows as He does.

Rahner writes beautifully of this relationship in his *Encounters With Silence:*

. . . it seems to me that knowing touches only the surface of things, that it fails to penetrate to the heart, to the depths of my being where I am most truly "I."

Knowledge seems more like a kind of pain-killing drug that I have to take repeatedly against the boredom and desolation of my heart. And no matter how faithful I may be to it, it can never really cure me. All it can give me is words and concepts, which perform the middle-man's service of expressing and interpreting reality to me, but can never still my heart's craving for the reality itself, for true life and true possession. I shall never be cured until all reality comes streaming like an ecstatic, intoxicating melody into my heart.

Truly, my God, mere knowing is nothing. All it can give us is the sad realization of its own inadequacy. All it can tell us is that through it we can never fully grasp reality and make it a living part of ourselves.

How can we approach the heart of all things, the true heart of reality. Not by knowledge alone, but by the full flower of knowledge, love . . . it is only in love that I am fully present—not in bare knowing, but in the affection engendered by knowing. . . . Then I have knowledge which is really myself, which abides as I myself abide.

Only knowledge gained through experience, the fruit of living and suffering, fills the heart with the wisdom of love, instead of crushing it with the disappointment of boredom and final oblivion. It is not the results of our own speculation, but the golden harvest of what we have lived through and suffered through, that has power to enrich the heart and nourish the spirit. . . .

Thanks to Your mercy, O Infinite God, I know something about you not only through concepts and words, but through experience. I have actually known You through living contact; I have met you in joy and suffering. For You are the first and last experience of my life. Yes, really You Yourself, not just a concept of You, not just the name which we ourselves have given You! . . . You made Yourself my poor heart's destiny.

You have seized me; I have not "grasped" You. You have transformed my being right down to its very last roots. . . . You have given me Yourself, not just a distant fuzzy report of Yourself in human words. And that's why I can never forget You, because You have become the very center of my being. . . .

You will be the final Word, the only one that remains, the one we shall never forget. Then at last, everything will be quiet in death; then I shall have finished with all my learning and suffering. Then will begin the great silence in which no other sound will be heard but You . . . resounding from eternity to eternity . . . then, I shall know even as I am known; I shall understand what You have been saying to me all along, namely, You Yourself. . . .

You Yourself are my knowledge, the knowledge that is light and life. You Yourself are my knowledge, experience, and love. You are the God of the one and only knowledge that is eternal, the knowledge that is bliss without end.[29]

GOD CHOOSES: HE IS ABLE TO BE CONCERNED AND TO LOVE

It would be a bizarre and frightening state of affairs, if this God who exists; whose nature is unified and singular, personal and love; whose knowledge is so deep and wide-ranging, were not able to choose in accord with His nature and knowledge. It would almost be, one might say, Kafkaesque to have a God whose awareness was limitless but whose power to choose were non-existent or limited. God would be victimized by anguish if He could not choose in accord with the personal and loving imperative of His Being.

Thus, Scripture shows God as a "Person" who desires, decides, and punishes. It sees God's will at work and it feels the effect of

God's will. It describes God in many ways which presuppose God's Will. God is power, justice, holiness, goodness, saving. God is able to do what He wills:

> The Lord does whatsoever he pleases, whether in the heavens or on the earth, in the seas and in all deeps. . . . He makes the lightning flashes for the rain, bringing forth the wind from his treasuries. It was he who smote the first-born of Egypt. . . . It was he . . . who slew mighty kings. . . . And he gave their land as a possession, a possession to his people Israel. O Lord thy name is forever. . . . For the Lord will give his people justice and will have compassion upon his servants. . . . O house of Israel, bless the Lord. . . . (Psalm 135, 6–19)

God's will is seen by Revelation in relation to the things God has made. It is not described as an abstract or philosophical will-power. When God deals with His creatures, He does "whatever he pleases, whether in the heavens or on the earth." But because God is a God of love as well as of power, He does not do anything at all but only what might help. He brings the rain and the winds, but best of all He brings salvation. It was He who protected Israel from her enemies and gave Israel a land in which to dwell. It is He who will give this same people justice and show His servants compassion. Therefore, Israel must bless the Lord. For he does not do anything at all with His will—He uses it to create and to save, to give life and to love, to speak and to gather us to Himself.

With a powerful and loving Act of Will, He creates and His kindness is everlasting:

> Give thanks to the Lord, for he is good,
> For his kindness is everlasting . . .
> Give thanks to the God of gods . . . to the Lord of lords . . .
> To him who made the heavens with skill . . .
> To him who spread out the earth upon the waters . . .

> To him who made the great lights . . .
> The sun to rule by day . . .
> The moon and the stars to rule by night,
> For his kindness is everlasting . . . (Psalm 136, 1–9)

God then creates from His goodness. One notices a slight difference in the description of God's Will-power in the Old Testament and the New. Although salvation is a constant theme in the Old Testament, the stress is more on the creative will of God. In the New Testament, the stress is more on the salvific will of God.

The Church has defined that God's Will is infinitely perfect.[30] Just as God's intellect is an infinite consciousness of God's fullness and a total knowledge of what He has made, so God's will is an infinite affirmation and possession of the absolute goodness of God and a total love for what He has made.

The mystery of God's irresistible Will becomes most bewildering for us in what seems to be our ability to resist. This God who does whatever He pleases in heaven and on earth can be contradicted by man alone. Scripture highlights the mystery and challenges us deeply when it has God comment:

> I called and you refused . . . I stretched out my hands and no one paid heed . . . (Proverbs 1, 24)

There are two problems we ought to consider before completing this section on God's Will. One concerns the reality of God's Providence; the other, the sincerity of His desire for the salvation of all men.

The God of Providential Concern

God's Providential care in the Old Testament is shown in all He does for Israel. Yet His concern for us is not the same as our concern for ourselves. God is not concerned with making the life of Israel easier. Scripture assures us that God's ultimate concern is our salvation. This is the source of our hope and our trust in Him. Because God is not only Creator but also Savior, His concern for us is depicted as a life-giving, grace-bestowing care. This concern, which is so emphatic in the Old Testament, is even more strikingly presented in the New.

> Look at the wild birds . . . your heavenly Father feeds them. Are you not of more account than they? . . . See how the wild flowers grow. They do not toil or spin, and yet I tell you, even Solomon in all his splendor was never dressed like one of them. But if God so beautifully dresses the wild grass . . . will he not much more surely clothe you . . . your heavenly Father knows well that you need all this. But you must make his kingdom . . . your greatest care. (Matthew 6, 26–33)

> Do not sparrows sell two for a cent? And yet not one of them can fall to the ground against your Father's will. . . . You must not be afraid; you are worth more than a great many sparrows! (Matthew 10, 29–31)

> Throw all your anxiety upon him, for he cares for you. (1 Peter 5, 7)

The First Vatican Council defined Providence as an article of faith in these words:

> . . . by his providence, God watches over and governs all the things that he made, reaching from end to end with might and disposing all things with gentleness.[31]

It is the Incarnation, however, which is God's ultimate demonstration of concern. It is Christ who gives us in the Incarnation the full Christian dimension of Providence. As one watches the actions of Christ, hears His words, witnesses His crucifixion, and accepts His Resurrection, he comes to some understanding of what Providence means. Sooner would a hen refuse to gather her young, sooner would a mother forget her son, sooner would an Israelite forget Jerusalem, than would God cease to care. All of creation and history point then to the Incarnation, and the Incarnation we must remember, is for us.

The Universal Salvific Will

The reality of God's Providential concern for us has never been seriously questioned in the Church's history. There have been few debates over this issue, which seems so much a part of the Christian message and can be grasped so easily and so beautifully.

Things are quite different, however, with the problem of what is technically called God's universal salvific Will.

When we speak of God's salvific Will, we mean that God wills supernatural life and salvation for all. God offers salvation and the means to achieve it to all men. He does this in virtue of Christ who was incarnate, died, and was glorified for all. There is no man, no moment of time, which has not been influenced by the fact that one Man, Christ, in one moment of time, saved us. This Will of God for our salvation in Christ is sincere, effective, and universal. The only thing that can frustrate God's salvific Will is man's decision not to be saved. God is powerless before man's decision to use his freedom poorly and to direct his power of love to self rather than others.

Therefore, when men such as Calvin teach that God has chosen some for salvation and others for damnation, a Catholic cannot respond sympathetically. Calvin says that man is free from external force, but that God's Will internally necessitates him to salvation or damnation. A Catholic cannot accept this. In such a situation, not only human freedom but divine justice perish. It says in effect that God uses some men well and mis-

uses others brutally. This is a classic example of preaching a
God whom no man should be asked to accept.

In order to put this problem into proper perspective, a definition of the terms "predestination" and "reprobation" is required.

By predestination, we mean that God predestines man to salvation from all eternity so that God remains sovereign over the
entire process of salvation both in its beginning and at every
step in the process.

There are indications both in Scripture and in the teaching of
the Church that this is indeed the state of affairs.

In *Ephesians* and *Romans*, Paul writes:

Blessed be the God and Father of our Lord Jesus Christ, who
through Christ has blessed us with every spiritual blessing in
the heavenly realm. Through him he chose us out before the
creation of the world, to be consecrated and above reproach in
his sight in love. He foreordained us to become his sons through
Jesus Christ, in fulfilment of his generous purpose, so that we
might praise the splendid blessing which he has given us
through his beloved Son. It is through union with him and
through his blood that we have been delivered and our offenses
forgiven, in the abundance of his mercy which he has lavished
upon us. He has given us perfect insight into his secret purpose
and understanding of it, in following out the design he planned
to carry out in Christ, and in arranging, when the time should
have fully come, that everything in heaven and on earth should
be unified in Christ—the Christ through whom it is our lot to
have been predestined.... (Ephesians 1, 3–11)

We know that in everything God works with those who love
him, whom he has called in accordance with his purpose, to
bring about what is good. For those whom he had marked out
from the first he predestined to be made like his Son . . . those
whom he has predestined he calls, and those whom he calls he
makes upright, and those whom he makes upright he glorifies.
(Romans 8, 28–30)

The Church has spoken most clearly on predestination at the Second Council of Orange, held in the year 529. The Council sought to ward off from the Church the influence of Semi-Pelagianism.

> And thus, according to the passages of Holy Scripture and according to the explanations of the ancient Fathers . . . we, with God's help, must believe and preach the following: The free will of man was made so weak and unsteady through the sin of the first man, that, after the Fall, no one could love God as was required, or believe in God, or perform good works for God unless the grace of divine mercy anticipated him. . . . We do not believe that some are predestined to evil by the divine power. . . . We also believe and profess for our salvation that in every good work it is not that we make a beginning and afterwards are helped through God's merrcy, but rather, that without any previous good merits on our part, God himself first inspires us with faith and love of him. . . .[32]

It is theologically certain that God so predestines us to salvation that He presides over every step in the process.

Another term whose definition will aid our understanding of God's universal salvific Will is "reprobation." We mean by this, that God permits our misuse of freedom from all eternity. It does not mean that He actually arranges for us to choose evil (positive antecedent reprobation). This too is an attempt to safeguard God's sovereignty over the process of salvation. He permits us to do what we do. He does not force us to evil. It is theologically certain that there is no positive antecedent reprobation, that is, God does not work for our destruction or damnation.

Very simply stated, what we are trying to say is this: God gives us supernatural life, and without God this life dies (predestination); God gives us freedom to refuse His offer, knowing that some may, but not arranging things so that any do (reprobation).

God does not so predestine that some must fail. To will sincerely the salvation of all, He must predestine all, directing reprobation to none. The truths that we must preserve from the issues we have discussed for an understanding of God's universal salvific will are these: God is sovereign over the process of salvation; man is able to fail in the pursuit of his salvation—his failure comes from his ability to choose un-freedom, to assert himself against God and man—his failure does not come from God, who in man's every contact with Him calls man to freedom, love and salvation. A correct understanding of predestination and reprobation is essential to a proper acceptance of what we call the universal salvific Will of God.

Both Scripture and the teaching Church make it clear that God's desire for man's salvation extends to all and effectively reaches all. Thus Paul writes:

> First of all, then, I urge that entreaties, prayers, petitions, and thanksgivings be offered for all men, for emperor and all who are in authority, so that we may live tranquil, quiet lives, with perfect piety and probity. It is right to do this, and it pleases God our Savior, who wants all men to be saved and to come to know the truth. For there is but one God, and one intermediary between God and men—the man Christ Jesus, who gave himself as a ransom for all men. This is what was testified to at the proper times, and I was appointed a herald and apostle of it—I am telling the truth, I am not lying—to teach the heathen faith and truth. (1 Timothy 2, 1–7)

There are a few points worth noting about this passage from Paul. Paul speaks of *universality* in terms of God's *Will*, which he insists is *salvific*. The universality of Paul's intent is clear in his words. Prayers must be offered "for all men," not just the brethren. In fact, one must pray even for emperors. This insertion takes on a greater cogency when one realizes that the emperor at the time was Nero who was persecuting the Christian community. One must pray for all because, Paul comments quite simply, God "wants all men to be saved" and to come to truth. The simplicity of Scripture can sometimes disarm the complexity of theology completely.

Paul furthermore speaks of a genuine *Will* in God for universal salvation. "God . . . *wants* all men to be saved." In the Greek text, Paul uses a verb which in Paul refers to a willed action and not a mere wish.

The universal Will of which Paul speaks is *salvific*. God wants all to be saved and the reason why He so wills is because "the man Christ Jesus . . . gave himself as a ransom for all men." Paul was appointed a herald of God before men to declare this sublime message. In this message, man learns serenity and hope and he comes to understand that God must indeed be love.

The theme that Christ and His salvation are for all is found not only in Paul but also in John. Thus, John writes:

> [Christ] is himself an atoning sacrifice for our sins, and not only for ours but also for the whole world. (1 John 2,2)

Christ, as John understands Him, is the "real light, which sheds light upon everyone" (John 1,9). He is the lamb "who is to remove the world's sin" (John 1, 29).

> For God loved the world so much that he gave his only Son . . . that . . . all should have eternal life. . . . God did not send his Son into the world to pass judgment upon the world but that through him the world might be saved. (John 3, 16–18)

Although the Church has never defined the fact that God's Will is universally salvific, she intimates this every time she speaks of salvation.

The early creeds of the Church state this truth in noble simplicity and with theological perception. Thus:

The Nicene Creed (a.325), promulgated at the first Ecumenical Council, reads: "For the sake of us men and for our salvation [Christ] came down, was made flesh, and became man."[33]

The Creed of Epiphanius (a.374) reads: "We believe . . . in one Lord Jesus Christ, the Son of God . . . through Him all things were made. . . . He came down and was made flesh for us men and for our salvation . . ."[34]

The Constantinople Creed (a.381) reads: "For the sake of us men and for our salvation [Christ] came down from heaven, was made flesh by the Holy Spirit from the Virgin Mary, and became man. . . ."[35]

The Athanasian Creed (fifth or sixth century) reads: "It is also necessary for eternal salvation that [we] believe steadfastly in the Incarnation of our Lord Jesus Christ. . . . He is perfect God and he is perfect man. . . . He died for our salvation."[36]

It was not only in its early creeds but also in its subsequent pronouncements that the Church comes back again and again to this theme. Thus in the sixteenth century at the Council of Trent:

> But even though Christ did die for all, still all do not receive the benefit of his death but only those with whom the merit of his Passion is shared.[37]

Again, in the seventeenth century, the Church continues to reject those who do not accept the universal implications of God's salvific Will. Thus she censures the teachings of Jansen[38] and issues, under Alexander VIII, a decree of the Holy Office repeating the same truth.[39]

It is a matter of faith (*De Fide*), though not defined, that God wills the salvation of every man He creates.[40]

The Scriptural statement and Catholic principle are so insistent on the point that God wants all men to be saved that the contrary is not even conceivable in the faith and preaching of the Church.

Only man's misuse of his power to be free and to love; only his misuse of his responsibility to create himself; only his abandonment of the imperative that he be himself, can frustrate God's desire for man's salvation. And one does not frustrate God's will easily. He must do this against the image of God in which he was made. He must do this against God's saving grace which all men are given.

In reflecting upon the issues and controversies of the last few pages, we can arrive at a few conclusions which will enable us to bypass endless discussion on predestination, reprobation, or the problem of knowledge in God as envisioned by Banezianists or Molinists. These few things seem clear:

We are saved because God gives grace. All men receive this grace. No one is denied it. (Against reprobation)

God and man now share the same life, a life that man cannot have without God.

That life must be continually given. (Therefore, the full sovereignty of God in predestination is preserved.)

We cannot seize God's life of grace and make it ours unless God gives it. (Against Pelagianism)

We cannot even start the life of grace by asking for grace or faith unless we are given grace to do this. (Against Semi-Pelagianism)

We know then that God knows us and loves us. He is concerned about us and wills that all be saved. His knowing and

loving us is a grace, his concern for us is providential; his Will
for us is salvific. What God creates in tenderness, He calls to
Himself for glory. God creates nothing without love and no one
without some reference to grace. Our world and our history are
graced and redeemed because of Christ and everything, absolutely everything, conspires for our eternal glory in God and
calls us to unending salvation in Christ.

In this final section, we have explored the complete-ness of
our dependence upon God. Yet to be dependent on a God whose
essence is love and freedom, whose Presence is grace, and whose
Will is salvific, to be dependent·upon such a God is to reign and
to conquer.

To sum up the issues discussed in this chapter, we considered
five defined positions of the Church:

1. Man can know God by the natural light of reason from
   things God made.

2. God is one and "possesses" some "attributes" of which we
   are aware.

3. God is limitless in knowledge.

4. God's Will confronts no restrictions or resistance.

5. God is providentially concerned.
One position we discussed is of faith (*De Fide*):

6. God wills the salvation of all men (universal salvific will).
Finally, three positions might be termed theologically certain:

7. Man can demonstrate God's existence from creation as a
   cause can be demonstrated from its effects.

8. God predestines us to salvation and influences the entire
   process.

9. God permits ʻour non-salvation but not positively and ante-
   cedently.

CONCLUSION: HOW SHOULD GOD BE
PRESENTED TO MODERN MAN?

God must be presented in terms evidently of Who He is, but
also in terms of our age's need for Him. A God who is infinite
can be presented to finite men in an infinite number of ways
without any fear of compromising God's identity. A God who is
ageless can be presented differently in every age and yet not
become another god in the process. The responsibility each generation faces is the need to understand itself and then understand
how God is speaking to it. The God of the Bible spoke to a
Semitic people in a Semitic manner. The God of the twentieth
century speaks to us in a twentieth-century manner. The God of
the Scriptures spoke of His splendor and majesty to men more
awed with God than with human problems. The God of this
generation speaks of our anguish and need of Him to men more
perplexed with the human situation than men have ever been
before.

A Christian or a theologian will never be effective in this
century unless he is involved with mankind and committed to
God. This is the time when the man who is not passionately involved with human concerns cannot speak relevantly of God.
This is not an age when bookish theology, worn-out clichés, or
complacent aloofness from man as man can serve Christianity.
It is true that such attitudes never got far with men in any
age, but in this age they are even more reprehensible. The
minister of Christ's message who has lost touch does not serve
the best interests of the Christian community. The priest or the
layman who is not in love with the world, attracted by it, eager
to do something for it, has not perceived the meaning of his
Christian vocation or understood Christ's incarnational approach
to life. God must not be something we foist upon man. We cannot present God as Someone you just have to accept. Yet we
shall find ourselves preaching this approach to God unless we

have been attuned to the human needs of our age. God means most to man when he does not accept Him as a duty or a responsibility, but reaches for Him as a need and a value. The need for God expresses itself differently in each age, not totally different of course, but at least distinctively different. A nine-teenth-century Christian does not need God in exactly the same way as a twentieth-century Christian does. Yet how does one who has run from mankind, who is bored or uninterested in the things which make men the type of men they are in any one age, who reads only the Catholics or only the theologians, who is convinced that there is no such thing as a theology of life in every generation, but sees theology only in terms of what theologians say or what Denzinger contains, how is he relevant to his age? How can he do justice to God and man in his profession of belief?

We said above that one must be effective not only in terms of involvement with mankind but also in commitment to God. A Christian or a theologian who is not a man of prayer and devotion is a repeater of Christian things rather than a preacher of Christ or a witness to the power of His message. A Christian who never contemplates, who never bows his head in speechless wonder before God, who never offers his confused heart to God, who never speaks to God in anguish or runs to God in joy, this man has no business teaching his fellow-men of God. A man who never reads the Scriptures, hears the Church, flees the egoism of life, studies the theologians, such a man also proves defective in' his witness. Thus we are faced with an antinomy. We are involved with God and man; with the theology of the schools and the theology of life; with an unchanging God and man's changing concerns; with hearing our fellow-men and speaking to our God.

There are some considerations of preaching or witnessing God which may aid our presentation of Him to our contemporaries:

God is the One who gives man the divine. Man needs Otherness. Yet if things only human are presented as divine, the tension and mystery of life is over and the need for Otherness has no hope of attainment. Man must come to see the unconditional character of God. He needs something more than man to reach for and possess. At times, it is helpful to urge man to goodness or God in terms of his human fulfillment or of an appeal to maturity or to selflessness. There are times, however, when the most effective thing we can do is remind man he is not his own master and that the Lord alone has dominion. There are moments when man needs most to hear not of a preservation of human values, but of Scripture's bracing message: "I am the Lord your God. Thou shalt not. . . ."

God is the One who gives man the human. Even when God comes to judge man, His coming is salvation and a grace. But God comes most often not to judge, but to bestow upon man creative development and transfiguration. For man with God becomes a blend of Creator and creature, of chaos and vital power, of anguish and peace, of sin and grace, of corruptibility and immortality. Accepting God, man gains a new energy, a nobler set of values, depth, and final purpose. He finds a God who sometimes says "Thou shalt not . . . ," but more often pleads "Father, forgive them. . . ."

God is the One who gives man love. God Himself is a joyous and suffering yearning for Otherness. This makes the Trinity and it makes man. Love is only real if there is a serious otherness about it. God's love is really real and infinitely Other. God tells us that Being-itself has the nature of love. Love is God's essence and man's image.

God is the One who gives man freedom. God gives man freedom and human freedom affirms God in every age. Man has never used freedom fully to banish God from this world. Man in his immense drive toward freedom, senses that only in affirming

God is there substance and object for his freedom. Man can declare himself autonomous of God, he is ever tempted to do this, and yet no age has ever done it fully or felt comfortable with the effort.

God is the One who gives man Christ. In Christ, all man looks for is realized: the divine and the human. No one was more loving and free than Christ. Christ had in Himself two natures and on this His love and freedom were based. The divine and the human both had to live in Christ for Christ to be Christ. Man too must have, as it were, two natures. Two worlds must intersect in him. The image of God and man must live in man if man is to learn love and to live in freedom. The dignity of man comes from his ability to live in the divine and the human realms, neither of which he fully knows or totally exhausts. Man must live in tension and harmony, in mystery and clarity, in turmoil and tranquility. He is never resolved or solved. He is ever creating himself. He is never settled, passive, or object. Like Christ the Man, man is ever a mystery to himself, ever aware of his divine calling, and his human concerns.

God is the One who gives man personhood. God speaks to man person-to-person. God acts differently in history depending upon how man reacts to God. Yet God is sovereign. We are not persons until we experience God. God does not first contact us as persons, but He makes us persons and then contacts us. In encountering God, we first experience what person is. The only value that man really becomes concerned about is a personal one. And God makes us completely personal.

If I might be permitted a personal reference, I would like to repeat a thought I wrote down a few days before my ordination to the priesthood. Searching for ideas on why I believe in God and need Him, I remember writing that of all the many reasons which fortify my belief, the one that most convinced me of God's existence was the realization that only God could have made a person.

THEOLOGICAL REFLECTIONS AND SPIRITUAL MATURITY

The implications of this theological study for an individual's spirituality are not easy to determine. If throughout the course of this endeavor, however, the reader has not felt a sense of devotion for God, then this study has been a failure. If theology does not come to a man as a call to prayer, if it is not a grace which makes God and Christ more real to him, then author and reader have been engaged upon a teaching effort and not a genuinely theological undertaking. If theology does not lead to worship, if it does not chasten a man with humility and fire him with love, then what it was meant to do has not been accomplished. It is not as though a study of theology is in itself sanctifying. This is a Gnostic or a Pelagian, not a Christian, position. Theology should, however, move a man deeply because it tells him of God and God's message, of God's Son and God's Church, of God's life and God's love. It creates an environment in which a man receives grace easily; an atmosphere where grace is ever near and where man's predisposition for sanctification is accomplished.

A number of insights for our spiritual growth should come across to us from this study. The critical importance of human values and social concerns for Christian development should be clear to us all. Heidegger's idea that man develops his personality and learns of Being in the world, is a profoundly Christian idea also. If spirituality must take humanity into consideration, then the impact of one's age on the way we pray and preach, on the way we express our faith and administer the Church, on the way we approach people and worship, should be taken for granted. God is found not on the solitary, isolated, unapproachable summits away from mankind, but in the city streets of Jerusalem or in the crowded Upper Room, or on the troubled waters of a well-travelled Sea in Galilee. And if one must pray by night, or alone in the mountains, or hidden in a garden, then one must take mankind there with him. Thus Christ chooses His apostles after His night of prayer and asks for human comfort in the loneliness of Gethsemene. Even on Calvary, the concern is for mankind: "Father, forgive them"; "You shall be with me in Paradise"; "Mother, see your son."

At one and the same time, this study should convince us of the need for mystery and reverence in our lives. The world is not something only to be discovered and conquered but to be sanctified and consecrated. One's fellow-men are not only to be aided but to be respected and loved. And one must realize he cannot do all things for them. They with him must learn together that life does not give all the answers as it poses questions, that it promises more than it bestows, that it enriches those who do not despair of it, and that it has a purpose for those who treat it seriously and recognize it not as a thing to be analyzed and known but a wonder and a marvel to be received in gratitude and some ignorance.

It should be clear also that our age demands relevance, sincerity, and simplicity in our approach to each other and life. This should characterize our spiritual life as well. Prayer should be born of our needs and influenced by our temperaments. It should be, as much as possible, something that fits and is distinctively ours. It is I who must approach God. I cannot send another or use another's thoughts or borrow someone else's emotions to pray. Spirituality should be filled with sincerity and simplicity. One should not pretend to have a faith which is not there, to love a God he will not serve, to accept a message he has little time for.

Our spiritual effort ought also to emphasize hope and personalism. This is an age of desperation and insecurity. It is a time of mistrust and hostility. Frequently our spiritual life recognizes faith and espouses charity, forgetting that neither grows without hope in each other and in God. Our approach to God ought also to be deeply personal. As life changes, so will our way of living faith. For faith is life. The protective faith of the child becomes the idealistic faith of the adolescent, the uncertain faith of the college student, the realistic faith of the mature man, the serene faith of the elderly. If God is approached personally, one must expect at times that faith will be demanding; that God is sometimes as near as Christ or one's neighbor, but sometimes as distant as the heavens or one's enemies. If God is approached personally then one does not give up faith because God disappoints, just as we do not end a friendship because a friend does not do exactly as we wish. Faith and friendship are not as far apart as they seem at first sight. God will not be found easily, we must remind ourselves, and yet His discovery is always glorious.

No book can ever tell us exactly how we should approach God. One's spiritual life must be lived with one's self and guided by the very few who know the individual well enough for this.

Yet it is well to remind ourselves that this is a splendid age and a vibrant time to be alive. It is a time when God and the Church may mean more to us than we have ever dared dream. It is a time when man's deep concern for existence and others may lead him to a new communication with God. It is a time when a Catholic can see his Church as a changing, imaginative, vital reality in the world. It is a time when Christianity seems more a community than it did a few decades ago and when it has become far easier to see a foreigner or an unbeliever as part of one's family. It is a time for so many things and a time of so much promise. Humanity seems to be on the verge of something new and different and the Church seems to be living almost her finest hour. It is a time when faith and reason, when God and man, when Church and world, when religion and science are beginning to see each other as partners in a great venture. This

is the time when the man of prayer is a man of action, when
atheists wonder about Transcendence, and when all see the
possibility of cooperation with each other and the eventual pros-
pect of a new harmony for mankind. This is the time when one
reaches heaven by renewing the earth, finds God at his neighbor's side, and accepts faith in order to live both as his brother's
keeper and his Father's son.

NOTES

[1] John Courtney Murray, *The Problem of God* (Yale University Press,
1964).

[2] Karl Rahner, *Theological Investigations* (Baltimore, Helicon Press,
1961), vol. I, pp. 88–89.

[3] The Latin word *tradere,* meaning "to pass on or hand down," gave this
system of thought the name Traditionalism.

[4] English translation of Council documents is taken from *The Church
Teaches: Documents of the Church in English Translation.* This collection
was compiled by the Jesuits at St. Mary's College, St. Mary's, Kansas (St.
Louis, B. Herder Book Co., 1955). Hereinafter, references to this collection
will be by the letters TCT with the respective number. The present TCT
number is 58. For those who wish to consult the original Latin, the new
Denzinger, entitled Denzinger-Schonmetzer, contains the document under
number 3004. Denzinger-Schonmetzer is also published by Herder. Hereinafter references to this collection will be written thus: D 3004. Thus Council documents will be cited in English translation and Latin original in this
fashion: TCT 58–D 3004. The document referred to above was issued on
April 24, 1870, during the Council's third Session.

[5] TCT 1806–D 3026.

[6] ". . . nam non simpliciter agitur in doctrina nostra utrum ab homine
prout nunc est Deus naturali lumine certo cognosci possit necne; sed agitur
in genere de conditione naturae humanae" (Mansi t.51 c.275C). The translation of Bishop Gasser's statements throughout is my own.

[7] "Nam si dicimus Deum cognosci naturali rationis lumine per creaturas,
id est, per vestigia quae creaturis omnibus impressa sunt; multo minus ex-
cludimus imaginem quae animae hominis immortoli impressa est; proinde
argumentum metaphysicum non excluditur" (Mansi t.51 c.276A).

8 "Quamvis aliquatenus 'certo cognosci' et 'demonstrare' sit unum idemque tamen phrasim mitiorem Deputatio de Fide sibi eligendum censuit et non istam duriorem" (Mansi t.51 c. 276B).

9 TCT 88–D 3538.

10 I have found Edward Sillem's book, *Ways of Thinking about God* (New York, Sheed and Ward, 1961), quite helpful for this problem.

11 John Courtney Murray, *op. cit.*, pp. 66–71.

12 Paul Tillich, *The Shaking of the Foundations* (New York, Scribner, 1948), pp. 159–160.

13 *Ibid.*, p. 162.

14 The reader may find helpful *Karl Barth on God*, by Sebastian A. Matczak (New York, St. Paul Publications, 1962).

15 John A. T. Robinson, *Honest To God* (Philadelphia, Westminster Press, 1963), pp. 54–55.

16 *Ibid.*, p. 58.

17 *Ibid.*, p. 81.

18 TCT 2–D 125.

19 TCT 3–D 150.

20 TCT 311–D 1330.

21 TCT 8–1862.

22 TCT 355–D 3001.

23 In the final pages of this section on God as personal and as love, I have found quite helpful, and refer the reader to, Karl Rahner's article, "Theos in the New Testament," *Theological Investigations* (Baltimore, Helicon Press, 1961), vol. I, pp. 79–148.

24 TCT 355–D 3001.

25 TCT 355–D 3001.

26 TCT 578–D 1101 (Council of Trent).

27 TCT 579–D 1102.

28 TCT 580–D 1103.

29 Karl Rahner, *Encounters with Silence* (Westminster, Md., Newman Press, 1963), pp. 29–33.

30 TCT 355–D 3001.

31 TCT 357–D 3003.

32 TCT 548–549–D 396–397.

33 TCT 2–D 125.

34 TCT 4–D 44.

35 TCT 3–D 150.

36 TCT 7–D 76.

[37] TCT 559–D 1523. The reason why the universal salvific Will is Catholic teaching and not defined doctrine from Trent is because what is here said of that Will is said *per transennam*, in passing and obliquely, rather than as the direct object and immediate intention of the Council Fathers.

[38] TCT 631–D 2005.

[39] D 2304.

[40] One must except from this statement, those who die without ever having attained the use of reason. The salvation of infants or of adults who are equivalently infants is another theological problem.

Bibliography

This bibliography is an attempt to recommend a few works, easily readable, most in paperback. It has in mind the reader who wants to add depth to the survey we have set forth in this book without undertaking an exhaustive and expensive study.

I EXISTENTIALISM

David E. Roberts, *Existentialism and Religious Belief*. New York, Oxford University Press, 1959.

This book is readable, perceptive, sympathetic and yet not uncritical. It is one of the finer studies of the religious problem as the Existentialists see it.

James Collins, *The Existentialists*. Chicago, Regnery, 1952.

This is a more critical and more philosophical evaluation of Existentialism. It will not read as quickly as the above-mentioned book, but it will explore the subject in greater depth.

Vincent Martin, O.P., *Existentialism*. Washington, D.C., The Thomist Press, 1962.

This is only a pamphlet of some 48 pages, but it treats rather well in a few words the thought of Kierkegaard, Sartre, and Camus. At times, the critical evaluation of these thinkers is not well done. The exposition of their thought, however, is effective and accurate.

Critical studies mean much in understanding thinkers as complex as Sartre, Heidegger, Jaspers, Kierkegaard, and Marcel. They cannot, however, substitute for a reading of these philosophers in their own words.

II LITERATURE

The recommendations in this area will be grouped under the names of the authors we studied. Some suggestions as to how one might become acquainted with these writers follow.

FYODOR DOSTOEVSKY

If one chooses to read Dostoevsky himself, *The Brothers Karamazov* will prove the best example of his style and religious thought. *Crime and Punishment* is easy to read but not as directly connected with the problems we discussed in this book. *The Possessed* and *The Idiot* are important but not easy reading.

One can begin a critical study of Dostoevsky with the article "Dostoevsky as Prophet" in *The Drama of Atheist Humanism* by Henri de Lubac, S.J., (New York, Meridian Books, 1950). A rather perceptive series of essays on Dostoevsky is published in *Twentieth-Century Views: Dostoevsky*, Rene Wellek, ed. (Englewood Cliffs, N.J., Prentice-Hall, 1962).

THOMAS WOLFE

Look Homeward, Angel has been the best received of Wolfe's books. *You Can't Go Home Again*, however, tells us more of the man and gives us a better insight into Wolfe's mature thought. *The Web and the Rock*, *Of Time and the River*, and *The Hills Beyond* have flashes of brilliance but not the sustained power of the other works.

FRANK KAFKA

The Trial and *The Castle* are required reading for an understanding of Kafka. *Twentieth-Century Views: Kafka*, Ronald Gray, ed. (Englewood Cliffs, N.J., Prentice-Hall, 1962) and the essay by Thomas Mann introducing the Modern Library edition of *The Castle* are both helpful.

ALBERT CAMUS

One ought to read at least five of Camus' works: *The Stranger*, *The Plague*, *The Fall*, *The Myth of Sisyphus*, and *The Rebel*. Two studies on Albert Camus are impressively done: *Albert Camus: A Study of His Work* by Philip Thody (New York, Grove Press, 1957) and *The Thought and Art of Albert Camus* by Thomas Hanna (Chicago, Regnery, 1958).

J. D. SALINGER

Three of Salinger's works are especially indicative of his approach: *The Catcher in the Rye, Franny and Zooey,* and *Nine Stories. Salinger: A Critical and Personal Portrait,* ed. Henry Anatole Grunwald (New York, Pocket Books, Inc., 1962) is a good survey of literary criticism.

WILLIAM GOLDING and GEORGE ORWELL

Lord of the Flies and *1984* are representative of the views of each of these authors.

III PSYCHOLOGY

Erich Fromm, *The Art of Loving.* New York, Bantam Books, 1963.

This study is well-done. It is appealing, informative, and accurate for the most part, though one wonders about its superficiality in speaking of God. *Escape from Freedom* by the same author (New York, Holt, Rinehart & Winston, 1941) is not as well-written, dated in parts, but still worthwhile as Fromm always is.

John Courtney Murray (ed.), *Freedom and Man.* New York, Kenedy, 1965.

This is a fine collection, though few of the essays have as much depth and insight as that of Karl Rahner. Rahner, in fact, is consistently impressive in his writings on human freedom. One might consult his essays in *Theological Investigations,* vol. II (Baltimore, Helicon Press, 1963) and in *Theology for Renewal* (New York, Sheed and Ward, 1964).

Dag Hammarskjold, *Markings.* New York, Knopf, 1964.

This is a contemporary religious classic. It is a book one reads more than once and reflects on often.

Four Screenplays of Ingmar Bergman, trans. Lars Malmstrom and David Kushner. New York, Simon and Schuster, 1960.

This collection helps one recall the power and poetry of Bergman's screenplays, though it does not include some of Bergman's finest work.

IV THEOLOGY

John Courtney Murray, *The Problem of God*. New Haven, Yale University Press, 1964.

Murray has written a thought-provoking and challenging book on the problem of God in different periods of man's thinking about Him. It is a work of a few pages, but its words are well-chosen and wise.

Edward Sillem, *Ways of Thinking About God*. New York, Sheed and Ward, 1961.

Sillem has some refreshing thoughts on the motives which led Thomas to speak as he did in his five "ways." He attempts also to show us how one might present Thomas to modern man.

Three works of Paul Tillich are most helpful in studying his thought on God's existence: *The Shaking of the Foundations, Dynamics of Faith,* and *Biblical Religion and the Search for Ultimate Reality.*

Sebastian A. Matczak, *Karl Barth on God*. New York, St. Paul Publications, 1962.

This is a readable and impressive study of Barth showing a sympathy for his thought though not a total acceptance of it.

John A. T. Robinson, *Honest to God*. Philadelphia, Westminster Press, 1963.

Both this and its companion book *The Honest to God Debate* are valuable for an understanding of a contemporary debate on God. Bishop Robinson is not always satisfying in his theology, but he is never uninteresting.

Name Index

Subject Index

Absurd, Camus' concept of, 104f., 118f.

Abyss, Barth's concept of, 241f.

Atheism, xiv, 174f.; of Sartre, 14f., 68, 200; in Dostoevsky's works, 66f., 75f.; Camus' problem of, 111

Being, in Heidegger's thought, 21f.; in Marcel's thought, 48f.

"Boundary Situation," 29

Christ, 158; in Dostoevsky's works, 74f.; in Wolfe's works, 89f.; -figure in Salinger's works, 142, 143f.; -figure in Golding's works, 154

Christianity, in Camus' thought, 134f.

Christology, 207f.

"Ciphers," 31

"Concerns," in Tillich's thought—Faith, 237; Courage, 239; God, 239f.

Conscience, in Heidegger's thought, 24

Courage, in Tillich's thought, 239f.

Death, in Heidegger's thought, 25f.; in Jaspers' thought, 30, 87; in Camus' works, 125f.

Despair, "of possibility," 40, 80; "of necessity," 41

Evil, in Golding's works, 149, 153

Exile, in Camus' works, 116f.

Existence of God, and human reason, 198f.; in the Old Testament, 202f.; in the New Testament, 207f.; proofs of, 228f.; in Tillich, 237f.; in Barth, 241f.; in Robinson, 244f.

Existentialism, 5–13; and rationalism, 8; and man, 8, 10f.; and truth, 9; weaknesses of, 11f.; of Sartre, 14f.; of Heidegger, 21f.; of Jaspers, 29f.; of Kierkegaard, 36f.; of Marcel, 48f.

Faith, 158; in Jaspers' thought, 33; in Kierkegaard's thought, 42f.; in Dostoevsky's works, 61f., 69f.; of Wolfe in the American spirit, 89f.; in Tillich's thought, 237f.

Freedom, xiv, 55, 157, 169; in Sartre's thought, 14f., 87, 108;

299